Ouida

Tricotrin the Story of a Waif and Stray

Ouida

Tricotrin the Story of a Waif and Stray

ISBN/EAN: 9783741170836

Manufactured in Europe, USA, Canada, Australia, Japa

Cover: Foto ©Andreas Hilbeck / pixelio.de

Manufactured and distributed by brebook publishing software (www.brebook.com)

Ouida

Tricotrin the Story of a Waif and Stray

COLLECTION
OF
BRITISH AUTHORS

TAUCHNITZ EDITION.

VOL. 1106.

TRICOTRIN BY "OUIDA."

IN TWO VOLUMES.

VOL. I.

"Better an outlaw than not free."
JEAN PAUL

"Sceptreless, free, uncircumscribed
.... unclassed, tribeless, nationless,
Exempt from awe, worship, degree, the king
Over himself."
SHELLEY.

"Love, and do what you will."
ST. AUGUSTINE.

TRICOTRIN

THE STORY OF A WAIF AND STRAY.

BY

"OUIDA,"

AUTHOR OF "IDALIA," ETC.

COPYRIGHT EDITION.

IN TWO VOLUMES.

VOL. I.

LEIPZIG

BERNHARD TAUCHNITZ

1870.

The Right of Translation is reserved.

TRICOTRIN,
THE STORY OF A WAIF AND STRAY.

CHAPTER I.

It was autumn; a rich golden autumn of France, with the glow of burning sunsets, and the scarlet pomp of reddened woods, and the purple and the yellow of grapes gathered for the wine-press, and the luscious dreamy odor of overripened fruits crushed, by careless passing feet, upon the orchard-mosses. Afar off, in the full noonday, the winding road was white and hot with dust; but here in a nook of forest land, in a dell of leafy growth between the vineyards which encompassed it, the air was cool and the sunlight broken with shade, while, through its stillness where the boughs threw the shadow darkest, a little torrent leapt and splashed, making music as it went, and washing round the base of an old ivy-grown stone tower that had fallen to ruin in the midst of its green nest.

There was no sound except one, beside that of the bright tumbling stream, though now and then there came in from the distance the ring of a convent-clock's bells, or the laugh of a young girl at work among the vines;—no sound except one, and that was the quick, sharp, gleeful crack of nuts in a monkey's teeth. There were squirrels by the score there in that solitary place who had right, hereditary and indisputable they would have said, to all the nuts that the boughs bore and the grasses hid; but Mistigri was no recognizer of rights divine; she loved nuts and cared little how she got them, and she sat aloft in her glory, or swung herself from twig to twig, crushing and eating and flinging the shells away with all that gleeful self-satisfaction of which a little black monkey is to the full as capable, after successful piracy, as any conquering sovereign.

"Mistigri, Mistigri!" said her companion, surveying her, "who could doubt your human-affinity who once had seen you pilfer? Monkey stows away her stolen goods in a visible pouch unblushingly; man smuggles his away unknown in the guise of 'profit' or 'percentage,' 'commerce' or 'annexation' —the natural advancement of civilization on the simple and normal thieving. Increased cranium, increased caution; that's all the difference, eh, Mistigri?"

Mistigri cocked her head on one side, but would not waste time in replying: her little shiny black mouth was full of good kernels.

"Why talk when you can take?" she would have asked.

Her owner did not press for an answer, but sung, carelessly, snatches of Goethe's *Millsong* and of Müller's *Whisper*, his voice chiming in with the bubble of the stream while he took at intervals his noontide meal, classic and uncostly, of Chasselas grapes and a big brown roll.

He was a man of some forty years, dressed in a linen blouse, with a knapsack as worn as an African soldier's lying at his feet, unstrapped, in company with a flask of good wine and a Straduarius fiddle. He himself was seated on a fallen tree, with the sun breaking through the foliage above in manifold gleams and glories that touched the turning leaves bright red as fire, and fell on his own head when he tossed it up to fling a word to Mistigri or to catch the last summer-song of a blackbird. It was a beautiful Homeric head; bold, kingly, careless, noble, with the royalty of the lion in its gallant poise, and the challenge of the eagle in its upward gesture;—the head which an artist would have given to his Hector, or his Phœbus, or his God Lyœus. The features were beautiful too, in their varied mobile eloquent meanings; with their poet's brows, their reveler's laugh, their soldier's daring, their student's thought, their many and conflicting utterances, whose contradictions made one unity—the unity of genius.

At this moment there was only the enjoyment of a rich and sunny nature, in an idle moment, written on them as he ate his grapes and threw fragments of wit up at Mistigri where she was perched among the nut boughs. But the brilliant eyes, so blue in some lights so black in others, had the luster and the depths of infinite meditation in them; and the curling lips that were hidden under the fullness of their beard, had the delicate fine mockery of the satirist blent with the brighter, franker mirth of genial sympathies. And his face changed as he cast the crumbs of his finished meal to some ducks that paddled lower down in the stream where it grew stiller around the old tower, and took up his Straduarius from the ground with the touch of a man who loves the thing that he touches. The song of the water that had made the melody to his banquet was in his brain;—sweet, wild, entangled sounds that he must needs reproduce, with the self-same fancy that a painter must catch the fleeting hues of fair scenes that would haunt him forever unless exorcised thus.

"Quiet, Mistigri!" he said softly, and the monkey sat still on her hazel bough, eating indeed, but noiselessly. He listened one moment more to the stream, then drew the bow across the strings. The music thrilled out upon the silence, catching the song of the brook in harmony as Goethe caught it in verse,—all its fresh delicious babble, all its rush of silvery sound, all its cool and soothing murmur, all its pauses of deep rest. All of which the woodland torrent told—of the winds that had tossed the boughs into its foam; of the women-faces its tranquil pools had mirrored; of the blue burden of forget-me-nots and the snowy weight of lilies it had borne so lovingly; of the sweet familiar idyls it had seen where it had wound its way below quaint mill-house walls choked up with ivy-growth where the children and the pigeons paddled with rosy feet upon the resting wheel; of the weary sighs that had been breathed over it beneath the gray old convents where it heard the miserere steal in with its own ripple, and looked itself a thing so full of leaping joy and dancing life to the sad eyes of girl-recluses,—all these of which it told the music told again. The strings were touched by an artist's hand, and all that duller ears heard, but dimly, in the splash and surge of the brown fern-covered stream, he heard in marvelous poems and translated into clearer tongue—the universal tongue which has no country and no limit, and in which the musician speaks alike to sovereign and to savage.

There was not a creature there to hear, save the yellow-winged lorioles and Mistigri who was absorbed in nuts; but he played on to himself an hour or more for love of the theme and the art, and an old peasant woman, going through the trees at some yards distance, and seeing nothing of the player for the screen of leaves, laughed and stroked the hair of a grandchild who clung to her afraid of the magical woodland-melodies: "The wood-elves, little one? Bah! that is only Tricotrin!"

Her feet, brushing the fallen leaves with pleasant sound, soon passed away; he played on and on, such poetry as Bamboche drew from his violin, whereat Poussin bowed his head, weeping with the passion of women, as through his tears he beheld as in a vision the "Et in Arcadia Ego."

Then, as suddenly as he had begun, Tricotrin dropped the bow and ceased; and struck a light and smoked,—a great Arab pipe of some carved wood, black and polished by long use. On the silence that succeeded there came a low laugh of delight—the laugh of a very young child. He looked up and down and among the ferns at his feet; the laughter was close beside him, yet he could see nothing. He smoked on indifferently, watching the bright eyes of the birds glancing out from the shadow; then the laugh came again; close at his side, as it sounded; he rose and pushed aside some branches and looked over a broken rail behind him beyond a tangled growth of reeds and rushes.

There he saw what had aroused him from his smoke-silence: more than half hidden under the moss and the broad tufted grasses, stretching her hands out at the gorgeous butterflies that fluttered above her head, and covered with the wide yellow leaves of gourds and the white fragrant abundance of traveler's-joy, was the child whose laughter he had heard. A child between two and three years old, her face warm with the flush of past sleep, her eyes smiling against the light, her hair lying like gold-dust on the moss, her small fair limbs struggling uncovered out of a rough red cloak that alone was folded about her. The scarlet of the mantle, the whiteness of the clematis, the yellow hues of the wild gourds, the color of the winged insects, the head of the child rising out of the mosses, and the young face that looked like a moss-rosebud just unclosing, made a picture in their own way; and he who passed no picture by, but had pictures in his memory surpassing all the collected art of galleries, paused to survey it with his arms folded on the rail.

Its solitude, its strangeness, did not occur to him; he looked at it as at some painting of his French brethren's easels, that was all. But the child, seeing a human eye regard her, forgot her butterflies, and remembered human wants; she stretched her hands to him instead of to her playmates of the air. "*J'ai faim!*" she cried, with a plaintive self-pity; bread would be better than the butterflies.

"Hungry?" he answered, addressing her as he was wont to do Mistigri. "I have nothing for you. Who brought you there, you Waif and Stray? Put down there and left, to get rid of the trouble of you, apparently? Well,—D'Alembert was dropped down in the streets, and found a foster-mother in a milk-woman, and *he* did pretty well afterward. Perhaps some dainty De Tencin brought you likewise into the world and has hidden you like a bit of smuggled lace, only thinking you nothing so valuable. Is it so, eh?"

"*J'ai faim!*" cried the child afresh; all her history was comprised to her in the one fact that she wanted bread,—as it is comprised to a mob.

"Catch, then!" he replied to the cry, dropping into her

hands from where he leant a bunch of the Chasselas grapes that still remained in his pocket. It sufficed; the child was not so much pained by hunger as by thirst, though she scarcely knew the difference between her own sensations; her throat was dry, and the grapes were all she wanted. He, leaning over the lichen-covered rail, watched her while she enjoyed them one by one. She was a very pretty child, the prettier for that rough moss covering, out of which her delicate fair shoulders and chest rose uncovered, while the breeze blew about her yellow glossy curls.

"Left there to be got rid of,—clearly," he murmured to her. "Any one who picks you up will do you the greatest injury possible. Die now in the sunshine among the flowers; you will never have such another chance of a poetical and picturesque exit. Who was ingenious enough to hide you there? The poor shirt-stitcher who was at her last sou?—or Madame la Marquise who was at her last scandal? Was it Magdalene who has to wear sack-cloth for having dared to sin without money to buy absolution?—or Messalina who covers ten thousand poisonous passions with a silver embroidered robe, and is only discreetly careful of 'consequences?' Which was your progenitrix little one, eh?"

To this question so closely concerning her, the Waif could give no answer, being gifted with only imperfect speech; but, happy in the grapes, she laughed up in his eyes her unspoken thanks, shaking a cluster of clematis above her head, as happy in her couch of flowers and moss as she could have been in any silver cradle. The question concerned her in nothing yet: the bar sinister could not stretch across the sunny blue skies, the butterflies flew above her as familiarly as above the brow of a child-queen, and the white flowers did not wither sooner in bastard than in legitimate hands.

"How the sun shines on you, as if you were a princess!" he soliloquized to her. "Ah! Nature is a terrible socialist; what republicans she would make of men if they listened to her. But there is no fear for them,—they are not fond enough of her school! You look very comfortably settled here, and how soon you will get life over. You are very fortunate. You will suffer a little bit,—paf! what of that? Everybody suffers that little bit sooner or later, and it grows sharper the longer it is put off. Suppose you were picked up by somebody and lived, it would be very bad for you. You would be a lovely woman, and lovely women are the devil's aides-de-camp. You would snare men in your yellow hair, and steal their substance with the breath of your lips, and dress up lying avarice as love, and make a miser's greed wear the smile of a cherub. Ah! that you would. And then would come age, a worse thing for women like you than crime or death; and you would suffer an agony with every wrinkle and a martyrdom with every whitening lock, and you would grow hard, and haggard, and painted, and hideous even to the vilest among men; and you would be hissed off the stage in hatred by the mouths that once shouted your triumphs, while you would hear the fresh comers laugh as they rushed on to be crowned with the roses that once wreathed your own forehead. And then would come the end,—the hospital and the wooden shell, and the grave trampled flat to the dust as soon almost as made, while the world danced on in the sunlight unheeding. Ah! be wise. Die while you can, among your butterflies and flowers!"

The child, lying below there in her nest, looked up in his eyes again and laughed: "Viva!" she cried, while she clasped her grapes in her two small hands.

"Viva? What do you mean by that? Do you mean, imperfectly, to ask to live in Italian? Fie then! That is unphilosophic. Take the advice of two philosophers. Bolingbroke says, there is so much trouble in coming into the world and in going out of it, that it is barely worth while to be here at all, and I tell you the same. He had the cakes and ale too, but the one got stale and the other bitter. What will it be for you who start with neither cakes nor ale? Life's not worth much to a man. It is worth just nothing at all to a woman. It is a mistake altogether, and lasts just long enough for all to find that out, but not long enough for any to remedy it. We always live the time required to get thoroughly uncomfortable, and as soon as we are in the track to sift the problem—paf!—out we go like a rushlight, the very moment we begin to burn brightly. Be persuaded by me, and don't think of living; you have a golden opportunity of getting quittance of the whole affair. Don't throw it away!"

The good advice of Experience was, as it always is, thrown away on the impetuosity of Ignorance. The child laughed still over her Chasselas bunch, murmuring still over and over again the nearest approach she knew to a name:

"Viva—Viva—Viva!"

"The obstinacy of women prematurely developed. Why *will* you not know when you are well off? 'Those whom the gods love die young.' If you would just now prefer to have your mother's love instead of the gods', you are wrong. What have you before you? You will be marked 'outcast.' You will have nothing as your career except to get rich by snaring the foolish; or to be virtuous and starve on three-halfpence a day, having a pauper's burial as reward for your chastity. If you live, your hands must be either soiled or empty. I would die among the clematis if I were you."

But the child, persistently regardless of wise counsel, only laughed still, and strove to struggle from her network of blossom and of moss.

"Your mind is set upon living,—what a pity!" murmured her solitary companion. "When your hair is white, how you will wish you had died when it was yellow,—everybody does, —but while the yellow lasts nobody believes it! You want to live? So Eve wanted the 'fruit of fairest colors.' If I were to help you to have your own way now, you would turn on me thirty years hence as your worst enemy. Were you able to understand reason,—but your sex would prevent that, let alone your age. Let us ask Mistigri. Mistigri, is that Wuif to live or to die?"

The companion and counselor, who lived in his pocket, and was accustomed to be thus appealed to, had swung herself down on to the grass, and was now squatted on the rail beside him. The child catching sight of the monkey, tried to stretch and stroke her, and Mistigri, who was always of an affable, and, when she had eaten sufficient herself, of a generous turn of mind, extended her little black paw, and tendered a nut, as an overture to an acquaintance.

"*You* vote for life too?" cried Tricotrin. "Bah, Mistigri. I thought you so sensible,—for your sex! When a discerning mother, above the weakness of womenkind, has arranged everything so neatly, we should be the most miserable sentimentalists to interfere."

As he spoke, the little creature, who had been vainly striving to free herself from her forest-cradle, ceased her efforts and looked up in piteous mute entreaty, her eyes wet and soft with glistening tears, her mouth trembling with an unspoken appeal.

He, who saw a wounded bird only to help it, and met a lame dog only to carry it, was unable to resist that pathetic helplessness. He turned and lifted his voice.

"Grand'mère Virelois, are you there? Here is something in your way, not in mine."

In answer to the shout there came out from the low broken door of the ruined tower an old peasant woman, brown and bent and very aged, but blithe as a bird, and with her black eyes as bright as the eyes of a mouse under the white pent-house of her high, starched cap.

"What is it, good Tricotrin?" she asked, in that sweet, singing voice that makes the accent of many French peasant women so lingering and charming on the ear; the voice that has in it all the contentment of the brave, cheery spirit within.

"A Waif and Stray," answered Tricotrin. "Whether from Mary Magdalene or Madame la Marquise is unknown, probably will never be known. Curses go home to roost, but chickens don't. The Waif is irrational, she thinks a mouthful of black bread better than easy extinction among the ferns. Claudine de Tencin has left a feminine D'Alembert in a moss-cradle; are you inclined to play the part of the foster-mother?"

Grand'mère Virelois listened to the harangue, comprehending it no more than if he had spoken in Hebrew, but she was used to him, and thought nothing of that.

"What is it I am to see?" she asked again, peering curiously with lively interest among the leaves. Before he could answer she had caught sight of the child, with vehement amaze and ecstatic wonder; the speech had been as Hebrew to her, but the fact was substantial and indisputable. Crossing herself in her surprise, with a thousand expletives of pity and admiration, she bent her little withered but still active form beneath the rail, and stooped and raised the foundling—raised her, but only a little from the ground.

"Holy Virgin! Tricotrin!" she cried, "look here! the child is fastened. Help me!"

He looked quickly as she called him, and saw that the withes of osiers and the tendrils of wild vine had been netted so tightly around the limbs, tied here and there with strong twine, that the infant could never have escaped from its resting-place; it had evidently been so fastened that the child might perish there unseen. His face darkened as he looked.

"Murder, then! not mere neglect. Ah! this is Madame la Marquise at work, not Magdalene!" he murmured, as he slashed the network right and left with his knife, and set the Waif at liberty, while Grand'mère Virelois went into a woman's raptures on the young beauty of the "petit Gésu," and a woman's vehement censures of a sister's sin.

Tricotrin smoked resignedly, while her raptures and her diatribes expended themselves; it was long before either were exhausted.

"Don't abuse the mother," he interposed at last. "Everybody gets rid of troublesome consequences when they can. We've done no good in disturbing her arrangements. We have only disinterred a living blunder that she wished to bury."

"For shame, Tricotrin!" cried Grand'mère, quivering with horror, while she folded the child in her withered arms. "You can jest on such wickedness! You can excuse such a murderess!"

"Paf!" said Tricotrin, lightly blowing away a smoke ring. "The whole system of creation is a sliding scale of murders. All the world over life is only sustained by life being extinguished."

Grand'mère Virelois, who was a pious little woman, shuddered and clasped the child nearer.

"Ah—h—h! the vile woman! How will she see our Lady's face on the last day?"

"How she will meet the world she lives in is more the question with her now, I imagine. An eminently sagacious woman! and you and I are two sentimentalists to interfere with her admirably artistic play. So you *would* live, little one? I wonder what you will make of what you have got! A Jeremiad if you are a good silly woman; a Can-can-measure if you are a bad clever one. Which will it be, I wonder?"

"Mon Dieu, it is an angel!" murmured Grand'mère, "such hair, like silk,—such eyes,—such a rose for a mouth! And left to die of hunger and cold! Ah, may the Holy Mary find her out and avenge her crime, the wicked one!"

"The vengeance will come quick if the sinner live in a garret; it will limp very slowly if she shelter in a palace. Well, since you take that child in your arms, do you mean to find her the piece of bread the unphilosophic castaway will want?"

"Will I not! if I go without myself. Oh the pretty little child! who could have left you? Wherever the mother dwells, may the good God hunt her down!"

"Deity as a detective? Not a grand idea that. Yet it is the heavenly office that looks dearest to man when it is exercised upon others! Grand'mère, answer me. Are you going to keep that Waif?"

The bright brown wrinked homely face of the good old woman grew perplexed:

"Ah, my friend,—times are so bad,—it is hard work to get a bit in the pot for one's self, and I stitch, stitch, stitch, and spin, spin, spin, till I am blind many a time. And yet the pretty child,—with no one to care for it! I do not know? —she must be brought up hard if she come to me. Not a lentil even to put in the water and make one fancy it is soup, in some days these hard times! But do you know nothing more of her than this, Tricotrin?"

"Nothing."

His luminous eyes met hers full, and frankly; she knew —all the nations where he wandered knew—that the affirmative of Tricotrin was more sure than the truth of most men's oaths.

"Then she must be abandoned here by some wretch to starve unseen?"

"It looks like it."

"Ah! the little angel! What does the barbarous brutal heart of stone deserve?"

"What it will get if it lodge in the breast that rags and tatters cover,—what it will not get if it lodge in the breast that heaves under silks and laces."

"True enough! But the good God will smite in his own time. Oh, little one, how could they ever forsake thee?" cried Grand'mère, caressing afresh the child who was laughing and well content in her friendly and tender hold.

"Then you are going to adopt her?"

"Adopt her? Mother of Jesus! I dare not say that. You know how I live, Tricotrin,—how hardly, though I try to let it be cheerfully. If I had a little more she should share it, and welcome; but as it is,—not a mouthful of chestnuts, even, so often; not a drop of oil or a bit of garlic sometimes weeks together! She would be better off at the Foundling Hospital than with me. Besides, it is an affair for the Mayor of the commune."

"Certainly it is. But if the most notable Mayor can do nothing except send this foundling among the others, would you like better to keep her?"

Grand'mère Virelois was silent and thoughtful a minute; then her little bright eyes glanced up at him from under their white linen roofing, with a gleam in them that was between a smile and a tear.

"You know how I lost *them*, Tricotrin. One in Africa,— one at the Barricades,—one crushed under a great marble block, building the Préfet's palace. And then the grandchild too,—the only little one,—so pretty, so frail, so tender, killed that long bitter winter, because the food was so scarce, like the young birds dead on the snow! You know, Tricotrin? —and what use is it to take her to perish like him, though in her laughter and her caresses I might think that he lived again?"

"I know!" said Tricotrin, softly with an infinite balm of pity, and of the remembrance that was the sweetest sympathy, in his voice. "Well—if M. le Maire can find none to claim her, she shall stay with you, grand'mère, and, as for the food, that shall not trouble you; I will have a care of that."

"*You?* Holy Jesus! how good!"

"Not in the least. I abetted her in her ignorant and ridiculous desire to exchange a pleasant death among the clematis for all the toil and turmoil of prolonged existences; I am clearly responsible for my share in the folly. I cut the meshes that her sagacious mother had knotted so hardily; I must accept my part in the onus of such unwarrantable interference. You keep the Waif; and I will be at the cost of her."

"But then, Tricotrin, you call yourself poor?"

"So I am. But one need not be a millionaire to be able to get a few crumbs for that robin. The creature persisted in living, and I humored her caprice. It was mock humanity, paltry sentiment; Mistigri was partly at fault, but I mostly. We must accept the results. They will be disastrous probably—the creature is feminine—but such as they are we must make the best of them."

"Then *you* will adopt her?"

"Not in the least. But I will see she has something to eat; and that you are able to give it her if her parents cannot be found. Here is a gold bit for the present minute, and when we know whether she is really and truly a Waif, you shall have more to keep the pot over your fire full and boiling. Adieu, grand'mère."

With that farewell, he, heedless of the voluble thanks and praises that the old woman showered after him, and of the outcries of the child who called to Mistigri, put his pipe in his mouth, his violin in his pocket, and throwing his knapsack over his shoulder brushed his way through the forest growth.

"Mock-sentiment!" he said to himself. "You and I have done a silly thing, Mistigri. What will come of it?"

The monkey cracked a fair-looking fat nut which she carried, with glee; and cast it forth in disgust: the handsome shell had dust and a maggot within it.

"Ah!" thought Tricotrin, taking the nut as a parable, "will that young innocent-looking life yonder ever reward us by corruption at its core?"

CHAPTER II.

THERE were two leagues between him and the nearest town, and this wanderer little loved any contact with the law or its officers, with the routine and details of citizenship and communities. But chance had brought him, and him alone, upon his little castaway. Bohemian though he was, he would not neglect the duty that the trouvaille, accidental and little welcome as it might be, brought with it. An evil thing had been clearly done; the search for it lay with the administra-

s of civil laws. He had no liking for them, and no faith
heir sincerity or their efficiency, but at the same time the
ndling's safety needed their interference. So he betook
iself straight through the vineyards across into the white
g road, poplar-fringed and without shadow, which led to
 small, still, gray town, whose peaked roofs and pointed
ers were rising far away out from a mass of autumn-tinted
hards.

It was a rapid progress with his light swift tread, yet
ature after creature stopped him, either of his own will or
their entreaty.

The women working in the fields; the vintagers at labor
ong the grapes; the meek-eyed cows looking over the stone
ices; the team of bullocks drawing a timber wagon wearily
ng; the children filling a pitcher at the roadside water-
out; the old women resting under the wayside crosses;—
had words from him, words which left them brighter,
aver, happier, than they had been before those kindly eyes,
ining so lustrous in the sun, had fallen on them. Man and
ild, woman and animal, felt the influence of glance and
ord, as the languid flowers feel the dew, as the shaded fruit
els the summer warmth.

"What makes thee so merry, child? Has any one given
ee money?" asked an old woman, deaf and blind, sitting
itting in the front of her vine-hung, rock-built cottage, of
c grandson, who came bounding to her side.

The boy laughed gayly.

"No, grand'mère. Better still. Tricotrin spoke to me as
 passed!"

"Ah, ah! Tricotrin? I wish thou hadst brought him hither.
e would have mended thy mother's spinning-wheel—and
ere are none like him for making dark things look bright."

"He was in haste, grand'mère. And he had loitered al-
ady, to look at Blasc Turgot's sick mare."

"And cured her at a touch,—is it not?"

"Not quite that. He says he cannot work miracles,
ough we think he can. But it is certain the beast let him

look at her wound as quietly as a lamb,—she who kicks and bites at all who go near!—and he has told Blase Turgot how to get her well in a week."

The old blind knitter nodded her head several times, with sapient comprehension.

"To be sure, to be sure! He can do what he likes. If he be the Wandering Jew, as they say, it was wise of the good Gésu to bid him stay so long on earth."

"You think he is that, grand'mère?" whispered the boy in awe, that subdued his mirth.

The old woman nodded her head again with meaning emphasis.

"It is said," she answered significantly. "And I have seen things——"

"But the Jew was wicked, grand'mère; and he is so good?" objected the boy, who loved little to think that the hand which had just tossed him a great golden-brown pear was a hand accursed of his Church.

The grandmother laid her knitting down on her lap, looking out at the sunshine as though her blind eyes saw its beauty.

"Pierre,—it may well be that a life led in atonement is the life nearest to God, and most blessed to men. Besides," —and she lowered her voice as one who speaks sacrilege fearingly, "besides—thou knowest he has no love for the priests, has Tricotrin."

Pierre nodded, but he remained unconvinced; in his secret soul he had no love for the priests himself, finding infinite weariness in his aves; and, moreover, the true instinct of the child felt, without reasoning on its instinct, that the brightness and the strength, the genius and the sweetness, of the life they spoke of were too unshadowed, and too unsaddened, to be the mournful though hallowed offsprings of remorse.

CHAPTER III.

"You get on ill, friend Turgot? Of course you do. You surprised? I am not. For a sou you give a sou's worth. oramus! how is that compatible with prosperity? You it a receipt for the philosopher's stone? I will give you . Stint the corn to the peasant's mule, and give overmea-
: to the rich man's fat stalled beast. Cheat the widow out an egg every time she sells you poultry, and throw a dainty bit gratis into M. le Curé's dinner. When the woman-np sits down famished give her the mouldy bread, and :n the Mayor of the Commune calls for wine serve him r best and oiliest. As soon as an inundation or a fire aks out far away in other provinces, let your name loom ge in subscription; when the ragged children creep in to t up the odd barley-corns thrown to your barn-door fowls, 'e them away with a crack of the whip. Do this and more wise, Turgot, and you will find the philosopher's stone ι you gold!"

Tavern-keeper Turgot, thus apostrophized, shook his d pensively in a sorrowful perplexity, standing at the :h of his good inn, the Golden Lion.

'Ah! it is well to talk, Tricotrin, and your lips ever melt laughter and irony. But you know me,—my receipts small, my compassion is enormous; the money runs, runs, s, like a scampering mouse, and never comes back again! hat would you? I have not the talent to cheat."

'And you became an inn-keeper? Imbecile!"

'An inn-keeper? Eh, monsieur! It is not only in an inn needs that talent to prosper."

'Oh no; it is wanted in imperial cabinets as much as in ·side ones; and the bills of a country want doctoring as :h as the bills of a café! If you cannot cheat, my Tur-——"

"What can I do?"

"Break stones. It is the general finale of honesty!"

The landlord, amused if not solaced, laughed a little despite himself, and went within to attend the wants of one of the few wanderers to the unprofitable though admirable Golden Lion, which stood so charmingly, close under the shadow of a noble old brown church, and fronting the market-place, then all ablaze with rich autumnal color, where the fruit-women sat with piles of melons, and gourds, and late peaches, and early grapes, and heaps of damp, sweet-smelling, gathered herbs.

Tricotrin left alone watched the market awhile, taking an artist's pleasure in all that glow and glory of confused hues, and thinking of the words of Antoninus,—"Whatever the seasons bear shall be joyful fruit to me, O Nature; from thee are all things, in thee they subsist, to thee they return."

For Nature was mother, mistress, daughter, deity, idol, teacher, friend, all in one to Tricotrin; and in all her protean shapes he loved her.

"What is it? All. What has it? Nothing," was the famous line anent the third estate which once, through Sièyes, convulsed a nation.

Much such a line expressed the social status of Tricotrin, philosopher, poet, cosmopolitan, artist, democrat, and wanderer. "Many-sided" as ever could be exacted by Greek zeal for mortal perfection, he could be everything by turns; but, for possessions, he had naught save his Straduarius, his Mistigri, and a well-beloved Attavante's Dante. He had the genius of a Mozart,—to make music only to a peasant's festival or his own solitude; the eloquence of a Mirabeau,—to remain a bohemian and be called a scamp; the sagacity of a Talleyrand,—to be worth no more in any pecuniary sense than one of the vintagers at work among the grapes; the versatility of a Crichton,—to shed his talents' luster forth on French hamlets' bridal feasts, Italian olive-growers' frugal suppers, Spanish muleteers' camp-fires, Irish cotters' wakes and revels, Paris laborers' balls and wine-bouts; the wisdom of a Boethius,—to laugh at life with the glorious mirth of Aristophanes, to need as little in his daily wants as Louis

Cornaro, to love all pleasure with the Burgundian jest of a Piron. Was this the reckless waste of marvelous gifts thrown away like diamonds cast on a sea? or was it a brave, joyous, wise adoption of a life without care and warmed by the sunlight of nature, careless of the gas glare of fame?

The world thought one way; the bohemian the other. "Judge no life until its close has been seen," says the sage; hence it had not yet been proved whether the world or the bohemian was most right.

That he was Tricotrin,—a most markedly distinctive personality moreover,—was all that any one knew of him. It was enough for the people who loved him; and they stretched from Danube to Guadalquiver, from Liffey to Tiber, from Euphrates to the Amazon, while in France, the land of his adoption if not of his birth, the hand which should have dared to touch him would have been bolder than the boldest of the iron hands which have seized and swayed her scepter.

His life was a poem; often an ironic, often an erotic, often a sublime one; a love-ode one day, a rhymed satire the next, now light as Suckling's verse, now bitter as Juvenal's, oftenest a Bacchic chant, or a Hudibrastic piece of mockery, but not seldom a noble Homeric epic. Life was a poem with him: he had as little sympathy with those who made it a wailing Miserere of regret as with those who made it a Monologue of self.

He stood looking out now on the fruit-market, enjoying its profusion of color as other men enjoy wine; and taking a peach from the basket of one of the girl-sellers, as pretty a little brown creature in the archness of her sixteen years as ever Florian or Greuze caressed ere transferring to celogue or easel.

"Have you had a good time all this summer, Ninette?" he asked her as they loitered in the deep oak porch of the old Golden Lion.

"Ah yes!" answered Ninette, ever loquacious, thrusting her tanned plump hands deep into the coolness of the vine-leaves as she rearranged her fruit. "You know that the château is open—bought by a great foreign lord?"

"Indeed? And you have sold much there?"

"Oh enormously!" cried Ninette. "The household has taken so much, though the seigneur is only just there. And they have made the place like a fairy palace,—mon Dieu! It is so beautiful, so beautiful; that old ruined desolate Villiers is now like a dream, Tricotrin! Valentin works in the gardens, and I have been over it once, before milord came;—and once since they let me look through a grating, when he was at his banquet, with a king's state all about him. And he is so handsome—that English noble!——"

And Ninette gave a little quick sigh as she replaced her peaches in their green nest. Tricotrin smiled, with a slight touch of pity in the amusement of the smile.

"Leave the noble alone, Ninette! His hand would only touch your soft cheek to soil it. The kiss of the eagle's beak kills the wild wood-dove. Do not let a glance of the aristocrat make you cold to poor Valentin."

Ninette flushed ruddily, like one of her own peaches; but she laughed with a frank, open laugh, that reassured Tricotrin on the fear he had entertained for her peace.

"Oh! there is no thought of that folly! Do you fancy I am such a little fool! Milord Estmere has never looked at me even! and they say he is so proud,—proud as a Bourbon!"

"Estmere!"—he repeated the name rapidly with an eager intonation.

"That is what they call him. He is a great man; he is nothing to me!" said Ninette, pettishly, shouldering her fruit afresh and going off to her stall in as near an approach to bad temper as the bright brunette could know.

Tricotrin's eyes followed her, without seeing her, to the tawny leathern awning under which her vivacious face gleamed so prettily; the look of interest and of eagerness was still upon his features, and the smile about his mouth had a certain sadness in it foreign to the careless, happy, humorous laughter common there.

"Estmere!" he repeated to himself. The name recalled many memories.

"Estmere at this old château!" he thought as he moved away from the Lion d'Or and through the checkered morning light in which the people of the little town were thronging, some to market, some to matins. "That is droll. He comes here in the vintage,—as if Beaumanoir, in those old cool green woods were not enough for one man! Has he aught to do with that little Waif, I wonder? No; not wittingly at least. Earl Eustace has none of these follies, and, if he had, would never drive a woman to desperation; such desperation as must have driven that one, whoever she be, to such a deed. He was betrayed, most foully, but he is no betrayer."

As the thoughts, disjointed and vague, passed through his mind, he made his way across the market-place, for once too absorbed in reflection and in memory to bid farewell to Ninette, or laugh an adieu with the dark, handsome matrons, and the old hardfeatured market-women, who were chaffering and chattering over the price of poultry and the ripeness of melons, while the Angelus rang from the belfry. That heavier and graver fit of musing lasted till he was out of the rampart-walls that still circled the small town with their relics of feudal fortifications, their ditches full of bulrushes and great campanula-flowers, their stones covered with lichens and with ivy. Then, when he was once more on the highway, with the noble champagne country stretching in vineyards, and rising in hills, around him, Tricotrin shook himself, as a big dog will shake his curls, and shook the alien depression off him; laughed his own mellow laughter at himself, and walked away at a swift, light pace, singing in the richest and most tuneful of tenors Béranger's

"Diogène,
Sous ton manteau
Libre et content je ris et bois sans gêne!"

till the browsing herds lifted their heads at the song, and the vine-laborers in the distance caught the air and hummed it back again, saying to each other, "Tricotrin must be near; you hear his *Diogène?*"

He went back to the place where the day previous he had lighted on the Waif.

The crumbled tower, so old that its history was lost in the days of Philip the Fair, with all the greenery clustering round its masonry, and the stream splashing under its base, had been abandoned to the bats, the owls, the hares, and to the widowed seventy year old Manon Virelois, who lived in its shelter very hardly, as she had said, maintaining life in her by sheer dint of the courageous, patient, hopeful thrift of her desolate old age.

The tower was approached by a perilous flight of stone steps which led straight into its interior; Tricotrin mounted them quickly, being as lithe and swift as a chamois, and entered the chamber. It was the only one that could be used for human occupance, but clean, and brightened with French skill, and with the radiance of the autumnal creepers that forced themselves through the crevices and grew profusely over the inner walls. In the center of the gray room, moreover, the old woman herself made a point of picturesque color, where she sat with an orange kerchief pinned under her chin, and the sun on the dark blue serge of her gown, as she spun on and on at her spinning-wheel, looking up with a cheery smile as he came to her.

"Well, my good friend? what news of the little one?"

"No news," answered Tricotrin. "Nobody knows anything about her, and to the best of my belief never will. I have told what we saw to the Mayor—good, stupid soul—and the police are on the lookout about it, but as yet there is no clew to who dropped her there. She must have been laid down very early at sunrise, before anybody was stirring."

"No doubt! Ah! the wicked wretches"—and grand'mère whirled her wheel with furious mutterings of horror and imprecation upon the unknown hands of the infant's deserters.

Tricotrin listening amusedly, let her wrath expend itself uninterrupted, while at the same moment an inner door that stood a little open was acting as an oaken frame to the subject of their speech, who stood like some old-world painter's cherub, with a large plume of white lilies in one hand, the other pushing back from her brow the clusters of her golden curls.

Tricotrin surveyed her in silence, and she surveyed him,—a singularly lovely child, with great, dark, meditative eyes, and limbs like a sculptured Cupid's scarcely concealed by the little loose linen shirt she wore, dropping off her snowy chest.

"So! there you are, my friend? Are you not ashamed to face me?" said Tricotrin, at length. "How obstinate is your sex! Now, if you were heiress to an empire, or if the fate of some great race depended on you, the first puff of cold wind would kill you, just out of the contradictory malice of things. A mere unowned bagatelle, a smuggled trifle of straw, a nameless, purposeless bit of drift-wood, without even your origin marked on you, a spurious coin without date or stamp of the mint, you flourish just because you are wanted no more than a stray mongrel puppy, and are of not so much consequence as a lost bunch of keys. Are you not ashamed of yourself?"

"Tricotrin," murmured the grand'mère reproachfully, "how can you talk so to that little angel, when you know your heart is full of pity for the——"

"Waif," interrupted Tricotrin. "Certainly I pity her. I pity every new creature tumbled, nilly-willy, into this ill-managed world. Besides, she must grow up a bad woman. Born under a contraband flag, there will be nothing for her but to join the pirates. She will not be to blame. The minute she was born the law drew a bar between her and the sunlight. She must, of necessity, steal the very few sugar-plums she will ever get, in the darkness of lawlessness. She is branded without deserving it. When she is old enough to see that ugly, unmerited brand, stamped there for no sin of her own, she will be one of a thousand if she do not do something to justify the scorch of the iron."

The child, who had stood as if listening, gathering confidence, sprang, in a sudden sunny impulse, on to the old woman's lap, and held up her lilies to Tricotrin.

"'Garde! si zoli!"

Tricotrin nodded assent to the lisped words.

"You would intend to say that though you are born without sugar-plums you contrive to console yourself with flowers; which is symbolical of the fact that nature is often kind to what man kicks? I concede the proposition. Nature is a shocking Socialist; that is why she is shut out from forum, school, and pulpit. She is a white-robed Hypatia, whom the saints stone, lest her teachings should unseat them,—and there is no venom like the venom of the Cyrils of the Creeds."

"Mon Dieu! to bewilder the precious infant with all that wisdom!" murmured grand'mère, concluding that it must be wisdom by a rule that often actuates the world's acceptance of unproved sagacity,—namely, that it was completely unintelligible. "Is she not lovely, the little darling? What a woman she will make!"

"Humph!" said Tricotrin, musingly; "she is well enough. Beauty, to a woman who has no name, no father, and no money, is much like the bloom to an unnetted peach—only a signal for the wasps to sting, and the flies to fasten, and the thieves to steal. Had she been ugly it would not have been such a sin against the future to have rescued her. You, and I, and Mistigri did a great wrong. I am afraid we owe her something."

"And you will help me to keep her, Tricotrin, if nothing is found?" cried the old woman, caressing the child's golden head.

"What does she call herself?" he asked, parrying the question.

"Only that one word, Viva."

"Viva? Not a bad name for a little pirate, and that is what she will turn, no doubt, out of vengeance for having been smuggled into this rough existence, like a bale of silk smuggled on to a rocky shore."

Tricotrin smoked in silence some moments, contemplating the Waif, who, leaving her protectress with all the ungrateful vivacious caprice of childhood, had thrown herself down within the doorway, laughing and playing with Mistigri, who had no aversion to a game at any time. She was perfectly happy now, whatever the future held in store. In her young form life was a rosebud just thrust forth into the light of the world; if in the bud a canker festered it would not be seen until leaf after leaf should have unclosed, and fallen beyond recall.

The old dame glanced first at one, then at the other; and set her spinning-wheel whirling again. She had a certain awe of Tricotrin; holding the credence prevalent in her country that he was the Wandering Jew, could turn dead leaves into gold at pleasure, could heal the sick and smite the healthy, call down storms and call up whirlwinds, become invisible and be always omniscient. So she did not dare attempt an interruption to his musing, but left him to his own thoughts,—thoughts ranging over a career filled with the mirth of Piron, the love of color and of fragrance of Dufresny, the philosophies of Diderot, the adventurous fortunes of Le Clos.

His erratic, careless, glorious open-air life was mellow as good wine, and radiant as noon; yet he too, like the child, was a Waif and Stray. It moved him with a certain sympathy for her, which tempted him not to cast her forth on chance. For the fragile porcelain of a female child's existence might perish on the rapids of that stream of hazard, where the strong gold-dashed bronze of a bold male life could float and vanquish.

Suddenly, still with his attention on her, he drew out his violin and touched the strings. It had belonged to Blanchini, and had often lulled Pauline Borghese to slumber, while its sounds floated over the orange grove at Rome. Tricotrin bent his head over it, and played one of those divine melodies of Lulli's, such as used to echo down the alleys of Versailles, and breathe over the voluptuous limbs of Coustou's goddesses.

He was a master of its melody, such as an age sees only once or twice in its generation. Laughing like some troop of revelers,—sobbing like some life worn out by pain,—rich as a carol of choristers' voices,—sad as the moaning of winds through the sea-pines,—the music followed his will as the souls that he moves follow the moods of a great poet, who wakes tears or raillery at his wish, and reaches now to heaven, and penetrates now into the darkness of hell.

As he thus played, the child, lying in a breadth of sunshine, glanced up and listened. Gradually the lilies dropped from her hands, her playmate was neglected, her face flushed with wondering awe, her eyes grew humid, her mouth parted in breathless delight. She never moved or made a sound, but heard, spell-bound to the last.

He laid the instrument aside and looked at her.

"You have a soul—a good deal of it for a female thing; though I am half afraid you have only just sufficient to get you into mischief. You will never be a saint, a martyr, or a heroine, my friend: but I should not be surprised if you develop into a Pompadour or a Cabarrus. Well, that was your lottery. If you had gone on playing I would have had nothing to do with you; as you answer to my music I will have something. I do not want you; you will be a nuisance; but saving your life is almost as bad as giving it you, and, after your unknown parents, I am the most guilty person toward you. I have not much for myself; I shall not have much for you; but, if nothing better come up for you, if nothing be learned of your rights, we will see what we can do to let Grand'mère Virelois keep you, since she has such a taste for the trouble."

"The Holy Virgin bless you!" cried the old woman. "You will adopt her?——"

"Far from it. No wise man binds himself. Though I am here to-day, I may be in the moon to-morrow. Life is a game of chance; so much the better. We should be stifled if chance did not now and then kick a throne into space, and give the accolade to a beggar, to redress the balance and clear the atmosphere. Adopt her? No. But, as I said, I will help you to keep her. She will not cost much yet awhile; and there may be sillier ways of spending coins than in floating a Waif,—though I doubt it. And I do not expect much of her future. She has a soul; but female creatures with yellow locks, and mouths like scarlet japonica buds, always kill any soul in them they may have been born with as rapidly as possible when once they are launched on the world——"

"Ah hush, Tricotrin!" murmured grand'mère, entreatingly. "All that I can do to teach her aright I will. You know that."

"Surely I do. But the teachers most likely to get hold of such a woman as the Waif will be, are two devils,—Vanity and the Desire of Riches. If you know how to exorcise them, Amie Virelois, you know what has beaten all the dealers in new creeds since the world began. Mademoiselle Viva!—you will not like Life. 'Plus aloës quam mellis habet,'—specially for your sex. All I say is, when you find out how much better it would have been to have embraced a golden opportunity, and died among the clematis, do me the justice to remember that it was your own obstinacy, and no lack of my good counsel, that made you prolong your existence."

With which farewell address Tricotrin turned to the old peasant, and in a few serious phrases explained to her the total ignorance prevalent through the district of any clew, or even suspicion, that could lead them to identify the deserters of the child, and settled to provide her with the small sum necessary for the young creature's maintenance, so long as nothing occurred to make it possible to enforce her maintenance from those on whom its duty rested. In the absence of this, the foundling, without him, would have gone to public charity. Partly out of the sympathetic compassion instinctive in him, chiefly out of the knowledge of the poor old woman's poverty and desolation, which his assistance would lighten and the infant's presence enliven, he promised to charge himself with the cost of the child, so long at least as nothing should be discovered of her rightful guardians.

Grand'mère Virelois knew well that the bond would never be broken, and that the money given her would come as surely as the spring or the autumn came; though she knew him also well enough to be aware that it was a thousand chances to one if he ever troubled himself to see again the thing that he protected. She knew his ways, and knew something also of his life, though it was clothed to her in that garb of fable, with which peasant superstition and exaggeration surrounded it.

The child, while her destiny was balanced and decided, played with Mistigri; something stilled by the effect the music had taken on her, but carelessly happy as only childhood can be, catching at the quivering sunrays on the floor with her hands, and burying her bright head in among her abundance of wood-lilies.

Tricotrin, as he passed away amid the old woman's thanks and praises, paused a moment beside his Waif, as the monkey leaped up to his shoulder.

"Mademoiselle Viva,—I wonder if you will ever make me repent having taken you out of your clematis coffin?"

Mademoiselle Viva laughed where she lay in the sunshine, pulling the snowy leaves impatiently to pieces of the lilies which she had found so fair, that she might reach their golden stamens.

"A bad omen!" said Tricotrin. "You are changeable and you are ungrateful:—of course you are, though, being feminine; you like that gold glitter, and do not care how the lilies die, so long as you get it. How early your sex shows itself!"

And with that he went out and down the crumbling stairway, singing his *Diogène*.

"What fools we are!" he thought. "Love freedom how we will, we are sure to bind ourselves with some unwelcome tie—a mistress or a spaniel, an Art or a Waif! Idiotcy! The child would have gone among the foundlings and grown up into a grisette or a nun; and now—she will look like a princess, and be reared like a peasant, and tease me I dare say all my life long!"

But pity, rather for the lonely tender-souled old woman, than for the stray child, had moved him to make the promise, and he would not draw back from it. Besides, one of the few sorrows of his joyous life had been when a young mother had lain dead in his arms with all her rich gitaña's beauty, colorless and breathless, like a broken pomegranate flower, and with his son of a day's life dead too in her bosom; for their sakes he had pity on this deserted thing, who also would be called a child of sin, who also might have vainly striven to find warmth at a heart whose pulse was still.

CHAPTER IV.

THE woodland nook in which he had found the Waif, and in which the old tower stood, was a piece of outlying forest-land, between the vineyards of one of the finest champagne districts of central France and the park of the château of Villiers, the chief, indeed for many leagues the only great demesne in those parts. It was a noble ancient place, that had once belonged to one of the highest races of the country, had passed through many owners' hands since the days of the Eighty-Nine, and had of late been purchased by the object of Ninette's homage, under whose domination it had again arisen to its long lost grandeur.

The park was like to that of St. Cloud; avenue rising above avenue on a steep hill-side, and Tricotrin ascended its broad winding roads beneath their succeeding aisles of trees, the Béranger chant rising also higher and higher, like the song of a lark, as he mounted the terraced slopes.

These stretched high and far; the forest and park of Villiers were of enormous extent, with the river flashing through them, on which the château itself looked down where it crowned the crest of the hill. Some two hours of swift walking brought him to the summit, and into the private gardens and avenues more immediately close to the house, which was itself a gray picturesque Renaissance pile, with many towers, many angles, much rich carving, much beautiful alternation of light and of shade.

He pushed open a gilded scrolled gate, looking up at the blazonry on the shield of its archway;—it was that of the arms of the foreign house of Estmere. He smiled as he saw them; and went through into the gardens.

A young man was at work among their gorgeous autumnal blossoms.

"Good day, Valentin," said Tricotrin, loitering a moment. "So you have a new lord?"

"A very good one," smiled the youth. "There is no lack of work here now, summer or winter."

"Good. And you have given up Paris?"

"I have, monsieur. I cannot be better than well off; and I am well off here."

"Quite right. It is a mistake, that over-centralization. Every soul rushing to the capital, and the country left a desert,—it is as if all the blood stayed in the heart: how would the sapless limbs move then? By-the-way,—why do you not marry Ninette?"

The young man colored, and destroyed a head of azaleas.

"Ninette is coy, monsieur,—she has seen these grand people here——"

"Pooh! Because you give the child time to think about them! She loves you, Valentin, but she wants to be more entreated to say so. Women scorn a timid lover; though shyness is the best tribute to their own power, you can never get them to appreciate it."

The gardener laughed and flushed with pleasure.

"Ah! you know how I adore her,—the little coquette! You know how my one desire is to win her as my wife!"

"Well,—tell her that boldly; you will conquer her. Give

her a wedding-ring and a hearth of her own, and she will think no more of the big people up at the château."

Valentin laughed happily.

"Ah! if I only thought she cared for me——"

"Simpleton! a man is not worth his salt who cannot get the woman he fancies. But if you let little Ninette think you only like her as well as you like Manon, and Rose, and Jacqueline, and Marthe, and all the girls of the village, why —of course she will begin to ponder on the '*beaux messieurs dorés*' up here."

Having left that suggestion to bear harvest in the good gardener's simple sincere soul, Tricotrin went onward; it was his way to scatter seeds of peace, and contentment, and reconciliation, and good counsel, in this fashion, without seeming to do more than cast light words most idly.

Valentin was the little peach-seller's first love; her fancy had subsequently been caught by the glitter of a life she could never reach, but Tricotrin knew enough of the village coquette's honest child-nature, through all her vanity, to know that her heart remained true to her early lover, and that she was of the temper, when once under the shade of her own vine, in the house of a husband, never to concern herself but about her fowls, and her flowers, and her Sunday earrings, and her spun linen, and the young children, who would play among the scarlet beans and yellow gourds of her garden. So,—a homely, innocent, pleasant life would be led in the fair grape country, instead of another lost one being added to the shoals of painted, drunken, ghastly, greedy lives, in the dens of Paris.

Through the gardens, with their statues gleaming white through groves of yew and cypress, Tricotrin passed on till he came close under the walls of the château, towering high above him, quaint, majestic, medieval, while from the peaked roof floated a standard, with the arms and coronet of the Estmeres on it.

He glanced up at the banner, then looked through a veil of flowering creepers that hung over a window near him;—a mullioned window, partially open, so that the chamber within could be seen. It was the old banqueting-room of the building; freshly restored, with rich deep hues of purple, and the soft gleam of dead gold, on panels, and floor, and ceiling; a splendid apartment, with its vast central table furnished forth as meals are set for princes. There were half a dozen servants, waiting noiselessly, but there was only one guest for them to serve. And he, as Tricotrin first saw him, made a motion with his hand for his attendants to withdraw, and as he was left alone sank back in his seat with a weary languor, his noon-breakfast scarcely tasted. He was a man some few years younger than the one who watched him, very tall, very fair, of a noble, thoughtful, northern beauty of feature, though his countenance was very grave, and shadowed with a look that had a restless, bitter, infinitely regretful melancholy on it.

He looked like a man on whom some heavy blow had fallen, and on whom its effects still endured, though striven against with all the strength and pride of a haughty and naturally tranquil temperament.

Tricotrin stood unseen, watching him in his solitude; and his eyes grew full of pity as he did so. He saw that this aristocrat amid his greatness was as weary and as desolate as a royal prisoner of state.

"Ah, Estmere!" he murmured, half aloud. "After all, how much happier am I than you!"

An impulse moved him to go within, to touch the hand that lay so listlessly beside the dishes of gold, to break the solitude that amid so much grandeur was lonely as peasants never are lone.

But though of a nature usually impulsive, he restrained the desire now; he remained quiet while gazing through the screen of foliage.

"I wish I could avenge him," he thought. "Four years have gone by, but the poisoned wound rankles still."

He turned away at length, after a long look, through which the man he watched never changed his position, but sat motionless and lost in thought, in the midst of his painted and velvet-hung chamber, on whose magnificence the noon sunlight of France was streaming.

"Ah, Mistigri!" murmured Tricotrin, as he passed out down the gardens, the one end of his visit thither accomplished. "Mine is the better choice. He is a prince in the purples, but under his ermine throbs the jagged nerve, wrenched by a vile wife's dishonor. You and I are happier, little one. If he have his grapes in a jeweled dish, we take ours out of their own vine-leaves, fresh from the vintage-feast. If he drink his burgundy under the shadow of costly frescoes, we drink ours under the green roofing of summer trees. If he have delicate patrician cheeks and hair diamond-studded to toy with, we have cheeks that bloom from the sun and the wind, and hair wreathed with the forest bowers. If he be great—we enjoy! Ours is the better portion, Mistigri. The only man happy is the man who is free. And the only man free is the man who is at once philosopher and wanderer. 'Sans pays, sans prince, et sans lois!' His country, the world,—his prince, his art,—his law, his conscience and his choice!"

And he went on, chanting once more the gay chant of the *Diogène* through the wooded slopes and down the terraces, while the distant joyous echo of his voice reached faintly to the ear of the solitary noble who sat within.

He heard it; and drew a deep breath that was almost a sigh.

"How carelessly that song sounds!" he thought. "Some vintager or forester, I suppose,—but surely a man who is happy!"

And the great man in his palace envied the careless singer.

CHAPTER V.

By the side of the Loire, on a wooded rock, stood a quaint little old building, picturesque, aged, cloister-like yet cottage-like, with an abundance of ivy clothing it from roof to base, in which so many thousand birds made their home that in the early summer the place seemed one mass of fluttering wings and joyous voices. Half of it had been knocked to ruins in the Fronde; the other half was worth very little, save to artists who loved its quaint nooks and angles, and the splendor of the panorama which stretched before it, of river, hill, and vineyard, with the towers and spires of Blois in the golden distance.

One of its gables held an oval deep-embrasured window, whose glass had long since perished and been replaced by coils of ivy hanging down across the aperture. The oval hole was high in air, in the topmost stones of the coping, beneath its red high sloping roof; but it served like a frame for a young face that looked out from it very often. The face of a woman-child of fifteen; a face with the richest of fair tints, with a beautiful scarlet mouth whose corners curled upward, with great dark eyes that were black with the soft glowing darkness of the antelope's, with a profusion of fair hair tossed backward, and tied with a blue fillet, to fall all over her shoulders at its own will.

It was a very lonely part of the riverside; Blois was only visible on a sunny day, and there were nothing but vineyards and peasant-proprieties for leagues around. Yet there had been no lack of the warmest, if not the most flattering, speakers, to tell the child of her beauty.

The old ferryman who would let her float for hours in his broad lumbering boat; the country people who when they passed her on their way to market would check their mules and give her their largest eggs, brightest fruit, sweetest honey; the vine laborers who would look up to catch a glance from her as they went to their work among the grapes; all

who came near her caressed her, spoiled her, lavished on
her all the kindliness and enthusiasm of their nation, and
christened her wherever she went "Le sourire de la Loire"
—"La Fille des Fées." And the smile of the beautiful
laughing river, beside whose banks all her short life had
passed, seemed caught on her face in its sunlight and beauty
where it looked out from the gloom of the oval embrasure.

She was listening with eager expectant pleasure, in the
stillness of the summer afternoon. All was quiet: her friend
the ferryman was mending an old brown sail under the shade
of his cottage, and the boat itself was motionless, casting a
long shadow across the water. Some way off, some children
in little blue blouses were playing under a sycamore with a
great gourd they could hardly roll. Very far down the stream
there was a barge, drifting lazily, with a load of hay, on
which the men who had mown it were stretched sound asleep
in the calm and the heat.

At every point where her eyes glanced there was a picture
of exquisite color, and light, and variety.

But the scene in its loveliness was so old to her, so familiar, that it was scarcely lovely; only monotonous. With
all a child's usual ignorant impatience of the joys of the
present—joys so little valued at the time, so futilely regretted
in the after-years—she was heedless of the hour's pleasure,
she was longing for what had not come.

Round a bend in the river a rowing boat came in sight.
The long straight stroke of oars in powerful hands sent the
little thing swiftly forward with pleasant and even pace. At
times it loitered while the rower let his sculls lie at rest and
gazed in peaceful indolence down the rush of the stream. At
times he brought it onward, gently and easily, down the rapid
current through the hot and fragrant day, between the landscapes of the vine-hung banks. Every now and then, from
under the shade of his sombrero, his eyes glanced up at the
distant cottage smothered in its chestnuts and its cork-trees;
and with the ripple of the waters his voice sung to the rhythm
of a Venice barcarolle, a rowing song of Turkish boatmen.

The Allah-hu! of the Golden Horn went echoing softly over the width of the Loire; and the bargemen looked up from their indolent rest in the hay, and the children left off their game with the gourd, and the old ferryman dropped the heavy end of his sail to shade his eyes from the sun with one hand, as they heard the song, and saw the boat, and smiled with one accord:—for it was Tricotrin.

The child saw and heard too; laughed with delight; balanced herself with an upward agile spring till her foot rested on the stone coping of her window-seat; and leaping lightly down off the jutting stones that formed a sort of crazed and crumbling irregular stairway from her casement to the ground, ran as fleetly as a young deer down the slope to the river-bank, and reached it just as the boat-keel grated there.

"Viva!"

He passed his hand over her hair with a tender caress as she threw her arms about him with the abandonment and welcome of an ardent, graceful child, lifting her lovely mouth, like a red camellia bud, up for the kiss which he gave it lightly.

"Viva!" he cried, "of a surety you have the most inherent pertinacity in living of any creature ever born! Nothing but a chamois—or a Waif—could have sprung down that wall by the jutting stones. You have a marvelous trick of thriving on what would have killed any other. Still—*tant va la cruche à l'eau, etc.* Take care!"

Viva laughed up in his face.

"If I had fallen, *you* would have been there! What matter then?"

"But—I may not be 'there' always! Do not lean on a reed, little one. To depend on another is to walk upon crutches: and the best crutch is but a sorry exchange for sound limbs. Ah! Mistrigi wants to get at you; take her. And you have been well all this while?"

"Why! I am always well!" laughed the child in the exultant security of her own perfect strength and health.

"I do not think I know what pain is. But for what a long time you have been away! I thought you would never come!"

Tricotrin shrugged his shoulders.

"Mignonne,—I cannot let even a Waif be a tie. I have enjoyed myself; and so have you, I do not doubt?"

"Oh, I enjoy myself," answered the child, with a certain disdain for the fact. "But Adèle says it is 'provincial' to enjoy."

"And who may this kill-joy and cynic of an Adèle be, I pray you?"

"She is at the convent;—a noble's daughter," said the Waif, still clinging to him with one hand, while she held Mistigri with the other. "But I forgot—you must be tired; you must want to eat?"

"Tired?—no. Hungry?—yes. I have been rowing three leagues, and have had only a draught of red wine on the way. Have you anything in your larder, little one?"

"Oh yes! There is some galette, and plenty of chestnuts; and a guinea-hen, though I am afraid she is a little old, and some fruit."

"Enough! It is a supper for a king."

"You will come in now?"

"To get it?—yes. To eat it?—*pas si bête!* Never spend time indoors when you can spend it out of doors. Stay. Run and bring me something, while I fasten the boat. Grand'mère is washing, I see; that is a sacred and solemn business. Tell her I will see her later on, when the linen shall have reposed in peace."

The child flew off on her errand, the cloud of her fair hair flying behind her on the wind, to where the little figure of the old peasant woman, older but none the less active, bent over a great washing-tub among the scarlet-flowering beans of her garden. Grand'mère had grown deaf, and the height of the beans had prevented her seeing the arrival.

Tricotrin dragged his boat up on the bank, high and dry upon the grass, fastened it to a tree, and had only just finished tying the rope when his Waif returned with both hands laden; the sunshine like a halo of gold round her head, her face beaming with delight, and the warmth of the day and the kiss of the wind.

"This is all I can find. Will that do? That gray cat of Sarazin's has stolen the fowl," she said, as he hastened to take her burden from her, with the courtesy he would sooner have omitted to a queen than to a foundling.

"Do? It is a meal for the gods! But you are feminine, Viva; it is not for you to serve me."

"I would serve none *but* you."

"Verily? Then you are wrong, my child. You should serve all the old and the poor. Nevertheless, I thank you for your preference. And now—let us go to your favorite tree."

The tree was at some little distance from the cottage where he had placed his Waif and her guardian,—a huge old beech-tree with wide-stretching arms of shelter and welcome, and moss-lined couches in the depths of its great trunk, and abovehead a broad crown of fresh green leaf. The tree stood some way from the river, yet close enough for all the babble of the water to be heard amid the deep-grown woodland wilderness that surrounded it; woodland ending only where the vineyards met it.

And here, in the hollows of the massive boles, was the Waif's favorite throne; a throne where the child would sit through many sunny hours, watching the birds' flight, and the movement of the insects in the blue depths of the aconite and the purple glories of the gorgeous belladonna; a throne without one care in its eminence, one cruelty in its embrace.

Twelve years had passed by since the Waif had been found among the clematis; and those twelve years had been full of the long, sweet, spontaneous pleasures of childhood. True, she lived simply in a river-side cottage, with an old and unlearned woman for her only companion, whose chief cares were the eternal wants of the *pot au feu*, and the health of the hens scratching in the garden. But then that old woman loved her with a passionate and most tender adoration; that cottage, with its little chambers that were like so many interiors of Teniers and Van Tol's, was the only home she knew. Fruits and flowers, and the singing of birds and of waters, and the picturesque life of the vine-fields, and the plenteous joy of the harvests, made up the golden sum of her young days; and from the night-time, when she fell asleep in her little white nest under the eaves, with prayers muttered above her, to the sunrise when she awoke, full of eagerness for the unworn innocent hours that the mere sense of existence made sweet to her as they are sweet to the young birds thrusting themselves forth in the spring-tide, Viva had led the pure bright life of a child in the country, and been happy in it as only children are.

She had thriven with marvelous perfection, as though in rebellion against the fate that had cast her out to perish. She had grown in grace and strength on her hard brown bread and her draught of goat's milk, as kings' daughters will not thrive in palaces. She had sprung up radiant, lovely, laughing, fearless, under the shelter of the crumbling roof, as a plume of golden-rod will blossom under the leaning wall of a ruin. And he who had first taken pity on her, had never since that hour deserted her.

He had seen her at intervals,—widely distant ones for several years, closer to each other as she grew older; but wherever he wandered, however long he was absent, the old dame, Virelois, was always certain that twice in the year would come, as sure as seed-time and reaping-time, the sum which he had promised her, to succor her poverty and maintain the Waif.

The child knew her history; he forbade her to be kept in secret of it. Nothing had ever been learned that could give a clew to the origin of her birth, or the motive of her abandonment; and Viva, fed on fairy-lore by her foster-mother, believed herself devoutly the offspring of elfin loves. She delighted to think herself not wholly mortal.

Any sense of shame, or of desolation, had never been permitted to touch her; and the kindly-natured peasantry of the district, sharing a little too in her own view of her fairy-parentage, caressed her, admired her, and treated her with a sort of homage that was due, partly to her own exceeding beauty, and partly to the reverent love in which they held her protector; and which did its uttermost to turn her childish head with vanity and willfulness, and persuade her that she was of very different mould to the common, sunburnt, toil-marked clay around her. For Viva—a Waif and Stray, nameless and homeless, found wrapped in a bit of red serge, and saved by a monkey stretching out a little horny, black hand—was as proud as though the blood of all the Cæsars had warmed her clear rosy cheeks.

The pride was fostered in her by many things: by the adulation of grand'mère, who incessantly fondled her, as something beyond earth in her loveliness; by the deference, of the few people whom she ever saw, to the charms and caprices of her graceful infancy; by the ignorance even of her own origin, which left her parentage a blank that could be filled up by imagination with every gorgeous and wondrous picture. This wayward and baseless pride had been nourished by every creature who approached her, save one; and that one Viva loved better than all others.

All the child's affectionate, wayward, contradictory little soul spent itself in love for Tricotrin. All she had that pleased her,—the blue ribbon for her hair, the bonbons in their silvered papers, the music that told her of such entrancing fables of unknown worlds, the pretty ivory chain that hung round her neck which was as white as itself,—all came to her from his hands, for though without riches himself, he could give what seemed riches to the fancy of a young lonely creature; and he who abhorred a tie—even a tie of love—had grown to feel an irresistible fondness for the thing whose life he had saved. Such fondness as was but an instinct with the warm, liberal, compassionate heart of the man for a being so utterly dependent on him.

The life that lay behind him had been filled with many

loves. His painter's eyes and poet's fancy had seen beauty in many female forms, under the suns of many lands; but nothing purer, and in its way, nothing deeper, had ever touched him than the tenderness that he had given his Waif. He had saved her as he would have saved a wood-pigeon from the trap, a hare from the netted snare, and had thought to concern himself no more with her than with the pigeon that flew, or with the hare that fled, away from him, rejoicing in release. But in his own fashion Tricotrin, who acknowledged no law but his conscience, obeyed what he deemed duty, even when obedience went hardly against him; and, to his own thinking, having brought this existence out from the death that had been assigned to it, he had a right bound upon him to see how it fared, and into what semblance it grew.

He loved the vine countries well, and with most grape-harvests came to them. Thus he had never wholly lost sight of his foundling; and Viva adored him with a passionate faith and reverence that she yielded to no one else, and which was rather increased than diminished by the rarity of his presence and the uncertainty of his visits. For these invested him in Viva's eyes with the grandeur of a king in disguise, and the miraculous advent of one who was not as other men are.

On the whole, the Waif fared better, having fallen to the hands of a vagabond-philosopher, than if she had drifted to those of a respected philanthropist. The latter would have had her glistening hair shorn short, as a crown with which that immoral and inconsistent socialist Nature had no justification in crowning a foundling; and, in his desire to make her fully expiate the lawless crime of entering the world without purse or passport, would have left her no choice, as she grew into womanhood, save that between sinning and starving. The former bade the long fair tresses float on the air, sunny rebels against bondage, and saw no reason why the childhood of the castaway should not have its share of childish joyousness as well as the childhood prince-begotten and palace-cradled; holding that the fresh life just budded on earth was as free from all soil, no matter whence it came, as is the brook of pure rivulet-water, no matter whether it springs from classic lake or from darksome cavern.

"A meal for the gods!" said Tricotrin, taking out the contents of Viva's basket. "Figs, pears, a melon, and white bread! Why, extravagant one, what were you dreaming of, to apologize for such a fair feast? Horace could not have wanted a better. This is my *fiambreras*, as the good Knight of Mancha phrased it. But the Don consoled himself for short commons with a long name and a vast show. We are wiser than that. We have the fruits of the earth, without bombast——"

"I wish there were something better though! That cat is such a thief!" said the Waif with a sigh, looking down on him from where she was sitting aloft in the curved trunk of the huge beech-tree.

"Better? foolish child! Ask Mistigri. There could be nothing better when I add my flask of wine, which it never does to leave to chance. Here is honey, sweet as that of Hymettus; bread to be the prose of corn to the poetry of fruit; and Rhenish that Schiller loved, with all the Rhine legends steeped in it. I would not change these, for all the cooks whose art consists in leaving you in ignorance as to whether you are eating fish, flesh, or fowl. And now, since it is no fun to look on at others' meals, and you say you have had your own, try some bonbons, *ma mie!*"

He tossed upward to her as he spoke several bright-colored packets of sweetmeats, gilded and silvered in the floral French fashion; and Viva caught each in its turn with a laugh of delight. She had just fifteen years, but she was a true child in heart, and if her mother had been a fairy, that fairy must have been French.

"I am glad they please you," said Tricotrin, looking up to catch the smile on her face where it beamed down on him through the beech-leaves. "Up at Blois last night Madame Dentrée's daughter was married. There was a grand bridal feast, of course. She has wedded well, to a rich young tanner of Sèvres, and I played for them till the dawn. *Dieu!* how they danced!—all those young men and maidens. The mother was pleased, and this morning she would have emptied half her bonbon-shop on me for you. She is a good woman, the Dentrée, and a rich tanner is a son-in-law to put one in good humor."

"I have never been to Blois," murmured the Waif, bending over her cornucopias of sweetmeats, which, though she would not have said so, were a little embittered to her by being the gifts of a pastry cook.

"No. Keep out of cities while you can. The range of old Sarazin's ferryboat is far enough for your wanderings at present. And how do you agree with the Sisters?"

"I hate them!" said the child, with flashing eyes.

"And wherefore?"

"Oh!—they hate me," murmured Viva.

"Indeed? Then I fear you must deserve it?"

"I dare say I do. They are so silent, so lifeless, so cold, so gray; there is no good in them! I love light, warmth, laughter, color,—*you* know!—and they talk folly, they say these are all vanity, that life should be one long psalm of humility, and denial, and sacrifice. Bah! it would be like living to wear tight bands of irons!"

"And you have a preference for rose-chains? Well— you and the Sisters look at life with the difference of eyes that have only been open for fifteen years, and eyes that have ached wearily for forty-five. A great contrast in vision,— that!"

"But *you* are forty-five?"

"And more. But I am a man, and any man who is not a fool or a criminal, can keep youth in him all the days of his life. But women!—and women behind the iron bars of a grating! But you only go to the convent to learn, Viva; why should you vex your soul at captivity you do not share?"

"Why?" replied the child, her pretty glad voice growing swifter and more eager. "They are forever rebuking me,—

not for learning; I *will* learn, though I abhor it, because you wish me, and because you say that knowledge is power,—but for frivolity as they call it, and impetuosity, and willfulness, and giddiness, and pride! They tell me I should be patient, and quiet, and lowly in mind, and as one in servitude always; that I have no right to be proud, and ought to think a vine-dresser as good as myself; that to be plain and virtuous is lovelier to God than to be handsome and wayward as I am!—that—oh! I could tell you for hours the tedious things that they lecture me on!——"

"Humph! So you are conscious of beauty, waywardness, pride, and frivolity, my friend? A nice quartette of qualities? 'Know thyself,' said the sage; certainly you obey him."

"But that is not all!" cried Viva, with burning cheeks, and eyes to which proud passionate tears started "There are two or three children there—that Adèle is one of them, a count's daughter!—and they are awkward, and heavy, and ungraceful in everything, yet they think themselves above *me!* And they are rude—very rude—grand'mère says because they are jealous of me; and they laughed in my face when I told them my mother was a fairy, and they twit me with having no name, with being only—as they say—a *thing* that is called Viva, like a cat or a dog!"

She threw back her head while she uttered the words that had wounded her, as though in haughty repellance of their power to sting. Nor indeed did they pierce with the humiliation which she would have felt had she not been guarded from all knowledge of possible shame in her birth, and had not her fancy-fed imagination genuinely believed the fantastic story of fairy origin, that grand'mère had woven to satisfy her eager questionings without pain.

Tricotrin looked up at her, and a smile of tender and infinite pity came on his lips.

"So soon!" he murmured to himself. "They might let you enjoy your bright brief dawn; it will swiftly be over! So the children cast shame ere they should know what shame is! We cannot wonder at the great world, then."

"Viva mine," he said aloud at length. "As for the Sisters' offences, they are nothing,—the good women mean well by you, and you have such willfulness and pride, *ma mie*, that you may well bear with some few sermons on your besetting sin. But for the rest, since you *are* proud, do you not know that the proud never let the barbed shafts of malicious tongues wound them? The words which hurt you are words of jealous mouths, you think; well, do you not know that jealousy is, and has been from all time, a liar and a slanderer?"

The child looked softly at him.

"But it is *true?* I have no name? I am not as others are?"

The fairy fabric of her elfin birth, although so devoutly and innocently believed in, was not wholly proof against the scoff and the taunt which had moved her. Already Viva was beginning to feel the power of that impalpable tyrant of "the world"—embodied for her in the small form of a little French girl, with a shrill mocking voice, and a "*de la*" appended to her name in voucher of nobility.

Tricotrin looked at her with pitying tenderness.

"Not as others? Why, my Waif? Is your foot less swift, your limb less strong, your face less fair, than theirs? Does the sun shine less often, have the flowers less fragrance, does sleep come less sweetly, to you than to them? Nature has been very good, very generous to you, Viva. Be content with her gifts. What you lack is only a thing of man's invention, a quibble, a bauble, a pharisee's phylactery. Look at the river-lilies that drift yonder, how white they are, how their leaves inclose and caress them, how the water buoys them up and plays with them! Well? are they not better off than the poor rare flowers that live painfully in hothouse air, and are labeled, and matted, and given long names by men's petty precise laws? You are like the river-lilies; oh child! do not pine for the glass house that would ennoble you, only to force you, and kill you!"

Viva smiled, following with quick fancy the picturesque metaphor; but she was not wholly content to be a river-flower, she wanted to bloom under the silver spray of palace fountains: she hung her graceful head on one side, in half arch, half pensive meditation.

"But—it is not pleasant to have no name. Only a nickname that means nothing; like the kitten Bébé, like the cock Roi Doré?——"

Tricotrin's humorous smile laughed on his lips; he had struck on a vein of amused thought that wandered away from herself.

"Is it not?" he laughed in answer. "Ask Bébé and Roi Doré;—they will tell you that so long as the voices they love call them, and the name serves to summon them to good food and good drink, it answers every purpose that a king's string of titles can do. Bah! little one! Be more of a philosopher. A name is a handle only; if the pot go soundly to the well, and if it bring back cool pure water for thirsty mouths, what matter how the handle be fashioned?"

Viva, accustomed to follow and catch the fantastic meanings of his phrases, knew well what he meant, but was not prepared to be convinced by it: she had a strongly-developed will of her own.

"That may be," she said, with a charming mutinous pout of her lovely lips. "Still—when one is a pretty porcelain pot it is ugly to have a broken osier handle, and to only go to the well as if one were of brown old earthenware?"

Tricotrin laughed more and more.

"So you think yourself of pretty porcelain, my dainty little bit of Sèvres? oh-hè! Well! I will warrant you will never be of so much use to others as if you were a homely brown pipkin. But to be proud of your uselessness is a thing that has not my sympathies."

The child colored; conscious of the satire and of the rebuke.

There is no pipkin that would not change, and be porcelain, if it could!" she murmured, with a certain pleading petulance.

"Well—that does not say much for the good sense of the pipkins then, if it be true. But I don't think it is true. There is many a sturdy, honest, sensible pipkin that would rather be going to the well twenty times a day, to have the children's thirsty throats, and the hot window-flowers, and the poor chained dogs, and the little feverish birds in cages, all grateful to it, and made happy by what it brings, than it would be a porcelain trifle, standing all the year round in a velvet-lined cabinet, only valued for the paint on its glaze, and liable any minute to be bought and sold as a chattel. I would rather be the pipkin, Viva; but you, I suppose, sigh for captivity and idleness among a collector's bric à brac?"

The child laughed too, but she gave a little quick sigh, and a hot flush for her chidden vanity and her own sense of its unwisdom.

"But is it so wrong to be proud?" she asked, dropping, female-like, the pipkin and porcelain symbol, so soon as she found it tell against her own argument.

"Proud? In what way, Viva?"

"Any way! To be impatient of grand'mère's friends because they talk such bad patois, and are only old ignorant women! To burn with hatred, and jealousy, and evil, at my first communion, because that Adèle had a wreath on of real silver, and scoffed at my beautiful lilies and lilacs because they were only real flowers!"—

"'Only!'" murmured Tricotrin.

"To be full of wrath with dear old grand'mère because she will bake, and wash, and sweep, though I know it is so good of her to do it! To be wayward and bitter, and long to avenge, when the children talk at me as though I were a peasant! To loathe to confess it when I know I am wrong; to long for sovereignty, and supremacy, and luxury, and power; to feel I would die rather than serve; and to disdain anything that is poor, and ugly, and meek, and without grace! Oh, how proud in all ways and at all hours!"

Tricotrin smiled as he heard her self-accusation, but he looked at her mournfully.

"Viva mine, you are not a philosopher: but it is a little early perhaps for that, and besides, nothing feminine ever was, I suppose. Wrong to be proud, you ask? No. But then the pride must be of a right fashion. It must be the pride which says, 'Let me not envy, for that were meanness. Let me not covet, for that were akin to theft. Let me not repine, for that were weakness.' It must be the pride which says, 'I can be sufficient for myself. My life makes my nobility. And I need no accident of rank, because I have a stainless honor.' It must be pride, too proud to let an aged woman work where youthful limbs can help her; too proud to trample basely on what lies low already; too proud to be a coward, and shrink from following conscience in the confession of known error; too proud to despise the withered, toil-worn hands of the poor and old, and be vilely forgetful that those hands succored you in your utmost need of helpless infancy!"

The sweet melodious tones of his voice, that grew infinitely gentle, almost solemn, as the last words left his lips, went straight to the loving, wayward heart of the child they rebuked. She threw herself down beside him in lowly passionate repentance; her fair face burning with contrition, her mouth trembling, her eyes brimming with great tears.

"Oh yes, yes! If they would only speak *so*, I would listen! I am wrong, I am rebellious, I am wicked, and I care too much for the things that are vain; but indeed, indeed, I am never ungrateful!"

Tricotrin, who would at any moment have sooner faced a flaming city, or a swarming barricade, than seen the tears of anything feminine, above all of anything he loved, passed his hand over her hair with a caress.

"To be sure not!" he said cheerily. "No one suspects you of such baseness! As for your desire for sovereignty.—

believe me there is none like the royalty of youth. Rejoice in that kingdom while it is yours; it will pass from you all too soon. And, for 'the things that are vain,'—you are feminine, as I say, and must love them I suppose according to your sex. But if you think a wreath of beaten-out metal produced from a jeweler's workshop equals the lilies and lilacs of a spring-blossoming earth, why,—you are no artist, my Waif, but a creature of acquired tastes, and innate vulgarities, as, judging by their choice of appareling, I often fear that all women are!"

The child laughed, but her tears were still on her long, curling lashes, and the words he had spoken had sunk into her heart.

She was silent, and he let her be so while she lay at his feet, her arms cushioned on the moss, and her head drooped on her hands, in the unconscious grace of a young resting stag.

"Proud as a queen, and among the base-born. Lovely as the dawn, and without a mother or a name. Willing to perish rather than yield, and a woman! It needs no horoscope to cast her fate!" murmured Tricotrin in English to the monkey, the language being one unintelligible to Viva, though familiar to him. "Ah Mistigri, Mistigri! shall you and I ever be reproached at the last? Had we better have let the thread of life be broken at the onset than have saved it to reel out, all glistening gold at first, all knotted tangles at the end? Porcelain?—yes! Such delicate, dainty, bright-hued porcelain! And how will it come out from the furnace?"

A certain sadness touched him where he sat under the broad beech-boughs, with the fruit and the bread for his noontide meal. He loved her well, loved her with patient and most gentle tenderness; but he knew neither whence she came nor whither she went—this young life that he had rescued—and it was possible that the time might dawn for both when each would deem it had been well if she had never awakened from her infant's sleep among the clematis.

"Want a palace while there is a forest! Little stupid!

What a thoroughly feminine animal you are, preferring the artificial to the natural—the lesser thing that is unobtainable to the greater thing that lies in your path!" he cried suddenly, rousing himself and the child from their mutual reverie.

"A wood is very nice!" said Viva, with her head on one side glancing under the boughs that had flung their green and welcome shadows on her through all the summers since she had been first trusted to their shelter as a Waif. "But—oh! to see those palaces of Paris! What would I give——"

"Your soul, little simpleton, to learn the madness of your barter too late!" he thought, as he answered her aloud.

"A wood 'nice'? Bah! you are a Goth, Viva mine. Why, there is nothing so beautiful on earth as the rich virgin growth of wild trees. Look yonder!—the squirrels flitting everywhere, the kingfishers over that pool, the huge boughs all moss-draped, the glimpses of green distance just caught between the branches, the exquisite stillness and freshness and loveliness! What would gilded rooms and marble stairways give in fit exchange for that? Wise was Scipio to leave the heat, and noise, and legions, and tumult, and clangor of the mistress of the world for the cool green shade of his leafy solitudes!"

"Wise? Oh no!"

"And why 'oh no'? you who condemn Scipio?"

The child laughed: she had little historic knowledge, little knowledge indeed of any sort, but she had caught up some stray gleams of classicisms from Tricotrin at intervals.

"Why? Well! Because I would rather have perished in my prime amid all the dignities of Roman rule than have lived threescore years in retirement——"

"Qui respiciunt ad pauca di facili pronunciant," interpolated her companion with Aristotelian terseness.

"I don't know Latin!" said Viva with the pretty disdainful gesture of a spoiled child. "But,—I should love to be great, and I do not believe Philosophy can ever bo sweet and grand like Power!"

"I do not suppose you do. Philosophy never was popular with your sex, who always go by externals."

"They must be the surest test to go by," said the child quickly. "If a thing *look* very handsome it is as good as *being* handsome, is it not?"

"Oh, you young sophist! So you are content with appearances? A bad indication that. Philosophy, Viva, is the pomegranate of life, ever cool and most fragrant, and the deeper you cut in it the richer only will the core grow. Power is the Dead Sea apple, golden and fair to sight while the hand strives to reach it; dry gray ashes between dry fevered lips when once it is grasped and eaten. Now you, my friend, having tasted neither, decide without a moment's hesitation between them; while men who have steeped all their lives in one, or another, die without having been able to settle the selection!"

"Still"—persisted the child with a laugh at herself, and she paused in her sentence, for in the forest-track, which bent round through the trees within sight, came some six or eight riders, who caught the eager fancy and the wondering eyes of the Waif.

Her river-side home stood in such complete loneliness that save for the craft that passed up the Loire nothing gladdened her sight from season to season save the droves of the cattle or the market-mules of the peasants. Her thoughts of the beauty of power and the charms of magnificence were purely innate in her; she had never seen anything whatsoever to suggest them; and she stood now gazing at the party as they advanced, with as entranced a delight as though she beheld some celestial vision such as she read of in the books at the convent.

They were returning from hawking in the woods of Villiers, and were going leisurely, after some successful casts at herons, with all the customary trappings of green and scarlet and gold, of attendants in the picturesque forester-costume, of noble hounds panting and triumphant, of, in a word, all the costly panoply of French falconry revived in its utmost magnificence. Breaking suddenly, like a Louis Quatorze hawking picture put into motion, on the woodlawn solitude around her, they looked to Viva like some group called up by enchantment: she stood breathless, a beautiful picture herself, with her feet ankle-deep in cyclamen and mosses, her hair flying backward in the wind like two golden wings, and her head crowned with a green wreath of oak-leaves and maiden-hair that she had woven as she had talked.

With one accord the eyes of all the riders turned on her, in amazed admiration, as they passed by through the forest-way. Some called a gay greeting out to her, all gave her the homage of bold ardent eyes; one alone uncovered his head as he passed her and bowed low in deference to her sex.

He was the last rider of all; a tall, slender, stately man, with a haughty carriage and a fair-hued face, grave almost to melancholy.

They were gone like the breath of the wind, lost to sight in a turn of the path; but Viva stood, still entranced; with a scarlet glow on her cheeks and her eyes full of delight and desire.

She turned breathlessly to Tricotrin.

"Who is *he?*"

"Which *he*, petite?"—he had watched the horsemen pass without rising from his leaning posture beneath the beech.

"The one who bowed to me?"

"Why that one in especial, Viva? There were others much younger to pleasure you."

"But he only did *that!* Besides,—they all looked noble, but he alone looked great!"

"Creditable to your discernment, Viva. He *is* great— and he is as tired as ever Scipio was!"

"But his name?" persisted the child.

"His name? Well,—Eustace Estmere."

"Estmere? And what is he?"

"You have said—a great man. Repeat your *exaudi nos* for him, Viva."

"He cannot want it. He looks strong."

"The strong suffer."

"But so proud too?"

"And the proud suffer more."

Viva gave a heavy sigh:

"How I shall suffer then!" she murmured. "But does he live here? How is it I have never seen him?——"

"He owns Villiers; but he is rarely there; and it is three good leagues away."

"He *owns* Villiers!"

To Viva it made him as a monarch; once, once only, one fête-day, grand'mère had taken her to see Villiers; one summer-time when the people were permitted free range over the park and the gardens and the terraces, down the dim never-ending splendid galleries, and through the orangeries and the palm houses and the wilderness of flowers; the glories of Villiers had never ceased to haunt her imagination, though it too rarely came within range of her friend Sarazin's boat for her to have had a second chance of beholding this Versailles of her province. The man who could own it looked to Viva as the sovereign of France.

"And he bowed to *me!*" she repeated softly and exultantly under her breath.

"Chut, Viva!" interrupted Tricotrin somewhat impatiently. "In what does the bow of a noble differ from that of a peasant?—it is a chivalry to your sex in both, nothing more! Your Lord Estmere and I are appropriate symbols to accompany my pomegranate metaphor. He is power: I am philosophy. I lie at my ease on a bed of mosses that have not a thorn; I find their true taste in plain bread and purple grapes; I am without bond and without burden; I take no thought for the morrow; my mind is my kingdom and mankind are my brethren; where I will there I go, and I have none to dictate to me. Now my lord there!—

he wears the purple robe with the steel corslet heavy beneath; he sleeps on palace-beds and State care lies down with him; he is the proudest man of his order, and his honor is stung to the quick where he cannot shield it; the garter ribbon crosses his breast, and his heart aches under it with a pain never quiet; he is a great man, *ergo*, he is never free, wherever he goes thither comment and curiosity follow him, and no sorrow can be sacred that befalls him, because the chattering world must have it as prey. I have the pomegranate; he has the Dead Sea apple. And yet—so eternal is the duello between philosophy and power, and so little will either of those rivals yield to the other, that I would wager he would no more change places with me than I would change places with him!"

And Tricotrin, who in those words had forgotten the child he addressed, sank back again among his mosses with a laugh on his lips,—a laugh infinitely humorous, something tender, and a little, ever so little, sad.

Viva did not answer; the young aspirant to Power remained unconvinced.

CHAPTER VI.

"You are content with the little angel, Tricotrin?" asked Grand'mère Virelois that evening in the porch of the riverside house which she owed to him.

"As little of an angel as may be," said Tricotrin. "But I am as content with her as man ever can be with a feminine thing; which is not much to say. I am well content with your care of her, if you mean that, good friend. The child thrives as—nothing but a Waif whom nobody wants ever could do."

"Ah, Tricotrin! everybody wants her who sees her. She is as beautiful as the morning."

"Oh yes," murmured Tricotrin; "and the young tribunes will shout *ad leones!* and she will get flung down in the sands of the circus, 'butchered to make a *Parisian* holiday!'"

"Paris?" repeated grand'mère, catching but one word she knew. "You mean to take her to Paris?"

"Certainly not; but she will take herself some day, no doubt."

Grand'mère sighed heavily. Paris was a word of terror to her. She had never been out of her own grape-country; but it was there, yonder in Paris, that the marble block, lifted up to adorn a palace, had fallen, and crushed into a shapeless mass the noble young form of her first-born son; it was there also, that, amid the blood and the smoke of the barricades of the Thirty Days, the youngest mouth that had once lisped its prayers at her knee had murmured with its dying whisper, "*N'en dis rien à ma mère.*"

"Paris! Paris!" muttered the old woman, whirling her spinning-wheel, with the evening light about her in the old oaken doorway; "God forbid the child should get to Paris. What could she do but perish there?"

Tricotrin smoked in silence. It was never his way to disturb himself concerning the future. It was waste of thought and time, he considered. Rattle your dice how you would, you could never tell what the throw would be; unless, indeed, you turned gamester, and weighted the ivory of circumstance with the lead of dishonesty: which was not in his manner of dealing.

"Do you know, Tricotrin," continued grand'mère, "do you know, I often wonder what her fate will be, the precious child! You see, I am eighty-three next month; I have not very many more years before me; and she is so young, and you—good as you are—are not really her father. What will become of the little one? I may die any day, and you—you wander so far, you are away so long! What would become of the Viva if I died in your absence?"

"Never ask what will become of anything, grand'mère. It shows a curiosity highly unphilosophic; and very impertinent, too, in a good woman like you, who thinks Providence looks after every little detail, from an earthquake that kills ten thousand people, to the nail that tears the slit in your blue gown. What will become of the world? Nobody knows. If it disappear to-morrow it will not be missed in the universe. "There is a falling star; look at it, my dear!' some man in Jupiter will say to his wife. That will be all the world's monody."

"You will ever jest, Tricotrin," said the old woman, with a little shudder over her spinning-wheel. If he were the Wandering Jew, as some said, who knew but what he might have the mission of the world's sudden extinction to execute!

"I do not care about the world!" she resumed, "I have lived my time in it, and it is cruel—cruel! But the little treasure has all her time before her; and look you, *mon ami*, I get anxious as she grows older. While she was a child it was all right enough. Let a child have the sun and the air, and sweet milk, and plenty of love, and a child is happy,— happy on a bare floor and in a wooden cradle. But a young girl is different; and sometimes I wonder what will become of her. She is proud, she has the ways of a princess,—she is not a creature you can set to scrub, and bake, and sew. Among the flowers, on the water, singing where she sets in the trees, dancing when she hears boats go by with music,— that is Viva's life. But it will not be a good life for womanhood, when there is no name and no mother."

There was a pathos in the feeble, aged voice, as the speaker shook her head over her wheel, with the sun so bright on her brown face and her white cap, and the brilliant child for whom she feared, fluttering like an oriole in the distance among the scarlet beans and the low apple-trees.

True feeling never spoke in vain to Tricotrin. He bent gently and reverently to the bent old figure, while his eyes glanced to the gay form of his Waif.

"Nay, grand'mère, do not disquiet yourself," he said, earnestly. "The child is brave, proud, truthful. These are three grand safeguards against evil. She has much vanity, many caprices, too fond a craze for things out of her reach; but her heart is of gold; these foibles are but the foibles of sex. For her future, we must leave it. How can we say whither she goes? we, who do not even know whence she came! But I have good faith in the Waif; faith that she will not decline into evil, even if evil tempt her, which it shall never do while I live. For the rest, if aught ail you, tell the good women at the convent to look to her. You know that I love no churches; and I was ill pleased that you steeped the child in the acid and the poison of Creed. While women are nurtured on superstition the men born of them will never reach their full stature. But I let you have your own way in that matter because thus you get shelter for her, and thus you set at ease your own conscience. Let the nuns know if you dread anything for your health; and for the years to come, we must trust Viva herself. If she choose Luxury, having known Love, she will not be worth a regret!"

A certain darkness passed over his face as he spoke. There was that which jarred on him in the child's inborn and ineradicable desires for a different life than that to which he had saved her.

"That is true, Tricotrin," muttered grand'mère. "Still, it is the stars that fall, you know, so fast, so fast, through August nights! And it is just the proud ones who have not gold at the back of pride; it is just the beautiful ones who have but cottage-roofs over their beauty; that Paris devours —devours. Ah! is she not filled,—that cruel, terrible Paris,— with the flowers of the country, that give their sweetness to her to be trampled dead on the stones of her streets?"

There was a tragic force in the eloquence of the aged withered lips. Grand'mère was a simple, credulous, innocent old woman, who had led her long life ever under the shadows of the vines of her birthplace, but she had suffered,—specially had she never forgotten her youngest-born, whom that beautiful, fearful, resistless Paris had drawn in, in his boyhood, and his ardor, and his fearless faith, and who had been murdered among the children of France, when the streets ran blood in the days of July.

"True!" said Tricotrin, gently. "Paris is beautiful, and she is terrible, very terrible! For in her the highest and the lowest forms of humanity meet; in her the perfection of Pleasure stands side by side with the culmination of Vice. She is beautiful, she is terrible: for she is the epitome of human life. You are right, grand'mère: none can say what flower she may not draw in—to bloom in unnatural brilliance a moment, and perish of the air that forced it, a trodden thing beneath men's feet!"

"Yes; and therefore the child——"

"*Allons donc!* The child is a child; leave her to the future. Sufficient for the day is the evil thereof. Why take thought for her womanhood? Thinking will not avert it. 'If the cucumber be bitter throw it away,' says Antoninus. Do the same with a thought."

"But it is not possible always."

"Paf! I think it is. There is no cucumber so bitter that honey will not put the taste of it out; and no cucumber so heavy that one cannot throw it over some wall. You have reared her well, grand'mère,—barring that little touch of church-superstition, which, woman-like, you could not help giving. You have taught her to scorn a lie; you could not arm her with a better shield. Do not disquiet yourself; *you* have done your duty, whatever the issue. There is no nobler crown to a life."

Grand'mère's brown cheek grew warmer with pleasure; though she was a brave old woman, and cared little for any one, so long as she "did her duty" in her homely, truthful fashion, she yet always held Tricotrin in a certain awe, as of one endowed with occult and omniscient powers, and it was with infinite relief that she always learned that he commended her.

With these words he left her and joined his Waif, who had just captured a sparkling azure butterfly in her hand.

"You are not going to kill it, Viva?"

"Oh no! only to look at it."

"Good! The Mussulmans treasure every little torn scrap of paper, because on it there may be some line of the Koran. So should we cherish every little ephemeral atom of life, because on it, however small, is the impress of God. Jean Paul has had that thought before me. Let the creature go; you wound its delicate wings, and you see it far better winging its way through the sunset glow. There!"

The child lifted her head, and watched it as it flew high through the golden warmth of the young summer evening.

"How I should love to roam like that!" she cried. He smiled a little sadly.

"Impatient bird, to long to quit the nest! Ah, it is always so with the fledglings! The old tree is so dull, the home wood so wearisome, and it looks all summer yonder! They know nothing of the plains of snow, the clouds of thunder, the driving winds, the storms of winter!——"

"But *you* roam!"

"Certainly I do. But I am not a woman."

"A woman! Because one will be a woman must one never see the world?"

The words were petulant and longing. Viva was happy, but she was not so happy but what she was also a little ill-content. She looked over at that sun-steeped distance, to which the butterfly was taking its flight with all the restlessness of curious desire. What could that "world" be which lay beyond? It was inborn in the child—that longing for forbidden knowledge; that aspiration after wider spheres.

"Was your mother an empress or a gipsy? Certes she must have been one or the other," murmured Tricotrin. "Nothing else could have given *you* birth. So you want to roam, Viva? And you do nothing all day long but live very much like that butterfly? Whatever shall we do with you, little one, in a year or two's time?"

"Take me with you! Let me roam too!" laughed the child, with her arms flung about him in gay pleading caress.

Tricotrin laughed also; then a momentary warmth rose over his face,—for the first time it occurred to him that his Waif, though a child now, would, in a year or two more, be no longer a child; and that, although he filled the place of her father to her, he had no kinship with this bright stray thing, whom, as it seemed to him, he had but the other day found left to die among the clematis.

"That is too much to ask!" he answered merrily, choosing his own thought not to touch her too. "I carry one thing feminine indeed, but then she is portable and exceedingly small; which you, my Waif, who will be tallest among tall women, never can be. Besides,—the essence of wandering is to wander alone. Oh! I dare say you will find some way of yourself to spread your wings when the time comes; but wait till they are full-grown, Viva, if you take my advice. To flutter a little way and then fall, will not suit you."

"No, indeed! When I soar at all I will keep above earth like a hawk!"

She tossed her fair head back as she spoke with haughty careless security; she might have been the daughter of some free victorious desert king.

Tricotrin looked at her with earnest scrutiny.

"And forget the lark's nest among the field-grasses that first sheltered you," he said to himself. "I dare say! That will be very like youth—and very like womanhood!"

But he did not utter the thought loud enough for her to hear, as he gave a farewell caress with his hand to her sunny brow.

"Well; adieu, for to-day!"

"Must you go? Must you?" pleaded the child, with loving entreaty.

"I must! I have promised Yvon Mascarros to play at his betrothal feast to-morrow, and his place is a dozen leagues from this."

"But when will you come again?"

"When? How can I say? I will not be long without coming,—unless, indeed, I go off to the Moon or the Shades, —for you are fair to see, Viva; and since we are both Waifs and Strays it is meet that we cling together."

"But then—if you love me, you will please me and not go?"

"Ah, ha! You have so much of womanhood in you already that you count the strength of love by the obedience it gives to your caprices, and exact its confession only also to exact its submission? How true to your sex you are, Viva! Nay—I love you, though I doubt if it be wise to love anything save Mankind and Doghood. And all I hope, Waif of mine, is, that you will never reproach me with having helped you to get out of your bed of clematis. Enjoy, *mignonne*, the utmost you can; the happier you are the less conscience-stricken shall Mistigri and I feel at our connivance with your escape into existence!"

Viva laughed—she always fancied herself that the little black Mistigri was a familiar of her own fairy-mother's—and she threw her arms fondly about him once more.

"I am always so happy when you are here, and so good too! Oh! if you never went away I should never have those wicked, envious, wayward thoughts; you are like my guardian angel!"

For she did in truth love him warmly; he stood to her in the stead of father, mother, brother, of home, and of kindred, and of the world; and though the child was vain, and like most children selfish, she had great affection in her, and spent it all on him.

Tricotrin's eyes smiled with exceeding tenderness on her, while over the fearless brightness of his face a flash of pleasure passed. So little had he of egotism or exaction, so little did he make count of his best actions, so quickly was he moved by any gleam of gratitude to him, that he felt himself the debtor of the child who owed him all, because she paid him in the rare coinage of a pure attachment.

"I thank you, Viva mine," he said softly. "Make me indeed your guardian angel, by letting my memory exorcise all evil things from your young soul. I ask no higher reward."

He touched her bright upturned forehead lightly with his lips, in his accustomed caress of greeting and adieu, and left her to unloose his boat from its moorings, and push it off into the stream, whose waters were flushing to violet, and russet, and golden hues beneath the glories of the setting sun.

There was a trail of light across the river like sheeted gold, into which the small boat glided; his form was full in its luster, as standing up and wafting it forward with one oar, he uncovered his head to her and laughed a last farewell.

That brilliance was shed still about the figure of the child, waiting upon the bank, among the scarlet flowers, while the boat passed onward into the shadows of the coming night, where the sun-rays did not follow.

CHAPTER VII.

"Nothing she does or seems
But smacks of something greater than herself,
Too noble for this place——"

HE mused, as his thoughts remained with her, while the strokes of his oars swept him away. He had never sought wealth; he was a republican to the core; he loved best the simplest forms of life; he deemed happiest those whose wants were fewest; and lo! in this foundling whom he had protected was a nature in the strongest opposition to all his views, requiring by sheer inborn instinct all that circumstances rendered it totally impossible he could ever give her.

Through the years of her brief existence, he had taken no heed of the child beyond the provision of her actual needs, and the kindly careless gentleness he would have shown to a dog or a cat; he had never regarded her in the light of a possible burden, a possible difficulty to himself in the time that was to come. The joyous and negligent temper of Tricotrin was not one that regarded the future; to rescue the child had been an impulse with him; that she would ever require more than the few easily granted wants of childhood, that the time would ever come when she would grow impatient of the life she led, had never occurred to him until now that her own words and those of the old woman had suggested the doubt. He was used himself, by choice, to live much among the people; his time, by preference, was much passed among the peasantries of divers nations. He was habituated to seeing young girls who were content enough if they got a new ribbon for their hair, or rode queen of a harvest on a bullock-drawn wagon: that the Waif would prove a young rebel, with the pride of a princess and fastidious tastes curiously inherent in her, was an additional perplexity to the whole dilemma of her maintenance.

The flower was fair, and was yet only in its bud; its hereafter had never risen before him as a matter of meditation and of possible future embarrassment. And even now he threw the fear from him: it was free to float on the air in its own happy fashion, sun-kissed and wind-tossed, it bloomed after Nature's own will with it, and all its fragrance was natural, like the sweetness of roses;—it was the best thing that could betide any opening blossom to be left so wholly to Nature. With Nature, therefore, he left too her future.

And he sent his boat up the stream with a swift strong impulsion, shaking the care from his thoughts as he shook the water-drops from his oars: he was something late for the feast of Yvon Mascarros, and Tricotrin never broke promises even in so small a matter as a vine-dresser's marriage-feast.

Care never waited with him; it will scarcely ever tarry where it is not entertained with welcome, and the rich sunlit nature of the man had no kinship with it as a guest. There had been times, inevitable in every life, when he had suffered with the intense passion of all vivid characters; but they had been few and far between, and the gracious gladness of his inherent temper had always resumed supremacy. Not for him the feverish unrest of ambition; the carking thirst of the seekers of wealth; the vacillating hopes and fears of those whose breath is the breath of the world's applause. He was not pursued by the haunting terrors of the hangers-on of public favor; he was not pressed by the uphill race of men who pant their hearts out in the struggle for gold; he

was not driven to find no sweetness in sleep, no beauty in
summer hours, no charm in women's smile, because greed
hunted him on and on, through dark and devious ways, seeking the rivers of gold. He sought neither riches nor renown;
he greeted each dawn without regret for its yesterday; he
saw the sun set and the night descend with happy Jean Paul
humor, saying in those words of wisdom, "I am content since
I have lived to-day!"

And he loved the people, and was loved by them; making
his home wheresoever men enjoyed and suffered.

Many wondered whence he came; many wove a thousand
marvelous histories to account for the anomalies which even
the least intelligent could mark in him: none knew anything
for truth concerning his origin, his nation, or his history.
Old people in this vine-country remembered him a bright boy
of twenty years, with the bronze of southern suns on his fair
skin, and the fire of a passionate youth in his blue eyes; who
had come no one knew whence, who laughed, and loved, and
played, and worked among them; and left them often for long
absences, and returned to them always the same, however
many years had passed, however slight the stay he made.
He was "Tricotrin;" all was said in that; he came and went
whenever it pleasured him, never questioned, ever welcomed,
like the swallows of the spring.

He was not wholly of them, that even the peasantry felt;
but he was *with* them heart and soul, and they loved him
better for that nameless difference, that intangible unlikeness,
which made them, while he toiled among them and feasted
among them, yet perceive a royalty in him that he never lost;
even as the shepherd-kings of the old east were none less
kingly to their people because they lived on pulse and water,
because they sheared the fleece and folded the herds, and
dwelt under the tents of their wandering people.

The people loved him in all lands; especially they loved
him in this beautiful France, which he had made his mistress
in preference over all the fair sisters of Europe. The people
caressed him, obeyed him, adored him, with a loyalty that

would have rendered him an irresistible power in times of revolution; and as he rowed down the river he knew well that there was not a cottage on its banks, not a water-mill on its shores, not a cabaret in its villages, under whose roof he would not have been welcome as is the summer sun in mowing time, when its early smile gives promise of the aftermath.

But he did not care to go ashore in that hot and lustrous summer night. Three miles down the river he overtook the hay-barge, slowly floating in the moonlight with its load of fresh-cut grasses, odorous as violets. It drifted through the broad, sheeted, silver radiance lazily, charmingly, with its great sail black against the sky, and the fragrant dews on its huge soft mounds of fodder that were tossed loosely together, with the wild clover and the white marguérites, scarcely dead, that had been mown with them. He hailed it, knowing its owner well, and the men recognized him with a shout of delight. The barge was stopped; in a second more he had leapt up among them, received with vociferous delight; they were to sail all night down the stream, and they took his little boat in tow with eager pleasure.

The skipper was a lithe, handsome, black browed Marseillais, with his broad chest bare, and a red sash knotted round his loins, and great gold earrings in his ears, who had taken the peaceful Loire traffic for love of a Loiret woman.

The skipper had earned a perilous repute for lawless piratical voyages in the southern waters, and was said to be as hot and as swift and as fierce as his own tramontana; hence the people of the woman he loved denied her to him with bitter words and loud revilings. Margot clung to her fiery southern lover, and refused to be comforted: there was misery for the child, and feud between her suitor and her brethren. At last, in one evil day, the latter heaped insult on insult till the Marseillais' blood of flame leaped up like a sword from its scabbard; his knife flashed in the sun, and would have darted down, first to be sheathed in her brother's breast and then in his own, had not an outstretched hand turned the blow, at price of a wound in its own palm, and Tricotrin's voice called out—"Has France no foes that her sons fight together?"

The offenders were passionately contrite, they wept like children to see his blood, they implored his pardon, they cursed themselves: he laughed and drew little Margot to him with his unwounded arm.

"Little one! Are you still not afraid of that sea-lion? No? You think he is so sure not to wound *you?* Well, then —if they are sorry for my hurt, your brethren must give you to me to give to him. You are the only lion-tamer for this wild beast of ours!"

And they gave her: so he made peace among them, and won for evermore the fierce, ardent, grateful soul of the Marseillais.

Margot's lion never harmed her; as her lion to Una, was Eudes Caros to the pretty, brown, soft, tender child of the Loire. He gave up the wild night roaming on the shores of the Riviera, for peaceful river-trading between the banks of her native stream; and now, in the little cabin of the hay-barge, where the solitary oil lamp hung above her lovely bent head, Margot sat, with a dreaming happy smile in her drooped dark eyes and on her thoughtful mouth, as she gazed at a picture of Christ hung under the lamp, and looked from that downward on the child that lay asleep at her breast.

"Did Mary know he would be God and yet die on the cross? Ah, how she must have longed that he had been but a mortal child who could grow to manhood, and live on obscure but unharmed!" thought little Margot, pressing closer the flushed cheek of her first-born; the thought was wholly a woman's!

Better an ignoble safety, an inglorious impunity, for the man that they mould, than the divinity of martyrdom, than the crucifixion of genius! Better that the soul, which is not of them, should die out in apathy than that the body they conceive and nourish should perish!

So they say—Margot and her million of sisters upon earth: and, of the sons they bear, none go up to Calvary, but thousands cumber the world as swine. Yet these women are good; their kisses are tender, their hands are pure: it is but their souls that are dead; it is but the souls of their children they kill.

Whether Margot's son were destined to become poet or swineherd, leader or servitor among men, he slept happily in her arms now, and she dreamt happily over him, while the barge floated in moonlight down the stream, and Tricotrin, nonchalantly cast upon the great sweet piles of hay, talked with the Marseillais, watched the shadowy landscapes drifting by, or touched now and then the Straduarius to fitful cadences full of river-song.

The night was very warm and profoundly still; one of the splendid nights of France, with stars innumerable burning through a cloudless atmosphere. The slow, calm passage of the barge with the fresh odor of its freight rising on the air, with the woods and vineyards and villages of the river-banks softened to an inconceivable beauty by the light, with the murmur of the water as it parted and met again, and with the occasional chime of belfry-bells from the land ringing some mellow monotone as they told the flight of an hour, was the fittest method for the passage of a summer night, and held a thousand poems and pictures in its indolent starlit voyage. Such pictures, such poems, as he best loved to fill his sight, and his heart, and his memory with; such as seen, and felt, and treasured, with the true instinct of pure love, had made his life itself the poem and the picture that it was.

As the evening wore on, Caros, prouder of the passenger his barge bore than he would have been of a king for his freight, went below to his Margot; Tricotrin remained stretched on the hay with all the fragrant dead flowers and saintfoin beneath him in a couch that was easier than the down of monarchs' beds. He fell asleep, sleep coming as lightly and as swiftly to him as it comes to a tired, healthy child; a night-bird's wing sometimes softly touching his fore-

head, a cadence from a monastery chime sometimes mingling
with his dreams. When he awoke it was night still; there
was a break of dawn eastwards, but the stars were still out,
the barge was still winding its tranquil way down the water.

Leaning his arms down in the yielding grasses he lay looking awhile, lazily, at the mark where the keel cut the stream,
at the dews that had fallen on the grasses, at the heavy black
sails swinging idly to and fro. His indolence did not endure
long; a face near him caught his eyes and his pity; and with
Tricotrin human sympathies were very keen and swift, human
woe and joy the sure chords to arouse and to move him. The
face he saw now was one of infinite pain; it was the face of a
man, who, like himself, had chosen that odorous mountain of
grasses and herbs for a couch; and who was lying there looking, with wide-opened eyes, down into the ebb and flow of
the water against the sides of the barge.

He was a man beyond middle age, with a rugged, homely,
weather-worn countenance, and large, black, pathetic eyes
that, out of the roughness of the other features, gazed, with
a piteous, sightless, yearning look, into vacancy;—a look as
of one startled and astray in some great agony. He wore
the usual blouse of the working-day, and his hair was un-
kempt, his linen soiled, his hand black with the pitch with
which he had that day caulked the sides of the barge; but
there was that in the mute, intense wondering anguish of the
eyes that gave at once grandeur and exceeding pathos to his
aspect. It was the look of a noble animal who has been
struck a cruel blow, and who will not hurt the hand that
struck it, even in just vengeance.

Tricotrin spoke to him gently, on some trifle of the night;
the man started, answered wearily, then lapsed into his former
attitude. No questions fared better; he replied to them with
a certain oppressive effort, but only an instant afterward to
fall afresh into the same apathy and absorption: he was but
a common sailor or fisherman, with nothing above the common in him, yet the patient, terrible despair upon his face—

a despair as of one incessantly seeking what was lost—lent him dignity, gave him greatness.

Tricotrin let him be; he knew how cruel is the kindness which forces itself in upon the silence and the solitude of calamity; and he saw too that here the mind was not wholly present, that in some sense reason had been dulled by suffering, though sufficient perception remained for the mechanical words and actions of daily existence. He said no more; but in the still, dark dawn, the music of his violin softly supplied the place of speech. There were many times when, through its manifold voices speaking in a universal tongue, he uttered to himself and others what the words of his mouth could not have phrased. Through it all the genius in him spoke; and in it all the heart of the player went out to the hearts of his fellow-men.

The music, unnoticed at first, failing at first to penetrate the profound self-absorption of the seaman, reached his ear gradually, as wave on wave of gracious sound broke on the air like the tide on a shore with rhythmical recurrent music. He did not note it as what it was; he did not make visible sign that he even heard it; but gradually consciousness of it stole upon him.

The music filled the quiet of the hour, that was only stirred besides by the lapping of the water as the vessel glided down; music low, and sad, and sweet; music like a psalm of consolation, with all the blind hungered yearning of a soul adrift upon a bitter world, told and answered in it. It pierced the lethargy that enshrouded a darkened, desolate mind; where the sailor leaned, with his chin resting on his hands and his eyes gazing down into the river, a certain change came over him, like the first quiver of returning life into one half dead through stupor; great tears started into his eyes, softening their vacancy; he moved with restless pain, then started from his bed of hay with a gesture of intolerable suffering.

"Hush,—hush! It reminds me of her voice!"

The music ceased even as he spoke; Tricotrin touched him.

"Of her? Of whom?"

The sailor's eyes turned on him with the tears floating in their weary depths.

"I cannot bear it! It is like her—like her voice as she sung her ballads!" he muttered, regardless of the question, lost only in the one memory that filled the darkened chambers of his mind to the exclusion of all outward sight. "I have lost her, you know, she went from me so long ago. One morning she laughed in my eyes, and kissed my mouth, and threw her white arms around my neck in play, with the sun all so bright on her face; and at night—at night, you remember?—there were only ashes on the hearth, silence in the chamber, darkness everywhere. Darkness that no light ever breaks; no light ever will break,—till I find her!"

He was ignorant that he spoke to one who had never ere then looked upon his face; he had no remembrance that the words he uttered had no meaning to the ear that heard them; to him his grief filled the world, his loss laid the earth desolate.

Tricotrin rested his hand gently on the other's shoulder; he saw that his music had broken the stupor of the brain, and stirred, though but to troubled shapeless motion, the locked thoughts of its solitary musing; he waited with patience to do more.

"To find her?" he repeated. "Then this one whom you love is not dead?"

"Dead? No—she is not dead," the seaman answered slowly, while his great eyes searched his companion's with a heart-rending look of search and of bewilderment. "That is it—see you!—she is not dead. Dead women lie cold and motionless, their fair limbs do not stir, nor their eyes unclose, nor their lips breathe, but they *are* there—you can hold them, though their heart does not beat on yours; you can caress them, though your kiss strikes on ice; you can wind their hair round your hands, though they know your touch no longer. They *are* there, though they lie lifeless on their bridal-beds. But she was gone, and did not leave even the beauty of her body to me. The chamber was dark, still, desolate; there was not even a dead woman to gather the sunbeams about her, and to seem to smile with their light on her mouth!"

There was an unutterable tenderness and desolation in the answer; his hearer knew all the meaning of those wandering pathetic words;—there is a loss worse than the loss that death causes. He divined what that loss had been; but he saw that the blow it had dealt had numbed the brain of the man who suffered by it out of all comprehension of its truth.

"She is not dead?" he said softly. "Then hope is still with you?"

The puzzled, aching eyes answered him with a look that struck him to the soul.

"Hope—hope! Yes—I hope. I suppose I hope, since I live on;—but the years are many, and I grow weary. It was in my youth that I lost her; and now I grow old. Ever and again I think I behold her; some girl's laugh on a grape-wagon, some girl's eyes that smile at me through the lattice that opens at dawn, some girl's round limbs where they bathe and float in the summer sea, has something of her, and makes me think I have found her. But it is never so;—they do not know me; they have no light in their glance when they see me; they have no place in their hearts for me. I wander far and wide; I go east and west, north and south, I seek her in the cities and forests, I watch before the palaces, I search in the hospital-wards, I look for her in the crowds of the streets, I wait for her in the loneliness of the plains—all in vain, all in vain!"

"Is it so many years since you lost her?"

"It is many. I cannot tell how many. I keep no count. The seasons come and go, but she does not come with them. Ah! it is terrible that!—in a throng to see but one face, in a world to hear but one voice, and the face forever eluding, and the voice forever mocking you! And the earth is so wide,

you know;—one may toil on and on and on and never reach
nearer! The house is ready for her just as she left it; the
flowers are dead, I cannot help that,—she is so long away,—
but all is as she left it. I try always to keep it so; I think it
will pleasure her when she comes back."

His head dropped on his chest with a heavy sigh, the
lethargy stirred for awhile by the power of the music returned; the brooding patience settled down again on the
features which for an instant had quivered and changed. He
was not conscious that he had spoken to a stranger; he had
only uttered the ever-present thoughts of his mind with the
wandering eloquence born of the intensity of one single and
dominant feeling.

A voice called him to the farther end of the vessel: with
the mechanical instinct of obedience he swung down from the
piles of the hay and went whither he was bidden,—become
only a common boatman, gone to the coiling of a rope, the
reefing of a sail.

Tricotrin watched him as he passed aft in the dusky
dawn that was now faintly reddened by the first approach of
day: his heart ached for this man who with his hard life and
his deadened reason could yet find strength and greatness for
such love as this.

"A woman!" he thought. "The same old story ever!
And the same blow which pierces Estmere's purples strikes
through the seaman's canvas shirt! There is no mail against
that stroke, either in power or in poverty."

The dark handsome head of the Marseillais looked up at
him at that minute from the cabin stair: Tricotrin signed him
to come higher and leant towards him.

"Who is that boatman of yours, good Caros?"

Caros raised himself with a sailor's lightness and swiftness
on to the height of the mounds of dry grass; he was a gentle-
hearted man, though the wild fire of southern pirates ran in
his blood, and to the one who had given him his Loirais'
bride he bore a passionate devotion.

"You speak of poor Bruno, my friend?" he answered.

"He is a good sailor on rougher waters than rivers, though his brain is gone for all but his work. I knew him well down in the south; he is poor, and so I gave him a berth and a turn on my barge."

"Bruno! Is that his name?"

"Jean Bruno: yes. We were lads together. And we were on the same craft for years in the Mediterranean days. He was a fine fellow—a noble fellow—till she ruined him."

"His wife?"

"Ay! His wife. We were lads together, though he looks so old, and I—I feel as young as Margot! He is scarce forty, Bruno. I remember her well; she was fifteen when she wedded him, and he a lad of twenty-two. She was the bastard child of some noble, a beautiful thing, all yellow hair, and smiling lips, and sunny eyes, and white soft limbs; she bewitched that black strong stalwart fellow, who was half lion, half lamb. He adored her—ah!—as those great, brave, mild natures always do love. It was almost terrible to see how that soft little piece of bright-colored life held the whole heart and soul of the man! Well,—he had one year of happiness, one year of a fool's paradise; he went short coasting voyages, no more, he could not bear to be away from the little cabin where she had everything he could get her—birds and flowers, and quaint Indian things that the Indian ships brought home. She was good enough to him; a gay, laughing, sweet-tempered, mindless thing; who could have thought she had been so cruel? One day he bade her farewell at dawn; he was going on a fishing trip to be absent only the day; I was waiting for him outside the cabin; I saw her laugh, and caress him, and wave her hands in adieu. We went out to sea. We were at sea all day. We got home with three boats' load by midnight. The light that always burned in her cabin was out: he flew like a madman the half league down the shore, and burst his door open,—Madelon was not there. Ah God! to this day I have never forgotten the sight of Bruno!——"

The Marseillais paused; the tide of recollection rushed

with painful force in on him; when he spoke his voice was low and full of pity.

"It killed the mind in him;—shattered it out of all sense of the truth. We found the truth soon. Favette had gone to shame; a shame that looked brilliant to her beside the innocent quiet sea-life that she led. The leaven of her mother was in her. She had gone to the stage; a great actor had made her his mistress. But Bruno never knew this. He could not comprehend when we tried to tell it him. She was lost; that was all he knew; that she had sinned against him he would not, or could not, understand. It was horrible!—he thought she had been stolen from him, he loved her so tenderly still! He has searched for her ever since. Time has not killed that love in him, though her crime has killed his reason. The little cabin down by the south is always kept ready for her return; not a thing is touched; and meanwhile he wanders all over France seeking what he can never find! You know who Favette is?"

"No. She lives then?"

"She lives. Lives in—Coriolis."

"Coriolis! Our great actress!—what?—the wife of that man?"

"Ay! How many such women own even as good a past as to have slept on the honest heart of an honest man they betrayed?" said the Marseillais bitterly. "Their nests are mostly fouler than that sea-bird's nest. Yes, she is Coriolis; but he does not know it, mind you. Though he seeks her, still his search is chiefly southward; he has never come on the dazzling sinner of Paris. Pray God that he never may! It is fearful enough, his quest for her, his task that can never be ended, his hope that can never be granted; but it is better, at its worst, than the truth could be to him if he ever looked again on the face of his wife!"

He said no more, but turned quickly, and busied himself with some ropes of the barge. He loved little Margot; he could feel now for his comrade as he had not felt in the years of their youth.

Tricotrin asked no more. He knew the comedian well, a lovely, heedless, heartless woman; full of laughter, of coquetry, of caprice; a soulless, brainless, beautiful thing; young still, fair still; with the beauty of the japonica or the azalea—beauty of hue and form, without a trace of the beauty that fragrance lends the flower and feeling lends the woman. Many a time had he seen the theater she graced convulsed with mirth at her gay and mischievous follies.

The story had a great pathos for him:—he who had seen the sparkling gayety of the wife felt the full force of the martyrdom of the husband. The cruelty and the crime had been rewarded by so shadowless a life of triumph,—the devotion and the fealty had been recompensed by so weary and endless an agony!

"Ah, Waif of mine!" he thought, "will you ever, I wonder, destroy a brave heart like that for the sake of your senses and your vanity?"

With sunrise the barge passed the village for which he was bound. He was pledged to the bridal feast of Yvon Mascarros, or his heart had inclined to follow the fortunes of that patient desolated life which had been ruined by a woman's infidelity. He went up to Bruno, and bade him gently farewell. The seaman lifted his head from the rough work on which his hands were engaged, and replied with mechanical courtesy; the momentary light and reason that the music had wakened there had died out from his features: the old, darkened, brooding, lifeless pain had gathered there again.

"There is nothing one can do him?" he asked of Caros.

The Marseillais shook his head.

"Neither God nor man can aid him. Who can give him back his wife, in her youth and without her crime?"

It was true. Solace for Bruno could only come with death.

Tricotrin watched him one moment more, sitting under the black shadow of the sail, with his fingers working at the cordage, and his eyes looking out at the sun, where it rose in all its glory. Then, with the hands of Caros grasping him in grateful farewell, and the bright face of little Margot looking, smiling and sunny, over the side of the barge, he dropped himself into his own little boat, and rowed himself straight across the stream to the landing-place. As he moored it to land, he paused a moment looking after the barge where it drifted slowly on down the river, with the glow of the sunrise, amber-hued and ruddy, on the waters around it.

"To have life killed in one at twenty-three by a woman! —and men call diseases that slay outright 'cruel,' while there are these blows which murder by means that draw out the torture through a quarter of a century. The plague is merciful compared with a woman without pity!" he thought as he watched the form of Bruno, dark and motionless, under the shadow of the sail.

That thing he himself had saved yonder, who was chasing the butterflies so joyously, with the sunshine on her fair brow, careless of the pain they felt—she, too, would soon be a woman. Had he rescued her from death only for her to deal death, like this fond, faithless wanton that the sailor had cherished? The thought came to him—well as he loved the child, well as all his years through he had loved her sex.

In some sense the weary, lonely, melancholy figure of the boatman, with his strong, massive frame that would not perish, and his jarred aching brain, to which death would have been so much mercy, stood out to him in painful contrast with his memory of the light, gracious, golden presence of the child, as he had left her among the scarlet flowers and the dewy leaves. These were both forms of the same human life!

But the thought was a bitter cucumber which Tricotrin threw away in obedience to his favorite Antoninus' counsel. He left the barge to pass on her way; and, after bathing in the river, walked through summer woods and green vineyards to the village of his destination, where, already in the early day, the peasantry were stirring, and the young girls and the children going out to gather wild lilies, and honeysuckles, and great branches of roses, to crown the head and strew the path of the prettiest among them, who was to wed with Yvon Mascarros.

And there, under the low eaves of the farrier's cottage, or under the blossoming boughs of the limes that sheltered the house, Tricotrin, with his mirth and his music, kept these innocent revelers gay from daybreak to nightfall,—gay with a zest they never had unless he were the Lord of Misrule. And the Loirois maidens, with their black laughing eyes, and their lithe robust forms, and their feet that flew like the flash of phosphoric insects, danced all through the sultry summer night to the same melodies, touched by the same hand which had awakened to momentary consciousness of its own agony the numbed and stricken heart of the boatman Bruno.

CHAPTER VIII.

UNDER the old sign of the *Cornemeuse* there was a gay after-midnight supper.

It was not the *Cornemeuse* of Dancourt, of Marivaux, of Piron. It was not the famous, well-beloved café of the poets, the artists, the epigrammatists of the eighteenth century; but it was a *Cornemeuse* as mirthful if not as traditional as theirs.

A bright, white-painted, gas-glittering little house, with gilded balconies and tri-colored flags, and tiny chambers, and open glass doors, with the perpetual color and movement of the Paris crowd under the trees before it, and the vivacious noise and music of a Paris night all around it. It was a resort of the bohemians,—of the painters, and the actors, and the rhymesters,—of those who make the laughter of the world, and of those who limn its manners for the age to come. Chiefly the artists came thither, and within the little building there was scarcely a single white panel, or a single piece of plaster, that was not covered with the charcoal or the chalk, the oil-color or the pen-and-ink of the master hands of France. The *Cornemeuse* had untold gold upon its walls; and the owner of it, a bright, hot-blooded man of the south, loved the pictured walls with all his soul, and had never sold a touch from his guests' brushes save once, when his daughter's dowry could not be found in any other wise, when he had taken down a shutter whose three panels were rich with three great masters' idle fancies, and had parted with it for its weight in francs. For half a century the *Cornemeuse* had thus gathered its wealth upon its walls and timbers; and among its treasures—the treasures its host valued most, though they were but the gifts of an amateur—were some half dozen female heads, with all the grace of Greuze and all the velvet hues of Boucher;—heads that looked out in charming coquetry from quaint dark corners, and laughed down from window-nooks, wreathed with flowers,—heads under which the brush of their creator had scrawled carelessly, "Tricotrin."

"You could have beaten us all if you would," had said once to their artist a painter whose name stood as the Velasquez of his modern time.

"Possibly; but then Art would have been my tyrant, whereas she is now my handmaiden."

"And serves you well. Yet, if you had let her rule you entirely——"

"I should have been her slave. He is a fool who is subject to his mistress. Can he ever wholly enjoy her? I doubt it."

"But is it not waste of genius?"

The wanderer shrugged his shoulders.

"I don't say whether it is my weakness or my strength to hate the bondage of anything,—even of Art. I only say—it is my temper!"

"But if every man had such a temper?"

"Well, if every bird were a lark we should get no useful fowls for the stew; but I do not see that the utility of stews to eat proves any argument against the right of the larks to sing?"

And the man who loved song, and light, and green meadow lands, and blue sunny skies, like the larks themselves, had taken up his friend's palette and sheaf of brushes, and had dashed in, in two hours, a female head that had all the brown glow, the voluptuous luster of the south in it,—a head that Titian might have painted.

He would create such in the caprice of free impulse; but he would have produced them as a trade no more than his fellow-bohemians, the larks, will sing in cellars.

It might be strength. It might be weakness. But it was, as he said, his temper.

Beneath that same golden, ardent, beaming Hebe face that he had there sketched in oils on the panel, he sat among his brethren now at the supper of the *Cornemeuse*, with the light on the leonine beauty of his head, and in the sparkling laughter of his eyes. He was the king of the revelry; revelry of wit and wine, where those whom nature had anointed with the same chrism that touched Rubens's brow and Shakspeare's lips, held joyous, lawless sovereignty; leaning to kiss ripe scarlet mouths of women because they were men, but rising to great thoughts that left far beneath them alike women and the world, because they were also immortals.

His laugh rang out, tuneful as the music of silver; his wit flashed through the speech like meteors through the night; his improvisations, full of irony, of raillery, of caricature, made the gay shouts of his listeners echo again and again. Ben Jonson odes, Beaumarchais rhymes, Béranger songs, and Breton carols, coursed each other off his lips, in a wild tournament of tongues; his own swift satires unhorsed all combatants, and as he drank he chanted Hellenic bacchanal hymns, with all the bright gay grace of Greece.

He would have lived as soon without light as without the freedom of unfettered mirth, the abandonment of unchained gayety, the debonnair enjoyment of the lord of misrule.

He loved pleasure; but he loathed debauch; when the former glided in its riot to the latter he left the *Cornemeuse*, as the morning dawn began to break, and went out into the air; the wine having only warmed all his poet's fancies, and only making richer and fuller still in its melody the ring of his voice as he walked through Paris, singing aloud the

> God Lyœus ever young
> Ever honored, ever sung,

of the wine-mellowed Elizabethan verse.

Tricotrin knew how to enjoy. His censors—and he had many—said that he deemed this too exclusively the only aim of life. At the least his enjoyment was of that free, liberal, and gracious fashion which sheds its light on all around it, and is never cramped into egotism, nor distorted into orgy.

None the less either because he came freshly from the lavishness of mirth and the pleasures of the senses was he awake to all that is terrible, to all that is horrible in the shame, the crime, the hunger, the agony that were hidden beneath the marvelous night-glitter of the city through which he went.

None the less because on his lips the carol was so mirthful of the

> "Stained with blood of lusty grapes
> In a thousand lusty shapes,
> Dance upon the mazer's brim,
> In the crimson liquor swim.
> From the plenteous hand divine,
> Let a river run with wine,
> God of youth!"

did he pause in pity at the sight of a wretched creature who begged his alms, though that pity was not heard in his first words.

"Charity?" quoth Tricotrin, to the appeal. "You ask for what men want, every one of them, but love little to give. Pass on, my friend."

"But bread—a morsel of bread at least?" moaned the man, who had stopped him in an obscure street, where there were few other passengers in the lateness of the night.

Tricotrin looked him through with his brilliant eyes by the light of the summer moon: he had no love for those who begged, and he knew thief from pauper at a glance.

"Off with you!" he said, amusedly. "If a man cannot get a bit of baked wheat for himself, in a world where there is so much to be done, he is not a fellow worth keeping in the world at all, to my fancy."

"It is hard to work!" muttered the other, who had the pure accent of education.

"Oh-hè! If everybody worked in moderation, nobody need overwork himself. It is because there are so many do-nothings—chiefly so many female drones—that those who do at all do overmuch. To say nothing, that the overseer of Greed drives his slaves at the devil's pace."

"But I am starving," moaned the beggar afresh. "And it is so bitter to die!"

"Not at all. Mere ignorant error. Hard to die? Is opium-sleep hard after racking pain? What fools men are! Writhing in famine and disease, they think it hard to be released from both!"

"Ah, you have not felt hunger!"—the poor wretch was longing for mere food; to be epigrammatized by a stranger in the desolation of the streets, little appeased the terrible desire.

Tricotrin's eyes softened greatly.

"Have I not?" he said, with infinite gentleness. "You mistake, my friend."

"Then for heaven's sake give me bread!" said the man fiercely; for his growing need made him ferocious, like a desert beast.

"Tut! Say for humanity's sake. Well—I have not a sou on me. I have spent them all at the *Cornemeuse* yonder."

Cheated in his hope, the starving creature shrank back with a shrill yell of grief, like a struck dog's; the sound went to the heart of his hearer, and outbalanced the predisposition against him, which his voice and his features had aroused.

He struck the beggar kindly on the shoulder.

"Unphilosophic man! Blind yet to the advantages of death? Come then—follow me."

With his quick, light step, and resuming his chant—Beau-

mont and Fletcher—Tricotrin led the way, through many
tortuous turnings, till he reached the quarter of St. Martin,
the starving wretch following him in dumb quiescence, shivering, though the night was warm with all the balmy sweetness
of a late French summer.

An impulse of trust had made him accost this stranger, so
utterly unlike himself, who had so dauntless a carriage, and
who had on his lips the carol of such careless revelry. All
that evening and night through he had vainly sought pity from
the crowds of Paris, from the beautiful painted women, the
men of wealth, the creatures of delight, who swarmed there
in such busy, heedless, glittering throngs; only this one man
had given him what he sought.

Tricotrin let himself in with a pass-key into a house of the
poor and crowded quarter, where he had fixed his dwelling
for the time. He was never stationary, scarcely for so much
as a week; he was yet freer and more completely unincum-
bered than the Arabs, for he had not even a tent to bear with
him, but made his nest where he would, as fancy took him,
like a yellow-hammer in a highway.

He wanted no home as he wanted no nation. Wherever
men dwelt he found both.

He went up a high wooden rickety staircase, very high,
for he always chose his room nearest the sky, and bade the
beggar follow him into the topmost chamber.

It was a very large attic, for he could endure no cramped
space; with bare floor and bare walls; Mistigri curled up on
a little straw bed, and his Attavante and his Straduarius lying
together on the deal table. It was perfectly comfortless; but
he was never in it except for slumber, and through the open
window there shone the sky, star-studded.

He wasted no time in words, but striking a light and going to a cupboard in the wall, drew out a great roll of bread,
some cold meat, an apparatus for coffee making, and a flask
of Burgundy, all he had in his possession. He set the food
before the beggar; made some steaming coffee in five minutes;
and poured him out as much wine as it was safe to give him

after his long fast. The man devoured as only starvation can, and Tricotrin, turning his back on him to spare him a witness of his voracity, busied himself talking to Mistigri, where she had thrown herself down on the mattress.

Now and then he cast a look at his guest, and the survey did not please him. There was a wolfish keenness in the way he ate which was of itself repulsive; but it was less this, than the cast and expression of his features that displeased his host. He was very delicately made, and his face was of beautiful type, with the hair cut short over the brow, and falling longer behind; he was not young, but the face remained youthful, though its clear olive skin was livid, and the jet black curls had many threads of white. Handsome he was, handsome as an Antinous, but the beauty was crafty, feline, cowardly, full of latent lust and cruelty, though such as would have been dangerously comely to the eyes of sensual women.

Something of remembrance came to Tricotrin as he watched him: but what the memory was he could not recall.

His meal over, the man thanked him with all the profusion of southern expletive, and all the grace of southern manner; there was that both in his speech and air which showed he had once been gently nurtured, though now fallen as low as this.

Tricotrin seated himself on the straw pallet, and listened silently; he was pondering what he could do for him; it was not his way to give men mere passing aid.

"No thanks," he said at last. "Sit down again a minute. I have done nothing for you. In Utopia there will be no want. But while we are as far from Utopia as we are now, we are bound to help one another. Tell me, my friend—what have you been?"

"Nothing!"

"Nothing! The best thing if you are a philosopher, the worst if you are not."

"But 'Philosophy bakes no bread,' as Novalis has it," murmured the stranger, with a mirthless and bitter smile.

Tricotrin eyed him more closely.

"Well—I am not altogether sure of that. At the least she teaches us to be content, in default of bread, with a handful of pulse. That is better than to have discontent and dyspepsia after a banquet. But, you are a man of education. Did your sense never tell you that it does not do to be 'nothing,' unless one has a million to be it upon?"

"I suppose it should have told me so, but I thought each day that the morrow——"

"Cras vives; hodie jam vivere Postume, serum est. Ille sapit, quisquis, Postume, vixit heri," murmured Tricotrin; he who enjoyed existence with the versatility of a humorist, the richness of an artist, and the carelessness of a wanderer, felt as much contempt as pity for those who were ignorant of the true secret of happiness—living in the present.

"Martial might have remembered," said the sufferer, quickly, "that there are some people who never get a chance of 'living,' worth anything at all, either yesterday, to-day, or to-morrow."

"Humph! The wise man compels chance. However, some want a good opportunity, as bad swimmers want an air belt. We will see if we cannot furnish you with one. But first be more explicit with me. What has been your career?"

The stranger hesitated.

"A checkered one," he said, bitterly. 'Now in sunshine, now in darkness. I have known what it is to be rich, successful, triumphant; I have known pleasure, and abundance, and women's loves. But—in a word—I have been a gamester; and the good fortune that crowned me so long has forsaken me for the last score of years, till—till—I have become what you see me!"

The tears stood in his eyes; he pitied himself with exceeding pity, and regarded his fate, as every gambler does, as the cruel result of a combination of cruel conspiracies.

"A gambler!" echoed Tricotrin. "How could you say you were nothing? You are of the trade that ruins more souls than any other, except the trade that women drive in love. A gambler! Bah! to peril all your brain, and your peace, and your future on the caprice of the turn of a wheel! Why, to pin them on the faith of a woman is not more foolish, and is far more poetic!"

"You are pleased to jest at my misery!" muttered the other, sullenly.

"Nay. I jest at no misery," said Tricotrin, earnestly. "God forbid! But if you have no other resource than play, it is difficult indeed to see how to aid you. Could I give you thousands they would all go in one night of hazard!"

"I used to have such luck! How could I tell that those devils of cards would only mock me as age came on me?"

The question was piteous and passionate—he deemed himself wronged as by some base treachery, by the change of the chance that used to smile on him.

Tricotrin looked at him in silence: his compassion for the evident wretchedness and dire want of the man restrained the scornful satire that rose to his lips on this folly of first trusting, and then recriminating, hazard.

"In what fashion would you most like me to aid you?" he asked at length. "I am poor myself; yet I could put you in many ways of earning bread, if you were one of those who were willing to labor for it."

"You recommend labor—but you follow pleasure, I believe. That is a common anomaly!"

The ingratitude of the graceless retort to the one who had just succored him in starvation, grated on Tricotrin's ear; but he did not suffer it to influence him. This man was in necessity; in Tricotrin's catholic humanity that fact excused all bitterness in him.

"You judge of what you know nothing," he said, simply. "Pleasure is but labor to those who do not know also that labor in its turn is pleasure. But we have to do with your concerns, not with mine. Can you tell me more of your life, —though you have epitomized it in that one word, Play?"

"What use would it be?" moaned the other, wearily. "I have said, I had my enjoyments, my conquests, my indul-

gences years ago—years ago! Of late—for many a long day
—I have done nothing save hang over the gaming-tables, on
which I had often not even a coin to stake! I have been a
fool—oh, yes! I know it as well as you can tell it me. And
why? Because I had never the courage to be wicked *enough!*
It is the man who is timorous in crime, who alone fails to
make crime a fair mistress, and a good paymaster!"

As he uttered the one-sided warped truth, his delicate
face worked and darkened with a spirit of evil which looked
as though only the power, but never the will, had been lacking in him to give himself wholly over to sin.

Tricotrin saw that, but he passed over the speech without
reply to it.

"What is your country?" he asked, simply.

"By birth I am Greek."

A darkness passed over his hearer's face.

"Slang has made Greek synonym for Cheat! Popular instincts rarely err. And you are 'noble' by birth too, I suppose?"

The stranger winced under the ironic and contemptuous
intonation of the sentence. He made no answer; feeling his
host's lustrous eyes were fixed like an eagle's on him.

"Every Hellenic scoundrel is descended from the Pisistra-
tidæ, or the Alcmœonidæ, if we believe his statement on the
matter!" said Tricotrin, with the same disdainful accent in
his phrase. "What may your name be?"

"Paulus Canaris."

"*What!*"

As the word leapt from his throat he leapt himself on to
the Greek, with his hand on the weakly and subtle form, that
writhed impotently in his grasp.

"Thief—traitor—hound!" he cried, with the intensity of
passion reiterating through the words, while to and fro in his
irresistible grasp he swung the stranger as easily as though
he held a dog. Speechless, breathless, paralyzed, the man
strove in vain to get free from this fiery and instant wrath,

which had thus broken up from the genial and sunny mirth of the one who had fed him and succored him.

"What have I done?" he gasped. "Is this your hospitality?"

Struck by the last word as by a lash, Tricotrin loosed and shook him from him.

"You have broken my bread—you are sacred. But for that—by God!"—

The oath was stifled in his throat; breathing fast and loud, controlling with strong effort the passion which possessed him, he fell back from the gamester, with his back against the casement, seeking the air by instinct, as a hound after combat seeks water.

"What is my crime?" murmured the other, halting, panting, blanched with fear. "What do you know of me?"

"I know you—as the paramour of Estmere's wife!"

The Greek's features grew livid, and all his delicate limbs trembled as with palsy.

"Estmere! Who are *you* then?"

"No matter that! I know all your life; adulterer, liar, betrayer, thief!"

The furious words coursed swiftly on each other; leaning back against the attic window, with his arms crossed on his chest as though to withhold himself from violence against the man made sacred by having eaten of his salt, Tricotrin stood gazing on him, with his eyes aflame like a lion's, and the night wind blowing his hair.

The Greek cowered under that look as under some physical torture; he had no conception of who the man was who thus arraigned him, he had no conception of why his wrath was thus aroused against the paramour of the wife of another, but he knew that the vileness of his own life had been seen by these eyes that pierced him with their accusation and their scorn.

"You use bitter words," he muttered at length, in the ague of fear. "Who are you—in God's name, who are you?"

"Blaspheme God, you who betrayed man!" cried Tricotrin, his passion once more striving for mastery. "No matter who I am—suffice it I am one who knows you. If you had not eaten of my bread I would choke your crimes down your throat with the vengeance on you that you merit. You are safe with me being under my roof, having sat at my board. But for that——"

He ceased; his breath came loud and hard, it went sore with him to let this man pass out in peace. But he would not break the bond that made the guest sacred to him, by the old grand law of nomad tribes; and he would not forswear his word. With a swift movement he turned, swept out the few gold coins his cupboard held, and threw them down at his debtor's feet, with a gesture of speechless scorn.

"I keep my promise even with things as vile as you. There is your 'chance.' Take it, and begone!"

The Greek cowered and shrank with shame, with terror, with repugnance. He hesitated an instant, the dire fear upon him conflicting with the lustful impulse for the gold, that moved him to take it even at this cost. For an instant even the debased nature of the man recoiled from accepting succor given thus. Then,—so low had he fallen,—he stooped, with a hurried, furtive action, caught the coins in the hollow of his hand, and slunk out in his ravening greed.

He was ashamed; but avarice conquered shame.

He went stealthily down the staircase, up which his preserver had so lately brought him, and out through the narrow door. The owner of the house was just up, in the dawn, and washing down his passages with broom and water, singing cheerily a rhythm of his old birth-country, Berri.

"Who lives in your fifth story?" the Greek whispered to him.

The gay, good-humored Berrois smiled.

"Ah, ha! The attic has a prince indeed! Do you not know him? Why, all Paris knows Tricotrin."

"Tricotrin!" murmured Paulus Canaris, as he slunk onward into the early daylight; the name told him nothing; he had never heard it. It increased his perplexity and his terror. He hastened to forget both in trying his "chance" at the nearest gambling den; but he registered the name in his memory.

When he was left alone, Tricotrin stood at the open window, his passion quivering still, hot and bitter, through his blood. It was rarely that rage or grief ever mastered the mellow, happy, and abundant life within him; but when he gave way to either, the emotion was terrible, the hour of his abandonment to it was very dark.

Forte è l'aceto di vin' dolce.

For a long time he stood there, combating the hatred and the remembrance that were so heavy on him. Then he shook himself, as lions shake their manes. The dew was wet on his forehead; his face was flushed red with the fury he had restrained; his chest heaved with quickened breaths. He stretched his hand out, and dashed to shivers the glass from which the Greek had drunk. As the pieces fell he smiled sadly, in rebuke of his own uncontrolled and boyish action.

"Mistigri," he murmured, "a philosopher should be as unmoved seeing his foes as his friends. A philosopher, decidedly, should not keep such a puerility as a Past. I am disgusted with myself, Mistigri. Scold, scold, if you like; that is a favorite way with your sex of showing sympathy: and I deserve it. Bah, Mistigri! even a philosopher is mortal when his personality is touched. I should have been vile enough not to have given that man food if I had known whom it was that I fed. How contemptible that! A clear human duty broken for a private sentiment!"

Mistigri made a murmuring, affectionate noise, as though deprecatory of his self-condemnation, and comprehensive that Man was still too near his progenitor Monkey not to instinctively give blow for blow.

"Clearly contemptible, Mistigri!" continued her owner with a smile, for his moods passed as rapidly as April days from storm to sunshine. "Lacedemonian Charellus was perfectly right. 'By the gods, if I were not in wrath with you I would have you slain.' He knew how wrath obscures reason. Wise man! And we degenerate moderns allege our anger as the very motive to strike! Let us banish the dark spirit, Mistigri. It is the ruin of all peace, and the foe of all philosophy!"

And to banish it, Tricotrin took up his perpetual consolers,—his violin and his meerschaum, and smoking the one drew music from the other. Whenever his joyous serenity was broken he restored its peace by the same spell as gave back sanity to Philip of Spain and Saul to Israel.

When does the artist ever so wholly escape from the oppression of the world around him as when he enters the world of his own creation?

The music stole out from the open casement into the warm gray dawn; and as it floated downward and upward on the quiet air, it breathed its beauty out over the crowded roofs of Paris.

Homeless outcasts, wandering footsore, heard it, and turned backward from where their steps were leading them to the brink of the black river. Lost women, desperate because they could not glean the foul wages of sin, caught the sweet fugitive echoes, and thought with a pang of long dead days, when they had leaned, in innocence and infancy, against their mothers' knees. And one little child in the street below, thrust out to steal with brutal blows, and fearful of returning because his hands were empty, listened where he lay, upon a doorstep, naked, hungry, sobbing,—listened till he fell asleep, with a smile upon his pale bruised lips, and dreamed of flowers and of sunlight, and of the pitying faces of angels.

Thus Tricotrin soothed other souls beside his own.

CHAPTER IX.

"GRAND'MÈRE!" cried Viva; "there is Sarazin! and he is going up to Villiers; and he says he will take us both there, if you will come; and we shall see all its glories; and he has a niece in the dairies, with whom we can stay and sup; and he will bring us back in the evening time. Say yes! oh, do say yes!"

It was very early morning. Grand'mère was boiling the breakfast coffee, and let the pot fall over on to the burning wood as she started and turned at the Waif's breathless and passionate exordium.

"Sarazin! Sarazin is a good creature, and it would be a pleasure for thee," she said, hesitatingly; "but then—Tricotrin?"

"Tricotrin!" cried Viva, with eager impatience. "Tricotrin says there is no better soul than Sarazin; and he always likes me to have pleasure,—you know that, grand'mère! And the sail there and back! and the sight of the château! Oh, come, come, come!"

"Call Sarazin in to breakfast, and I will talk with him," answered grand'mère, evasively, but knowing well in her heart that the child always got her own way.

Sarazin entered willingly. He was a little wizen, sunburnt, hardy creature, with a shell as tough as a cocoanut, and a temper as sweet as its milk. He was the only ferryman near for leagues, and was devoted to the service of Viva, who was as capricious and exacting as most fair mistresses are, and who owed the sunniest hours of her sunny life to him and his clumsy old boats.

One of the peasant proprietors had hired him to take up a load of wheat that had been purchased by the stewards of Villiers. He was to leave his grandson in charge of the ferry, and himself conduct the corn barge to the great château: nothing loth, for it was rarely that he had a chance of quitting his lonely boathouse; and to go up to Villiers was a great event in the lives of the scattered river people of the neighboring hamlets.

Grand'mère, troubled with an indistinct remembrance that Tricotrin had once expressed a wish that Viva should never be taken thither, but unable to recall it plainly enough to be satisfied in opposing the child's entreaty, yielded with a certain disquietude, and locked up her dwelling, and went down the towing-path with a worried conviction that if she were not doing rightly he would hear of her action from the swallows that lived by the hundred under her eaves.

"Why do you always watch the birds so?" she had asked him one day.

"Because I have found out what François d'Assisse did not, that they can talk better to me than I to them. They tell and teach me many things, though the art of flying remains uncommunicated."

And grand'mère had received his speech literally; and had never since then seen the swallows fly in and out of their nests under the ivy without a certain awed conviction that they listened, and saw, and took tidings to their fellow wanderer.

"However, there can be no harm," she thought now; "the little one is with me and Sarazin."

The big brown sailing boat, with its load of corn, was ready; the horses of the wagon that had brought the wheat stood half asleep upon the shore, hock-deep in grass and rushes; the little quaint ferryboat peered out of a nest of vines and fruit-laden pear-trees, and tall leafy poplars. The whole was a lovely study of morning light and peaceful labor.

But Viva heeded little of that; rejoicing in it, after a vague, unconscious fashion, as a plant rejoices in sweet air, but never pausing to think of it with any poet's deep, inborn delight. This was not in her. She was too essentially feminine; too radiantly self-engrossed. What she thought of was, that the peasants who had brought the wheat, and the boys who were in the boat, and the very ferry dog asleep in the sun, all gave her welcome because they found her fair.

Under the shadow flung by the sail, beneath the yellow pile of the corn, while the old woman sat knitting, and scarce looking up as the shores drifted by, Viva, lying full length on a plank, passed down the river,—slowly, dreamily, as before her Tricotrin had done on the hay-barge.

She loved nothing better than these long summer sails; and to her fancy, in that lustrous sunshine, the old boat became a gilded galley, the brown wheat golden treasures, the torn tarred sail a silken canopy, the gliding banks her kingdoms, and she a Cleopatra or a Catherine of Cyprus, sailing onward to land at the marble steps of matchless palaces. For she had the one enchanted power—Youth—with which the linen folds seem robes of purple, the chaplet of cowslips becomes a monarch's crown, the wooden bench is as an ivory throne of empire.

"She dreams,—that child!" murmured grand'mère to the ferry-keeper.

"The young always dream," answered Sarazin. "That is their kingdom of heaven."

"Whose end is hell!"

"Nay, not so. Look you, there are holy dreams, and they end mostly in the cloister; and there are happy dreams, and they mostly fold their wings in their husbands' chimney-corners; and there are——"

"Such dreams as hers," said grand'mère, with a motion of her head toward the child. "And they—if they do not end in an empress's diadem, which cannot be, people all say, out of fairy stories—*they* end in misery, and sin, and shame!"

Little Sarazin looked affrighted.

"What then?" he whispered; "you think the devil talks at that pretty rosy ear?"

Grand'mère shook her head in doubt.

"Sarazin, how that may be, I know not; but I do not think there is any cause for the devil to talk when a woman-child that is fair dreams of her own face."

"That is true," said Sarazin: and he went to the steering of his boat, while the old woman drooped her head over her knitting; and Viva watched the gliding shores with eyes that only saw the dim and glorious shapes of some imagined future.

They had started so early that Villiers was reached by noon, for the tide served them, and the wind also. Sarazin went about his errand; but he first asked permission for the old dame and the child to wander through the park, and gardens, and building; and, since his niece had some favor in the household, obtained it.

Through the sunny alleys, the fragrant avenues, the sweet, still, orange-shaded ways, and the beds of gorgeous blossom, the little bent figure of grand'mère, in her white headgear and blue gown, with Viva's bright, gay, ever-moving form at her side, passed in the sultry August noon.

The voluble dairy-girl was their guide, chattering endlessly: but Viva paid no heed to her. She was absorbed in contemplation; in wonder as to the great man who dwelt here; and in fugitive fancies as to the possibilities of her own right to some such superb domain as this. "Estmere—Estmere—Estmere!" she repeated over and over again to herself. "Is he a king, I wonder?"

She had the haziest ideas as to ranks and habits. There were, to her own thinking, but two classes—the peasants, with whom she was assured she had no link in common; and the princes, with whom she was certain of affinity.

"Does it not make thee afraid?" whispered Sarazin's niece, in an awed whisper, as she led them through the splendors of the banqueting-hall.

Viva tossed back her sunlit head.

"Afraid! I am in my native air—that is all!"

The dairymaid, daughter of very poor and abject charcoal burners of the forest, looked at her and crossed herself; it was true, then, she thought, that this Waif of Tricotrin's came of no mortal mould. What Viva said was true: although she had never known but the simplest mode of existence, though her milk and bread had been served in a wooden bowl, and though her restless feet had danced over a bare brick floor ever since they had first danced at all, the child felt born to greatness: and things of beauty, luxury, or splendor always seemed to her to belong to some native and beloved sphere from which she had been banished. There are daughters and sons of cotters who feel thus; and it is they who give the world its magnificent actresses, its merciless adventuresses, its heaven-born statesmen, its Russian Catherines, its victorious Rienzis. As likewise there are daughters and sons of monarchs that wear their purples in uncouth clumsiness, and cling to swinish tastes and ways, and look like boors amid their own court circles.

"*He* is not here? not the great lord?" she asked once, with a pang of disappointment.

"Silly one!" cried the dairy-girl. "Should *we* be in these rooms if he were?"

"Why not?" said Viva in haughty wrath. "He would let me be at the least: you should have seen how he bowed to me!"

And little by little she dropped aside and wandered away from grand'mère and Sarazin's niece: when she glanced at the great mirrors that they passed she saw how utterly unfitting to the place looked the little brown shriveled figure of the good old woman, and the plump, coarse form of the milkmaid, with their serge gowns, and their linen caps, and their heavy, wooden shoes; and she grew impatient and ashamed of her proximity to them. She liked best to roam through the château alone, and when she met any of the household, glide by them unseen; and so she got away by herself and strayed at ease, dreaming a thousand dreams through the halls, and chambers, and corridors of Villiers.

Once, twice, thrice, she noticed portraits of its owner; and stood before them with rapt, uplifted eyes and folded hands; his face had a strong fascination for her, but the chief spell of his power lay in the fact that he was the first "great prince" she had ever seen. For Viva, the offspring of hazard,

who had no more ancestry than any blue cornflower that
opened to the sun, and knew no more whence she came than
any gold-spotted moth fluttering up in the starlight, was, by
instinct, a passionate aristocrat; and adored what she did not
possess with all the half-envious, half-generous obstinacy of a
thoroughly feminine nature.

No one interfered with her: she went where she would;
and, absorbed in her own thoughts, which were a curious,
vague mixture of pain, pleasure, wonder, desire, irritation,
and enjoyment, unanalyzed as a child's thoughts are, she
never remembered that her "grand'mère" might be uneasy
at her absence, or vexed by her abandonment. Things of
Viva's type very seldom do think of others.

Straying about thus by herself, she came at last into the
picture-galleries; she had an instinctive love of pictures, born
partly of her passion for color, partly of her impulses toward
graceful form and fair ideals.

Except the sketches of Tricotrin she had never seen any
paintings save those in the nunnery-chapel; and hour after
hour went by with her like enchantment in the presence of
the Cuyps and Claudes, Salvators and Titians, Liberis and
Van Horns. To the eyes of a young and imaginative creature
the painter is as a magician, and each picture becomes a mirror of gramarye.

The works that appealed to the soul, the beatitudes and
the martyrdoms of spiritual art, of divine aspiration, were
dumb to her; but the works that were full of fragrance, of
color, of splendor, of magnificent fancy, the works that appealed to the senses by the highest forms of sensuous beauty,
filled her with a rapturous delight.

A tall, frail, white-haired old man, the custodian of the
galleries, seeing her enter, watched her long himself unseen;
it was so seldom that any footfall was heard in his solitude,
that the presence of this vivacious, beautiful, unknown child
was very welcome to him.

He approached her at last, and spoke: Viva, wakened out
of her trance, and ever ready with speech, answered him

gladly, and told him how she came thither, and all else that he chose to ask of her; while in turn she rained questions upon him. To these he replied cautiously: he was a devoted servant of the house, and there were things in their lord's life of which the servants never gossiped. But of the pictures he discoursed readily: and told her what she would of their histories.

Though gifted with the charming facile talents that make, under culture, bewitching and brilliant women, Viva was very ignorant: almost as ignorant in knowledge as she was intelligent in perception, owing less to the nuns' mode of teaching than to her own radiant idleness, and her incurable hatred of trouble. The old custos was pleased to find a listener for his lore, and she was well amused with his stories: to the genealogies and histories of the works she lent indeed but a listless ear, to the anecdotes he told her of the portraits she gave an eager attention. Human life interested her more than any other thing: she had seen so few forms of it; it was environed to her sight with such magical mystery; and it lay in her hands like an unopened casket from which all the gifts of the gods would one day arise to her.

One portrait attracted her in especial.

It was the portrait of a boy, quite young, standing up to his knees in shallow water and flowering bulrushes, with a wounded water-bird in his hand. The singular charm of the picture lay in the union of his sunlit and fearless radiance of boyish beauty, and the tearful, tender, wistful compassion in his eyes as he regarded the stricken bird. She was of too heedless a temper to be very pitiful herself; yet the study moved her and riveted her gaze: it was life-size, the work of a great artist, and bore surety—which some portraits do even to those who know not their subjects—of being a faithful resemblance of the original it re-created.

"Who is that boy?" she asked softly, at length.

The old man sighed:

"One who died long ago."

"Died!—oh, he looks so full of life!"

"'The brightest flowers are always the quickest to fade: how long the brown wallflower lives, but the purple convolvulus withers with its noon."

She was used to such fanciful speech, and it heightened her interest in the portrait.

"Will you tell me of him? was he well known to you?"

"Yes: long years ago, in another land than this. Move you into the shade—there, the sun falls still on *his* face. I will tell you the tale if you wish. There is no shame in it."

He stopped; there was one history in his lord's life that was dark with shame, a shame that every soul in his great households had felt as their own dishonor when it had touched their master's name.

"'Tell me!" cried Viva, happy in her new companion, eager for a new history, forgetful that the anxious heart of the old woman Virelois would be ere this palpitating in wonder and terror at her absence. "Tell me!" she cried, with her bright eyes fastened on the fair eyes of the boy.

And the old man told her:

"It was long ago that yon lad lived. I was young myself in those days. My lord—not this lord, but his father—was a wild and lawless man; proud beyond all, but given over to his passions, which were stronger yet than even his pride. He was always known as the Mad Earl. The world thought his madness surely proved when in his travels he wedded a fisher girl,—from the sea-cabins away to the west, there, by the Biscay Waters. I have heard that they are very proud also—those fishing people of the sands of Olonne; that she refused to him to be aught save his wife. But you know nothing of these things—I forget. Well, he brought her home; there were none to say him nay: she was a magnificent creature, daring, beautiful, free of limb, carrying herself like a fleet forest doe. But of course there was a strange difference betwixt her and the women of his own rank. She was as a wild mare of the desert, and they as the stalled, slender, pampered Spanish jennets, and the trammels of splendor were chains on her, and the tyranny of pomp was a curb that forever fretted and galled her.

"In her own national garb she looked an empress: but in a patrician's robes she was—a noble thing imprisoned, that made one ready to weep. She bore a son in the first year: and I think the only happy moments she knew grew out of the boy. For her husband, repenting his act, took a hatred to her; and he was passionate and hot and cruel, and would scourge her with many hard words of scorn. And that hatred for her spread to her son: he would scarce bear the sight of the child,—yet a nobler little lad never breathed. The child loved his mother, and felt the cruelty to her, though he was but an infant when it came to an end:—she died when he was only a few years old, worn out by futile pain and loss of liberty, like a captive leopardess.

"My lord went into distant lands, and took another wife in her stead,—this time the daughter of a Russian prince; and when in time she also brought him a son his bitterness grew greater yet against his heir who had sprung from a race of French fishers. He would scarce ever see the boy; and never saw him without a mocking taunt or a brutal glance. But the two children grew up together with some seven years between them, and nothing could exceed the love in which they held each other. The difference of age only seemed to serve to draw them closer together. My lord and his wife were seldom with them; they lived in the great world, and the boys were left, with the care of able scholars, in the heart of the old Beaumanoir woods. Only, at such rare times as the castle was filled with guests, it was always the younger that was displayed and caressed and adored, the elder was almost banished. But no venom came between them; there was naught of the Cain in the one, there was generous childish love in the other. Lord Chanrellon—that was the heir's title —had much of his mother in him; he was too proud to complain, and he gave back scorn for scorn with his father. One day when he was fifteen,—he was younger when that picture you see there was painted,—my lord and he came in collision.

The quarrel was brought about by a noble dog that the Earl commanded to be killed, under some specious pretext, but chiefly, it was well known, because Lord Chanrellon loved the poor brute. Wild words came on that score between them: Chanrellon was mad with rage and anguish, and said fiery and furious things in his dead mother's name; and my lord cursed him aloud, and prayed that he might be struck dead rather than ever enter into his heritage. It was an awful scene;—but the whole household were for the boy, and pitied him, and honored him only the more, for he was the beloved one of us all, and we knew that he was in the right, and mortally stung, and wounded, and incensed. Well,—the night of that day some rare jewels were missing:—they required to be reset, and had been left in a casket: great search and demand were made for them: and my lord, blind with wine and with hate, charged his eldest-born with the theft of the diamonds. Ah!—if you had seen the lad's face in that hour! I never beheld a thing so beautiful! its unutterable scorn, its speechless amaze, its luminous truth and honor that any dolt must have read in its gaze! He never made answer to the foul foolish charge;—he only drew himself straight as an arrow, with his head proudly poised like a stag's, and looked his father hard and full in the eyes. Then without a word he passed from the chamber.

"It was near midnight then:—when the sun rose he was missing. We scoured park and forest and hamlet, we hunted through brake and plantation, we dragged water, and we loosed his own bloodhound out on the track. His young brother said that he had been wakened by Chanrellon leaning over him and kissing him on his mouth, and murmuring, 'You shall have it all, my darling—be brave and noble and true;' but he had been still half asleep, and had thought it only a dream. However, it had been no dream—it must have been a terrible truth. For toward eventide we raked up his cap entangled among the water-lilies on the moat, and a poacher crept forward and confessed that about the dawn he had heard a dull splash in the water and had stolen away—

frightened, not daring to see what caused it. So then we knew he was dead:—and the young one grieved for him as a lamb for its mother."

The old man paused; his voice failed him; the time of his sorrow seemed fresh to him as that of a day just gone by, and his gaze was fixed on the fair tender face of the boy that looked down from above in the sunlight.

Viva listened; hushed and wondering.

"Why do you think that he died?" she asked at length.

"Why? why? Child! does not your own heart tell you?"

"But to leave such a splendid heritage?" she murmured.

"Well,—there are some to whom there is no heritage worth aught save their own stainless honor. Lord Chanrellon was one of them. He had the sea-lion's blood of his mother's race, and taunts had lashed that wild, brave, untamable blood into fury——"

Viva mused awhile wistfully; the history touched her, and yet she understood the impulse of the dead heir as little as young Pompeius, with his insatiate and dazzled vanity, could understand the supreme scorn and sacrifice, half contempt half generosity, of the Sullan renunciation.

"And you never knew more of his fate?" she whispered, with a certain sense of dread as the light died off from the portrait while a passing cloud swept over the sun.

"What more was there to know? We searched for his body; but we felt that the search was useless, for the moat was fed by subterranean waters whose channels ran deep, and passed out to the ocean. The child had been pierced to the quick by the scorn cast on his lost mother and the bitterness flung on himself. He had been falsely accused. To tempers like his there is no more unpardonable wound. He was ever impetuous and warm to passion, though those who knew him aright could lead him by his affections with a cord of silk. Well,—the Earl felt remorse, I know: he suffered keenly for awhile; but the boy that he loved was heir now, and this soon sufficed to console him. The lad himself—my present

lord—felt far more enduring grief. For a long time he was
as one who had lost all the treasure he owned. He had
worshiped his elder brother: and the tragedy left its sorrow
on him for so long that I think his nature never wholly recovered its elasticity; it made him grave beyond his years,
though he was so young when it happened."

"Does he ever think of it now?"

"Ah! who can say? My lord is a great man, and lives in
a great world. He may have utterly forgotten—I know not.
For thirty years none have ever heard him allude to his dead
half-brother. Men as high as he have fleeting memories.
Yet—sometimes I fancy he remembers his playmate, for when
he purchased this place and selected it as his favorite resi-
dence, he ordered this portrait among others to be brought
hither. That would look as though all remembrance had not
perished?—however, that also is many years ago now, and
recollection withers under eminence."

"I saw him once, not long ago," whispered Viva, "and I
thought that he looked like a sovereign."

"He is a great man," said the old servant briefly:—her
sympathies were chiefly with the lofty and brilliant life whose
power and strength and dominion allured her fancy: his were
with the young, rash, noble life snapped in twain so early,
like a young pine broken by the first autumnal storm.

He looked at her half curiously half angrily.

"You have not much heart, you fair thing!" he muttered
as he moved away: Viva laughed a little to herself,—she
remembered that the Count's daughter at the convent had
said it was "provincial" to feel emotion, and she accepted
his remark as a compliment to her own aristocracy.

The sun was still clouded, and there was a gray shadow
lying across the face of the portrait, as she gave one lingering
farewell glance to it, and fluttered on to gaze in entranced
delight at the velvet beauties of Boucher, the pictured pageants of Versailles, the rose-wreathed laughing goddesses of
Watteau.

The old man, disappointed, went back to his nook in one

of the embayed casements, and bent afresh over a manuscript catalogue of his beloved collection, which had been a labor of love with him for many years; he took no more heed of her, but when later on she passed him with a gay farewell, flying with swift feet down the long galleries, he murmured after her:

"*You* will never harm yourself for another's sake, you handsome, wanton dragonfly, though many may suffer for yours, like enough!"

Viva did not hear: she was out of the picture-galleries and pursuing her adventures through the building, with her long, fair, tumbled hair flying behind her like a comet's golden train.

"Oh how foolish he must have been to have given up this!" she thought: the boy's face haunted her, but his history failed to touch her because it seemed to her a madness so absolute and so insensate to fling away such proud inheritances for the mere sake of a stung honor and a dead mother's memory. She had been always caressed, indulged, adored; she had a charming innocent vanity that made any doubt of herself impossible; she was never wounded by any shame at her fate, because she was so perfectly assured that her birth must be royal at least, if not more than mortal. To comprehend the sensitive pride that had refused to accept honors begrudged; the fiery impulse that had refused to remain a burden to a race that had rejected his mother; the childlike chivalry of tenderness that had chosen rather to perish than live, barring out the brother he loved from his heritage; was impossible to her: their nobility, indeed, she saw; but what she felt far more clearly was their overwrought and headlong self-ruin.

She wandered on, through the reception-rooms and conservatories, as idly and as gayly as a bird wanders through a rosiery, and paused once more in breathless amaze of wondering delight in the midst of the tropical houses. She who had never beheld any flowers save the flowers of the field and the woods, had never seen aught in her dreams equal to these glorious blossoms of purple and scarlet and amber, these gigantic perfume-breathing lilies, these marvelous parasites with their net-work of color, these palms like the columns of some Solomon's Temple.

She was in perfect solitude: there was nothing living beside herself save the canaries and lovebirds and cockatoos that made their home amid the profuse vegetation. She sank down on the marble steps of the entrance, entranced; scarcely breathing, yet almost laughing with ecstasy. As the hues of the Bouchers and Watteaus had enchanted her eyes, so this wilderness of color, this delirium of perfume, intoxicated her senses. She clasped her hands above her head in rapture.

"Ah!" she cried aloud to the wandering birds; "ah, this must have been the world I belonged to!—this was the kingdom of my birth!"

To her it seemed far likelier that she had sprung from the violet chalice of some superb flower, such as those that hung by the thousand around her, than that anything of want, of humiliation, of human care or human shame, should ever have weighed with her.

Her origin was a mystery; her existence was dependent upon charity; her only recollections were of the homely hearth of an old peasant woman: but this made no difference to Viva. She believed devoutly in the splendor of her own descent, and gazing down the maze of tropical color, and drawing in the delicious odors of the magic flowers, it seemed to her that she only revisited the place of her birth, that she only breathed the air that she had used to breathe in her native land.

And whether this was in truth the awakening of dim infant memories and associations long lost but unforgotten, or whether it was but the fancied glories of an imagination steeped in fairy lore and legendary fantasies, she never asked herself. To her own persuasion, lying on these marble steps, under these wondrous coils of blossom, she was like the slumbering princess of the enchanted forest, who waited for her coming hero, for the advent of her empire. And dreaming thus in the hot atmosphere, in the intense perfume, in the lulling of the fountains that played near, the sultry fragrance overcame her, her head sank down upon the marble, and she fell asleep.

Lying thus, canopied by the purple-flowering vine of the Pacific, with her flushed cheek on the white stone and her lips lightly parted, and the cambric of her boddice half open, showing the rise and fall of her snowy chest, a youth, coming in through the orangeries, saw her, and started and paused. He was a handsome boy, with brown delicate features, and dark slumbrous eyes, that lighted and smiled as they fell on her.

"A little peasant with a princess's face! Where can she come from, I wonder?" he thought, as he stooped down from the stair above her on which his steps had been arrested, and looked long and closely at her as she slept. He was moved and thrilled with her loveliness; but he did not hesitate to study it mercilessly in its unconsciousness: he only hesitated as to whether or no he should waken her.

He could learn who she was without her aid; and she might raise some alarm if she were startled.

He guessed that she came from some one of the hamlets, and had strayed in thither, and fallen asleep through the heat of the day and the hot-houses. He bent down one moment, on an impulse to awaken her by kisses on her cheek; but some look on her face, even in its ignorance of slumber, repressed the impulse as it rose. He scarcely dared to adventure that mode of calling her back to the sentient world. He gazed at her long, and drew some of her curls through his hands. She was unlike any one of the peasant girls whom he had ever seen among the vineyards or on the river barges: he felt a difference that he could not have analyzed.

Then, moving very softly, he gathered some of the finest fruit from the grapes and oranges that hung abovehead, laid them down on her blue kirtle without wakening her, and drawing off a ring from his hand, slipped it over a branch of yellow jasmine, and left it with the fruit on her lap. Then, laughing to himself, he moved away, and out of the tropical houses.

"The pretty fool will think they came from paradise!" he mused. "It will be the best mode to rouse her to interest: nothing allures a woman like a mystery! Who can she be? but that can soon be learned."

Viva slept on, unconscious of her gazer and her gifts. The day was far advanced when she awoke with a start, as a loriot flying past her brushed her forehead with his wing. Her eyes were barely opened ere she saw the fruit and flower and jewel on her lap; she gave a loud cry, half of terror, half of delight. By her they were believed to be as surely fallen from a supernatural hand as Dorothea's roses and apples which were sent from Eden to convince the scoffer and the skeptic.

The place filled her with a sudden affright. The birds seemed elves, the flowers seemed like glistening eyes. The odors and the heat stifled her; the cadence of the fountains sounded like fairies' music. She gathered all the presents up in her linen skirt, and fled headlong out from the winter-gardens, and under the colonnades of orangeries, and forth into the fresh air, hardly knowing what she did, but believing that she bore some fairy's treasures with her; calling aloud on Sarazin and grand'mère, and half delirious with the wonder of her own greatness, that thus marked her out for such especial favor from this elfin world which was unseen by common eyes.

She had some recollection of the way she had come from the out-houses where Sarazin's niece had her dwelling; and she rushed on and on, across the gardens, down the terraces, over the lawns, along the avenues, all on fire with her marvelous story, panting and thirsting to gain a listener. Instinct took her right, and she dashed headlong into the wide cool chamber, with its blue and white Dutch tiles, and its sweet, wholesome scent of cows and of milk, of thyme and of clover, where the dairy-women were clustered around the old Virelois who was sobbing and wringing her hands, and calling on the Virgin and Tricotrin to aid and forgive her, for she had lost the child.

Viva, utterly regardless of the woe that she had caused, bounded into their midst, and held the jasmine branch, with its yellow stars, before their astonished eyes.

"Grand'mère, grand'mère! Look here! You and I knew that I was not as others are. See what the fairies have sent me!"

The old woman, breaking from the circle of her sympathizers, threw her arms round her recovered treasure, scolding and caressing her, praising the saints and reproving the wanderer, all in one breath: but Viva shook aside her embrace with a certain impatience.

"I had a right to go where I chose!" she cried; "and look here! were not these well worth the straying for? Oh, you do not know what I have seen,—such things! such things! And I fell asleep at last in the temple of the flowers; and while I slept it was all changed, and every blossom turned into a fairy, and every bird into a wood-elf; and when I awoke there were these in my lap, and the magic ring hung on the great amber jasmine!"

Her audience were dumb with solemn amaze. Viva, unconscious of her own exaggeration, and working herself into the full credence that all had been as she told it, stood in their circle proud with all the pride of one selected by fate for an extraordinary distinction, and smiling on them with contemptuous benignity.

"Oh! you have never known such a wonder—you!" she said, with scorn at the mutterings of the awe-stricken dairywomen. "Of course you have not; one must be of that world ere one beholds it. Your cows chew the daisies and buttercups, only tasting in them food to make milk: but none the less do fairies and elves live under the grasses for those who have sight that can see them. Yes; it was all as I tell you. The place was full of a glory, and I heard the most exquisite music—so soft! so soft!—and you can feel the fruit, and smell it, and eat it, if you doubt; and you can take the jasmine in your hand, if you like, and watch the ring on it sparkle and flash!"

"It is very strange!" murmured Grand'mère anxiously, while among the women the myth soon grew into an article of faith, with the giant growth of any popular delusion; but they held aloof from touching either the fruit or the flower.

"You are afraid!" cried Viva, with more and more cruel disdain. "Do you suppose they would give what would hurt me?"—and she pressed a peach to her curling red lips.

Grand'mère caught her hand with a scream.

"Child! child! If the fruit be unholy!——"

"Pooh!" laughed Viva, setting her pearly teeth in the luscious, juicy pulp.

They watched her, expecting some horrible change; what they knew not: but all they saw was a child enjoying a fruit. Viva, however, had only done it out of bravado. She was not by any means secure herself that some extraordinary transformation might not take place in her, though she had too much of the Eve to resist the temptation of trying; and she felt a sense of relief that she would have scorned to have acknowledged when the peach was eaten down to its stone, and no awful results had ensued.

Encouraged by her exemption from evil, the women ventured at length to stretch timid hands out for the jasmine bough, and gaze at the ring that hung on it, and babble among themselves with voluble excitability. Grand'mère's face alone remained wistful and anxious, and her tongue was mute.

"It is truly a noble bauble," was all she said; "but how canst thou tell, child, whether it will give thee pleasure or pain? It came to thee for an act of disobedience."

Viva, infuriated, and full of outraged dignity, seized the jasmine out of her hand, and went off by herself to a distant nook of the dairy, and began counting her grapes and her oranges.

"You are a set of senseless peasants!" she muttered, the brown bright mouse-like eyes of the old woman were dimmed a moment with tears she would not shed; but Viva, engrossed in making the sunset rays play on her jewel, never saw that dumb reproach.

The milk-women were very angered, and called her a spoilt insolent baby, and jabbered hard things of her in under-tones, and began to believe all this magical story a lie. She cast one glance of supreme scorn upon them, then turned her back to them where she sat on her stool, and put the jasmine on her hair, and the ring on her finger.

There was a pleasant meal set ready in the dairy chamber, of honey, and cakes, and coffee, and hard eggs; a meal whose enjoyment her absence and the anxiety it had involved, had spoiled and postponed. Sarazin's niece came kindly though shyly to her and pressed her to join in it; Viva was extremely hungry, having eaten nothing since her forenoon bread and chestnuts in the boat, but she was too proud to deign to acknowledge it, and would have died of starvation rather than have shared in their supper. She shook her head in petulant negative: and sat alone eating her fairy grapes, which were delicious indeed, but unsatisfactory, save to her pride.

When the time came to leave the dairy-house for the boat, she vouchsafed them never a word, but swept out through the huge brass pans on the floor with the step of a young sovereign, and passed into the soft gray evening with the jasmine crown glittering like a wreath of golden stars upon her head.

"If that be how jewels change the temper, they must be the curse of the world," muttered grand'mère.

Viva heard: but she would not deign to reply.

"She is a vain wicked thing: she will bring the Virelois to shame," said one of the dairy-maids, standing with arms akimbo, on the lintel of the door.

"Do you believe in that story? She told it like the truth?" asked another.

"It may be; such things have been known," said a third, cautiously.

"But we have lived here all our lives, and never heard of the like at Villiers," responded the skeptic from the doorway. "If the young lord were here, I should say it was one of his tricks."

The conclave laughed, the suggestion was agreeable: to have traced an envied distinction to a fount of evil is the sweetest palliative to jealous mortification.

"She called us peasants," continued the cynic in the porch. "I had a good mind to tell her we were not bastards, but knew who our mothers and fathers were, which is much more than she can say, and I would have said it too, if it had not been for the poor old grand'mère,"—and she plucked a spray of honeysuckle from the outside wall and bit it spitefully, regretting her excess of good nature.

Over the broad green pastures that stretched around the dairies, two herdsmen came driving up some of the cows to their stalls, pretty smooth-hided lowing creatures with sweet-toned bells that sounded pleasantly through the evening stillness. Both animals and men were well at Villiers; they were never overtasked, and they were ever gently treated.

"What news, friend Jourdan?" called out the girl from the doorway, to the cowherd nearer her. There was very little news at Villiers at such seasons as its lord was absent.

"Piffirie has foaled," said Jourdan, meaning a favorite farm mare.

"Ah, bah! And what else?"

"The mill people say their son has got a first-class medal at Paris for his painting. Thou rememberest him?—that idle simpleton who was forever chalking over the stable walls, and staring at dirt and stones and mosses?"

"A medal! And the fool could not drive a cow straight!" laughed the woman, with her hands in her side. "What else?"

"Nothing. Yes, wait,—the bull Georgeo broke his feeding tether, and led us a fine dance this morning; and they tell me the young seigneur has come back unexpectedly, and will stay here some weeks. He is in disgrace for some freak; so they say——"

And he passed on with his herd to the fresh-smelling, fresh-foddered stables away to the left.

The dairy-girl in the porch clapped her hands above her head, and shouted with gleeful triumph.

"I said if he only were back! Do ye hear, Paule, Claudine, Lisette? He is back! Ah, ha! So much for the tale of the fairies! so much for the worth of her truth! The ring, the ring! It is not a marriage ring, I guess—ha, ha!"

And she laughed till the rafters rang where she stood under the honeysuckles;—for jealousy is cruel as the grave.

The boat went home in silence. Sarazin was tired; grand'mère full of thought; the child's heart swelled with rage and pride where she sat with her hands full of the magic fruits, and her eyes watching the star-rays play on the jewel she wore. Save their good nights, none of them spoke a word.

The dog barked, the white cat purred, even Roi Doré woke on his perch to crow a welcome; Viva took no notice of any one of them. Was she who came back dowered with elfin gifts to heed such common sounds?

Moreover, she was not quite at ease with herself. And one must be very much at one's ease to enjoy such tender, homely, innocent things as these.

Grand'mère got some bread and some honeycomb and some milk, and brought them to her in silence; but Viva left the food almost untasted, though she needed it: she knew she had been wrong. They went up stairs in the clear moonlight, needing no other light, and the child undressed herself slowly, with the moonbeams falling about her fair round limbs, and shining shower of hair.

The Virelois, still in silence, opened her book of hours and read—knowing the words by heart, and forgetting to turn over the pages.

Suddenly Viva sprang to her, and threw her arms about her.

"Grand'mère, I was wicked! I am sorry!"

The old woman's firm lips quivered.

"That is enough," she said, softly; then she laid her hands on the girl's shoulders, and held them there, looking straight down into her face as she knelt.

"That was a true tale you told us this day?"

Viva's eyes met hers full and fearlessly.

"Quite true, grand'mère."

"It is strange!" murmured grand'mère: then she stooped and kissed the Waif's flushed, wondering, eager face.

"The saints take thee in their holy keeping! Go—say thy prayers."

CHAPTER X.

Viva, two days later, was lying wide awake in her little white nest, under the eaves, while still the first tittering of her friends, the swallows among the ivy, was the only sound of the coming day, and Roi Doré, in the shed hard by, was giving his first challenge to the yet unrisen sun. Her heart was in a tumult of glad excitation: for the first time the romance, befitting such a fairy princess as she, had touched her life; for the first time those long-careless elfin ancestors of hers had bethought them of her, and had sent her a visitant from their immortal home. The first page of that bright-scaled book of Fœrie, which she called her Future, had been opened to her gaze; the charmed reading of the mystic volume had commenced. A terrible loss had come to her, which wore to her enchanted eyes the brilliancy of an immeasurable gain: her childhood had gone forever.

Viva, lying awake there in the dullness of the dawn, was dreaming of the wonderful things that had glorified the days gone by; decidedly those fairy progenitors had remembered her, and sent her a Fairy Prince at last!

It had happened in this wise:

The previous morning had been very hot—hot to tropical fervor, even in the cool old convent gardens, with their deep lush grass, their silent darkened flower-filled ways, their noiseless air syringa-scented, and moved by the silent wings of countless birds.

The child had been in some disgrace, and given a Latin canticle to learn; and, banished into solitude, had learned her task with random quickness, knowing nothing of its meaning, and then resigned herself to indolent delight, lying half covered with the thyme and plumes of speargrass, and doing nothing in sublime content. Hours had drifted over her uncounted, when the boughs above her bent, their leafage rustled, and close beside her dropped—a Fairy Prince, as Viva instantly concluded,—a youth of two and twenty years, or somewhat more; dressed in dark velvet, like an old picture, delicate, gracious, very fair to look at, and with a voice like music. He had let himself fall from the convent wall—climbed by the ivy's aid—and for the first time in her life, Viva, long caressed by the voices of honest affection, heard the dangerous voice of adulation.

The innocent but supreme vanity of the child made her, though startled, amazed, perplexed, and a little frightened, quickly grasp the flattering truth that it was her own loveliness—seen on the highway road he told her—which had incited him to this adventurous experiment; and her visitant commanded a soft, sweet eloquence that won its way at once to her hearing. She did not comprehend one-half that he said, nothing that he implied; but she knew the one fact: that he thought her very beautiful—and was too well content with it to refuse to hear him ring the changes on it.

Nature had planted in her an innate coquetry, as thoroughly instinctive as a bird's flying, and the instinct moved her now without her knowing it. Flushed, startled, infinitely fair, half risen from her bed of fragrant grasses, she gazed at her young adorer, and listened breathless to his utterances; but the coy, proud, arch, malicious, feminine nature in her, taught her to parry his words, and play with his worship, in an impulse to defend herself and torment him, that astonished one who had thought to find her some shy, simple, pretty idiot of the peasantry.

Viva—by nature wholly free from shyness, and proud of herself from her conviction of her lofty birth—thought nothing more charming than such an interruption of the too even tenor of her days; all the more charming because of the atrocious crime the stranger's presence formed against all the laws of her detested foes, the nuns. She was perfectly aware that she was sinning against all their rules in not fleeing instantly from this intruder; but the rebellion was just what she enjoyed. His oratory was most silvery sweet on her ear, for it told her only of herself; and, half willing, half reluctant, she listened.

It was just what suited that old, shadowy, luscious-scented garden, and such an enchanted princess as herself, to be thus beset under the mulberry shadows by such a wooer!

Of love, in men's and women's meaning, the Fille des Fées had no conception; this was only worship, she thought, such as in her fairy stories the captured Prince always gave the sovereign Beauty. The youth was facile of tongue; in very brief space he had filled her brain with intoxicating images of herself, learned all she had to tell of her short history, and conjured up before her magnificent visions of the world from which she was shut out; he might have progressed yet further, but that the voice of Sœur Séraphine calling for Viva and the Latin canticle interrupted his success. Not caring to be caught in that rookery of women, the young stranger murmured his hurried and tender farewell, swung himself lightly by branch and ivy coil up the steep wall, and disappeared, leaving her in a tumult of excitement, which sent her with scarlet cheeks and dancing eyes to the call of Sœur Séraphine, and reduced all memory of the canticle to chaos.

She awoke the next morning, feverish with wonder and

expectation; he had begged her to meet him at the beech-tree, and had promised to tell her of a thousand marvelous things. She had told grand'mère, and grand'mère had not been as pleased as she had anticipated; grand'mère had not taken her view of the stranger; grand'mère had scornfully suggested that if he were a fairy prince he would not be under the necessity of climbing earthly walls; grand'mère had finally stated that it must have been he who had had to do with the ring up at Villiers, and declared that she thought Tricotrin would not like her to go to the beech-tree. Whereupon Viva, self-willed, but frank as the day, had declared that she would go, that nothing should prevent, and had been fiery, and wayward, and, as she well knew, naughty. She had gone to bed with naughtiness in her soul, and awoke with it.

When she threw open her little lattice, close under its sill, where a robin's nest had been made in the spring, and was still there though the young redbreasts had all flown, there gleamed something of all colors with a shimmer of gold and of silver. It lay on the nest; trembling with delight she drew it up through the casement; it was a collar of exquisite workmanship wreathed with forget-me-nots in turquoises and opals—ten thousand times more beautiful than the silver wreath of that odious Adéle!

With the self-same action as poor Gretchen's, Viva, laughing, and almost crying with joy, clasped the lovely thing round her own white throat, and gazed enraptured at her own reflection in her tiny glass, and rushed down stairs to where the old woman was busied with the breakfast-coffee!

"Grand'mère! grand'mère! Look! Was he not a fairy prince after all?"

Grand'mère looked, and, to Viva's amazement, seemed troubled; even while woman-like she marveled at the beauty of the toy.

"The only fairy prince the world holds—a rich man," she

muttered. "Your throat is more graceful without it, my little one!"

"Grand'mère!" cried Viva, in supreme scorn, "that is because I am dressed like a child—like a peasant! If you saw me with silks and laces and all that one ought to have!"

"Ought to have!" murmured the old woman as she set down the brown rolls and the steaming milk. "There is no one from whom you could claim even *these* as your right, Viva."

Viva did not hear the rebuke; she was standing in ecstasy before a great burnished copper caldron that served as a mirror, watching the sunshine play on her necklace. Grand'-mère was very silent during the breakfast, though her cheerful loquacious tongue was generally never still over her coffee. Viva was silent, too, angered that her splendid possession had not met with more enthusiasm. Already the jewels on her throat had cast a shadow on her young soul; they were so costly and so brilliant that all the dear familiar things of her home—even grand'mère's brown face in its frame of white linen—looked common and unwelcome.

"You will go to the beech-tree?" asked the old woman.

The child tossed her spirited head.

"Of course! I said so!"

But when Viva came in the late afternoon to her tryst, under the beech boughs, knitting her scarlet worsted, sat grand'mère.

Viva could have cried, and her prince, when he came also, could have cursed, with vexation. But he was not so frank as the Waif, he showed no displeasure; on the contrary he talked so softly and charmingly, showed so graceful a respect toward the old age of the Virelois, and evinced such interest in all he had heard of Tricotrin, that even grand'-mère's prejudices began to dissolve.

"She is so lovely; she is fit to be a princess in earnest, the little angel!" thought the latter. "The young man speaks well—he has a fair face—who knows? ....."

And her thoughts drifted on building castles almost as aerial and baseless as Viva's.

He, when he left them and sauntered away to where his servants and horses waited in the shadow, mused to himself:

"The old fool will give me more trouble than the young one. But the child is so handsome—I never met with her rival—she will be worth some patience and some strategy!"

For the boy, with his delicate face and his tender voice, was at heart the coldest of sensualists; and youth is not seldom the most cruel of egotists.

"Is he not a prince now, grand'mère?" laughed Viva, in triumph. The old woman mused.

"He is well spoken," she cried, cautiously. "But I misdoubt if Tricotrin will wish you to keep that pretty toy; and, —do you like this one as well as that great lord of Villiers that you told me about?"

"Oh, no!" cried Viva, fervently, careless of how her confession hurt her present hero. "*He* looked like a king, a Charlemagne, or a David, or an Arthur, you know. This one is only like a Prince Fainéant!"

And she laughed mischievously at her own merry conceit. She was delighted that "this one" should worship her, but she had no inclination to worship him.

"It is dangerous," thought the old woman, anxiously. "Ah, if Tricotrin were only a man in a house, like a Christian, instead of always wandering, wandering, wandering, like a gipsy, one could let him know, and he would come. M. le Curé would write for me. But he is like the wind, going all over the earth, no one knows why or whither. Well! the good saints have her in her keeping;—though to be sure one does not know whether she was ever baptized, which may make them indifferent. But I do not think they would forsake an innocent child for that; and—Tricotrin is a sorcerer, he will come if any real peril touches her."

So she comforted herself with the remembrance of the occult powers of Viva's guardian, and did not try to discover

who the young man was, lest she should find him of a rank
that would dazzle with still more fatal effect the eminence-
seeking eyes of the ambitious Waif.

To the best of her power the good old creature tried to
screen the child from the sight or approach of this dangerous
stranger. But the resources that riches command, and the
subtilty of such love as the young voluptuary had conceived
for the "Light of the Loire," were more than a match for the
Virelois' honest and simple endeavors.

He made no more trysts since Viva so innocently revealed
them, but over and over again he waylaid her, in the woods,
on the high-road, at the ferry, or in the convent garden when
she was condemned to solitude for inattention or insolence;
and such faults were now more common than ever. Viva was
of necessity often alone; and he had many opportunities to
gain her ear. He filled it with many hyperboles about her
own loveliness, with many asseverations of his own homage to
it, and with what was yet more alluring to her, many pictures
of the "world" for which she longed. Cities of Italy all
glowing with flowers and wild with festivals; masked balls
all a-glitter with rich hues and shining jewels; summer-fêtes
with the toy-boats drifting on summer-lakes to palace-steps
hidden in myrtle and oranges; Paris itself in its nights of
rejoicing, with the churches all domes of sparkling fire, and
each street a stream of laughing life—all these he painted to
Viva, and, relying on the child's absolute ignorance, promised her deathless roses, royal power, every manner of
glory and delight, if she would go thither with him. But
Viva resisted this: she would have dearly liked it she told
him for sake of all those wonderful things which he promised
her. But then—Tricotrin, grand'mère, Roi Doré, Bébeé, all
that there were to leave!

He could not make her reconciled to flight from them all;
and he soon found that in her love for Tricotrin, whom he
held in light scorn never having seen, as some vagabond
scoundrel—lay the stoutest foe he had to encounter. Without this he might easily have lured her to her own ruin by

those chief agents of her sex's destruction, vanity and the desire of wealth. It was in her love for her protector that lay the only shield she had, unconscious as she was of her own danger. It was in vain that her wooer promised to acquaint Tricotrin of her presence in Paris if she once would but go there; Viva would shake her head and ask him mournfully how could he do that when no one knew where Tricotrin lived? It was no less in vain that he strove to persuade her that Tricotrin could not be angered, but would rather be pleased that she should have any pleasure. Her heart was too loyal to her only friend to let her be induced to go from the home that he gave her, unknown to him. Moreover, Viva was rather deterred by her consciousness that grand'mère did not approve of the stranger, or of his jeweled toys, or of any part of the business; and the disapproval of the good indulgent old woman was so rare on any project of the child's whom she loved so well that it had a weight with Viva that none of the sermons of those Sisters, who were always scolding her, would have possessed. Her young suitor was irritated at the slow progress he made, he was used to conquer quickly, and the unforeseen difficulty he had here piqued his pride and his self-admiration.

"We must come to a climax," he thought one evening as he sauntered to meet her. "It is no use playing the Faust any longer for nothing; and if ever there were a Gretchen whom jewels will tempt and console it is this little vain ignoramus!"

As he mused he came near her; standing beside a waterspring with the jug she had come to fill hanging empty in her hand, while she dreamed of—not himself, though he flattered himself that she did so—but of her own perfections as he had mirrored them to her.

They were young; but both their loves were as egotistic and as insincere as though they were two subtle courtiers playing at sentiment for the sake of intrigue. It is not always in youth that the loves are the strongest and purest. The insincerity and the egotism were unconscious in her, in him they were part of his system; but with both they were there.

"Viva!" he whispered as he stole behind her. "That is too much Cinderella's work for my Princess!"

The poor little princess colored angrily: she was only too quick herself to disdain useful errands.

"Grand'mère is old, and the water is far to fetch," she said, hurriedly, apologizing for doing what duty, and affection, and veneration for age alike demanded. So soon had the poison he had sown borne fruit.

"You can do these things and look a princess still!" he murmured. "Still, I would see you where slaves should obey your slightest word."

"Yes!" sighed Viva.

He always spoke in hyperbole to her, and the child's imagination was intoxicated by it.

"Well! Come, then! I must leave your province with to-morrow."

"Leave it!"

She turned a little pale, and looked up startled: she was not prepared to lose this generous eloquent visitant, who had come to break, with the charm of so much mystery the too tranquil tenor of her days.

"Leave it? Yes. Will you regret me?"

"Oh indeed! I should miss you so much!"

Her face grew very sad and earnest. She felt her lips quiver a little. She did not like to think her fairy-story was going thus soon to be broken off without any more wonder-flowers blooming for her.

"Then you love me, my fairest?"

"I try to do so, monsieur," said Viva, softly.

It was the truth; she did try. She thought he deserved her love, he was so good to her; but, in real fact, she did not give him quite so much genuine fondness as she gave Roi Doré. He bit his lip with irritation; he knew the total absence of love that spoke in the answer. Still, the chagrin and the mortification only made him more resolute in pursuit.

"All I dare hope is to make you love me one day!" he murmured caressingly. "To be loved as I love were too much to desire; but, if you would but trust yourself to me it should go hard but I would win your heart. Come! Come to that world I have so often painted to you. Come—to be its idol, its empress, its treasure!"

"I should dearly love it!" sighed Viva, wistfully; "but——"

"There is no 'but,'" murmured her tempter. "How lost you are here! A ferryman, a swineherd, a postillion by hazard, the only creatures that see what a king must adore! If this man whom you speak of cared really for you, would he keep you in poverty and obscurity thus? Come with me, my fairest. You shall be queen of Paris, I swear to you!"

The child sighed again. Her cheeks were burning, her eyes glittering, her whole soul intoxicated. Was he a prince of France? she thought. Why not? And then to refuse him when he was willing to take her to share all his glories!

His arm stole round her, lightly brushing the hanging profusion of her fair curls.

"Come! come! to have France for your sovereignty, and all men who look once in your beautiful eyes for your slaves!"

Viva glanced up, half vaguely terrified, but still in a trance of incredulous and dream-like rapture. With the next moment she might have said yes,—she might have rushed to her own ruin, blind with the longing for change and for power,—she might have fallen headlong into the abyss opened beneath her;—but one word was her savior.

That word was;—"Viva!"

Under the trees stood Tricotrin.

With a bound like a deer's she sprang to him. Her young lover stood, sorely discomfited, gazing in blank amaze-

ment, in bitter annoyance, at this man of whom he had heard
so much, and whom he had never seen; who came so unwel-
comely, in so untimely a moment, between him and his
prey. Tricotrin's bright eyes swept over him, and a great
wrath gleamed in them; but he stroked the girl's hair caressingly.

"Who is your friend, Viva?"

"A stranger; a prince, I think!" she whispered eagerly.
"And he has given me beautiful toys, all covered with jewels,
lovelier than the gold things they have on the altar; and he
says if I will go with him he will show me Paris *en fête*, and
give me roses that will never die, and diamonds, and riches,
and the life of an empress! May I go? and will you go too?
and we can make grand'mère so happy! And he says that
kings' daughters will not be noticed when *I* pass through the
streets!"

The breathless words, poured out in all their childish
mingling of selfishness and generosity, of innocence and
vanity;—Tricotrin listened, then laid his hand gently on her
shoulder:

"Go to grand'mère, Viva. I will talk with this good
friend of yours, and hear a little of all these wonderful things
to which he invites us. Do as I tell you, my child. You
shall not lose the deathless roses by obedience."

Viva looked at them alternately a little wistfully; she was
loth to go.

"He has been so kind!" she murmured softly; "and I
should like to go, if I may!"

Then she obeyed, and passed from them toward the
cottage, her head turning still wistfully back to them, with
the empty jug still hanging in her hand, her errand to the
water-spout forgotten.

Tricotrin stood in silence, waiting till she should be beyond hearing. The youth stood his ground, too proud to
turn away, but livid with chagrin, rage, and mortification;
marveling also at the aspect of the man who had come thus
between him and his soul's desire. He had thought with

light contempt of the wanderer, whom the old peasant deified and the child adored, as of some poverty-stricken, folly-steeped vagabond; some strolling musician, since they spoke of his art; some half-outlawed eccentric, whom he could quiet with coin. He was bewildered at the royal and splendid beauty, the careless, fearless bearing, the magnificent manhood of this bohemian who stood before him in the linen blouse of the people, and with a little black monkey peering, witch-like, from over his shoulder.

Viva once out of sight, Tricotrin swung round, his eyes like blue lightning in their wrath.

"So, Lord Chanrillon! this is the thief's work in which you spend your villegiatura!"

The young man looked at him in silence, startled into speechless amazement at the sound of the name that he bore, a name he had carefully concealed through the whole of the siege he had laid to Viva. He recovered himself with an effort.

"Since you know my title," he said, with chill languor, "you know also the respect due to it. Know still further that I have no wish to parley with you on any subject."

"That I will warrant you have not! But your wishes are not what I shall consult. Do you know that I could kill you where you stand just as easily as I could break that slender sapling asunder; and,—by God!—I have a mind to do it, too, you beardless libertine, you smiling sensualist!"

His height towered above the young man's slight stature; his voice rolled out in sonorous passion; his chest heaved with his quickened breathing. A momentary horror seized his hearer, who shrank back with an involuntary impulse, while his clear, brown cheek turned white like a fainting woman's. Who could tell, he thought, what the vengeance of this lawless republican might be?

Tricotrin saw the fear of him, and laughed bitterly in his wrath.

"Pshaw, child! Men do not kill such things as you, though it is dangerous to spare adders because they look so small; a wound unto death is one's common reward for the misplaced compassion! Well, what plea do you raise in defense of your villainy?"

The youth laughed coldly and scornfully.

"I am not accustomed to raise pleas for my actions; still less should I do so to an inferior. If I needed one, however, the easiest would be found in the overtures that were made to me by your——"

The lie faltered and died unfinished on his tongue. He knew that as little might a lion be enraged with impunity as this man be goaded with safety. He replaced his falsehood with a scoff.

"Pardon me! I can understand your annoyance. The annoyance of losing the one ewe lamb! But; if I remember the Bible story aright, the ewe lamb went with much eagerness to the sacrifice. Your Viva does not differ from Bathsheba! Besides, I mean very well by her. The charming little fool is wholly lost here."

Tricotrin's hands fell on his shoulders, and shook him to and fro, as the jaws of a lion can shake what they seize but forbear to destroy.

"Another word like these and I will fling you out into that water, to sink or swim as you may!"

The youth freed himself from the grasp with difficulty, growing pale with rage and fear.

"It would do you too much honor to resent your outrage myself," he said insolently; "I will send my grooms to the task."

Tricotrin, even in the tempest of his wrath, laughed at the threat with his old ironic amusement.

"You will? Indeed! It will be a mistake—for your grooms! For the rest, my lord, as you term yourself———"

"I decline any more speech with you!"

"Pshaw! You will listen as long as I choose," answered Tricotrin, with contemptuous command. "Honor you have none; good faith you have none; but your father has both. If you do not swear that from this hour Viva is free from your vile temptations, and keep your oath to the letter, Estmere shall learn what the heir to his name can become!"

The young man broke in on the words with a laugh of insolent ridicule.

"The earl will not aid you much! He and I are very distant acquaintances. Besides, Estmere has quite youth enough in him to be no saint himself."

A darker storm swept over Tricotrin's face.

"Europe reveres your father; cannot you do so much?" he said sternly. "That you please him ill, I doubt not. Eustace Estmere is a gentleman, a just man, an upright man, a man of noble temper and pure honor. You must degrade him bitterly—you!—the son of such a mother!"

The young man's features flushed duskily with a flush of shame, even while absolute amaze possessed and held him silent.

Tricotrin's eyes softened a little as he saw that reddened, painful shadow on the insolent young face before him.

"I would not have taunted you by your mother's dishonor if you had not sought to lure a creature, innocent as the very doves, into dishonored life," he said gravely. "But—you make me doubt, you make me disbelieve that you can come of Estmere's race."

"Estmere!" echoed his hearer, in bitter impatience of his father's name; "Estmere! You prate of Estmere! What can he be to you?"

"What he is to all the world,—what his son will never be —a gentleman! He bears you no love, my young sir. You outrage, offend, incense him at every turn and every phase of your worthless life. What mercy do you think he will show you if I tell him of some of your pastimes, of some of your vices? of your fashion of spending the last night of April, in Paris, this very year?"

The youth started and grew deadly pale.

"Good God! What are you?" he muttered. "Devil, or sorcerer, that you know these things?"

"One needs to be neither to know how you steep yourself

in the foulness of orgies that many a debauchee would recoil from in disgust!" answered Tricotrin with the sonorous force of his voice ringing loud in disdain. "Pshaw, boy! Do you think I cannot tell the truth of even such pitiful things as your valueless years? I know the shame of your vices—of your crimes—my young Commodus. Your father does not: well for you that that eagle soars far too high to see where you riot with the carrion birds! Your mother lay in his bosom to rend his great heart with her treacherous talons; you, fit son of the traitress, claim his race and his name to sully them both and drag both through the mud of the foulest of license! He cannot tear his name from you; he cannot rescue his race from your mother's pollution of it; he cannot prevent your present rank or your future succession. But you know what he is,—you know how he can judge and how he can punish, —now,—shall he hear the whole vile truth of his heir's brutal orgies? Or will you purchase my silence by leaving in peace what I cherish?"

Viva's lover stood irresolute, pale, tremulous with rage, with wonder, with baffled hatred, with ignominious submission. Above all the contesting emotions which shattered his insolence and broke asunder his self-control, was one supreme all-absorbing amaze at this man who arraigned him with the authority of a king, with the disdain of a superior, with the omniscience of a god!

Even in that moment of humiliation and powerless passion, a curious dreamy speculation came on him, and made him wonder how, if such men as these were the people, it arrived that the people did not govern and rule?

"Choose!" said Tricotrin simply. "Do I know too much of you for you to oppose my will any longer? Or must I take sharper means to protect what is innocent from your toils?"

He did not answer: he was irresolute. A galled pride, a vacillating fury, combated with him the impulse of prudence and fear. He loathed to bend and surrender; yet he dared not provoke vengeance from one who knew his worst secrets.

"Choose!" said Tricotrin with fiery impatience. "No matter to me the choice that you make! Do you renounce your pursuit?—or do I go to Estmere?"

"Were either Estmere or you such anchorites in your youth?"

The mortified pride, the ignoble fear of the young man's heart took refuge in a feeble taunt and evasion.

Tricotrin smiled contemptuously.

"Neither of us. Think you that I blame a boy's ardent follies?—a young man's lawless loves? Think you I do not know how sweet women's lips are in our youth, and how hard to resist the soft glance of their eyes? I make excuse for the swift unthinking sins of young years; I can pardon error where warm passion blinds conscience and tempts all the senses. But that is not your crime. You,—cool, cold, and wary; not loving, only desiring; not seeking a heart to beat echo to yours; but only seeking new prey to first seize, then throw away;—you,—weave lie on lie to trap a child in her ignorance, you—with all a boy's cruelty have all the graybeard's slow science, you—are a traitor, a thief, and a liar!"

The young man, stung beyond endurance, sprang on him to strike a blow for each word; Tricotrin caught his arm and held it there, the arm uplifted, the blow unstruck.

"I like you better for that," he said briefly. "There is some touch of the old race in you, though very little. But it is hardly worth while to resent what is true. It were better to admit it with apology and remorse. Now—make your choice. Leave France for a year on any pretext you will;—or stay and see what your father says of the things I can tell him. It is no matter to me which you select. Either course will equally serve me."

With that he loosened his hold on the boy's arm, and turned from him, leaving his foe to an impotent and feverish rage—the rage of a proud, self-engrossed, pampered, imperious nature against the only creature who had ever crossed its purpose or arraigned its actions.

Calmly as he had spoken to his antagonist there was no

calmness on his face as he walked on alone; walked on, away
from the river, and toward Viva's home. Tempestuous pain,
and anger, and many mingling unanalyzed emotions, had
been awakened in him. Wrath was rare with him, and when
it awoke was as the wrath of the lions; moreover, many things
of bitterness, many memories long buried, stirred in him
under the suddenness of this peril to the one he had chosen
to defend. He had needed to ask no questions; he had told
what the young man's object was, and what her danger, the
first moment that his eyes had lit on them together under the
trees about the water freshet. And it had filled him with an
almost ungovernable passion. The insult, the jeopardy, for
her, would have been from any one outrage enough to make
his blood in flame; but from the son of Estmere, they took a
darker color, they dealt a deeper blow.

"Must they have even *her?*" he said in his soul.

At any time it would have been painful to him to know
that the risk of womanhood so nearly approached the child
who to him was but such a child still; that the corruption of
worldly wishes and worldly temptations had so soon found
her out in her solitude to assail her; that the insidious graces
of youth and of love had crept in to assault and to taint the
young heart, whose transparency and whose pureness from
all evil knowledge had been his delight. He had saved her
from death, and sustained life in her through all the years of
her sunny existence, which, through him, had never been
darkened by a single cloud;—and his reward was, that the
first beardless stranger who took the trouble could lead her
away with a few honeyed words!

The desertion struck a heavier pang into Tricotrin's heart
than he, the laughing philosopher, cared that anything should
do. He would have given up much for Viva—nay, had given
up much many a time to be able to send gold enough to maintain her in ease and in some sort of grace,—and she! She
was willing to go away from him to the first handsome heartless youth that entreated her!

There was a tinge of jealous pain in him, which made

the caprice and the ingratitude in her strike him doubly sharply.

But as he had done when in wrath with the Greek Canaris, so he did now,—he strove against and shook off the alien regret. He lifted his head and looked at the sunset which was burning, rich and red, low down in the west.

"So I and his son have crossed!" he murmured. "Ah! That is droll, Mistigri. What is not droll in this world? Tragi-comedy everywhere. How we waste our time in wrath! —and neglect all that might raise our souls. How many men will look at *that* to-night? Not one in a million; the sun sets every day,—who cares? God has cast beauty broadcast all over the earth, the gentlest teacher we can have;—and who thinks to thank God for it?"

He stood awhile looking with eagle eyes at the glorious spectacle;—the broad field of glowing light, the clouds sun-flushed to scarlet, the blue sky deepening into purple, the shafts of the dying rays slanting upward like golden spears: —stood till all the radiance sank away into the deep peace of the early night.

Then having thus exorcised his darker spirit, he moved away with his head bowed like one who turns from that which is holier and greater than himself, and from which he has sought both counsel and consolation.

CHAPTER XI.

He went back to Viva.

At the door of her home she met him, lifting her face full of eagerness.

"May I go with him? Do you like him? Did he tell you all he told me?"

Tricotrin looked a moment away from her.

"You wish so much to go with this wonderful new friend, then?"

Viva gave a longing sigh.

"Oh, yes! To see Paris illuminated!"

"Ah, capricious and true to your sex! Change—that is all you want!" he murmured impatiently. "So! It is for the sake of Paris illuminated, is it? Would you go with him to a desert? To a dreary sun-burnt place?—to the sand-plains about Marseilles for example?"

Viva opened wide her large eyes in horror and sheer perplexity.

"Oh, mon Dieu! No!"

Tricotrin smiled; his worst dread was dissipated, he saw that love had not even left its first breath here, that what had beguiled her was the city in its festival season.

"Listen, Viva," he said gently, "you love me well enough to believe what I tell you and to be content with it without asking its reason?"

Viva looked up a little stilled and startled.

"Oh yes!"

"And to be sure that my pleasure is in your joy, and that if I deny you aught, it is because I know that thing would be hurtful?"

Viva's eyes grew graver and less luminous.

"Of course! You are so good to me!"

"Then, Viva, it will pleasure me best that you should not talk more with this friend, and that you should not see Paris till you can go with me. It would not be well, and this young man would not be a wise and fitting guide for you there. Now, if you love me as I imagine, you will be content that because *I* say so, therefore it is true and right. Can I count on your trust thus far? It is much to ask, for I am disappointing you; but it is not so much that I think you will deny it me?"

There was an infinite sweetness, and a shadow of anxiety, in his eyes; that this creature owed him all, to the very saving of her sheer existence, the man was too generous even to remember:—far too generous to base on it any claim to her gratitude or her obedience. He waited for the assurance of her faith and allegiance, as though he were her debtor, and not she his for every crust she ate, and every draught she drank.

Viva was silent a moment; the tears were in her eyes, the tears were in her voice, she could not trust herself to speak, for she was very proud, and could not bear to show emotion; —the disappointment was bitter, very bitter to her. The great world had seemed to open its gates to her, and disclose such gorgeous and untold glories. With the words of her tempter such a pageant of splendor and wonder had spread before the vivid dreaming fancy of the child. Such lands of enchantment had risen before her, all for her sovereignty, and lit with a light that never shone upon earth! To behold these swept down suddenly, as impossible and forbidden, was a trial terrible and poignant.

Tricotrin watched her mutely.

She stood quiet, the tears she refused to let fall standing on her long drooped lashes, her face at first very flushed, and then equally colorless, all the keenness of her disappointment and something of her haughty willfulness and resistance, spoken on a face eloquent of every thought, with the eloquence of the southern nations.

She looked up at length and caught the gaze of the eyes which watched her: their look touched and won all that was generous, noble, and loving in her temper, all that was grateful and all that was unselfish; she saw that he to whom she knew that she owed life, home, protection, her very food and bed, grieved to be compelled to pain her, and asked her allegiance, not as his right, but as her free and gracious gift.

Then all that was best in her awoke. She threw her arms about him with grateful caressing affection, in a passionate repentance for that moment's disloyalty and hesitance.

"What could you ask that I would deny! I would give you my life, and you would have a right to it, since you saved it! I do not care for the diamonds, or the roses, or Paris, or the Fêtes, if you think I am better without them. It is enough that you wish me, your wish is my law!"

Tricotrin stroked her hair tenderly, where her head leant

against his heart; he was silent for the instant, and his face lighted with the frank warm joy which had come there once before at the expression of her affection;—he was as rejoiced at her faith in him as though he had never done anything to merit, or give him title to demand, it!

"I thank you, Viva mine!" he said, with a force which gave almost a tremor to his voice. "That is generously and bravely said. You have given me the best gift there is in this world—Trust. In after-years I will tell you why I seek it now."

Viva leaned against him, speechless; she had given her allegiance loyally, and with love, but she was a child, and her disappointment was great; the tears were still in her voice, and her eyes, and she could not bear to betray them, lest he should be pained to see that the trust which he asked was fraught with sorrow to herself.

"And now—another point," pursued Tricotrin. "This stranger friend of yours gave you costly golden presents?"

"Yes!—beautiful ornaments!"

Her voice was very tremulous, and her eyes looked up with pitiful beseeching appeal; her lovely jeweled toys, with which in a thousand day-dreams she had fancied herself a Marquise, an Empress, Marie Antoinette in the brilliant days at Versailles, Louise d'Orléans in the gorgeous gatherings of the Palais Royal, anything, everything!—she should not surely have to part with them!

Tricotrin read the look; and smiled.

"Nay, child; for anything I take from you, you shall have as good. You are feminine, and I would not break your heart by robbing you of your first jewels! You are a child of the Fairies, but they forgot to dower you with Philosophy —*tant pis!* But the jewels your friend gave you must go back to him, though you shall be no loser."

Viva's eyes glowed and dropped with shame.

"Was it so wicked to take them? I did not know—he said it would be cruel and discourteous to refuse? I had no one to tell me, and—they were so pretty!"

"Wicked? No!" said Tricotrin, promptly: his chief desire in all he said was to conceal from her any hint or glimpse of what had been her tempter's motive and end, and to dissipate in no iota the innocence of her own danger which she enjoyed. "It is nothing to cause you shame, Viva; it was most natural that the pretty toys beguiled your sight; are you to be wiser than all your generation, or stronger than all your sex? But now that *I* know, they must be returned to your friend; because I accept obligations from no man, and neither must you. We spoke of pride when we were together last; there is a pride that you may cherish in your heart's heart, Viva; the pride which will never be laid beneath a debt. There was no one to tell you, and you were a child, pleased with beautiful bagatelles, and there is nothing to grieve or to blush for, at all, in the fact that you were won into taking these adornments. But remember in the future that the woman who is proud, and honors herself, must take the gold and the gifts of no man. You would give your cheek to the caress of no stranger; never take from him that for which he might, were it only in mirth, ask you for a caress as his payment."

Viva listened, the flush deep upon her forehead, her eyes drooped in humiliation, all the haughty pride of her temper was roused by and followed his words, and the bitterness of the golden ornaments was far exceeding now the sweetness they had given.

"Send them back to him! Send them back! I hate them now!" she said, passionately, while the hot color burned painfully in her face, and her lips quivered. "He wanted to kiss me once, and I told him I was no peasant girl; but it showed how low I had fallen in his sight, how I had given him the right to despise me by taking his presents!"

Her voice broke down, she flung herself upon the grass, and sobbed aloud half in grief, half in rage; her heart was not even touched by the loss of her tempter, but her pride was wounded to the quick. In the stead of the diamonds and the deathless roses, and all the wondrous, glorious, unknown world, this Waif and Stray of the Loire, who had the hauteur of a child-queen, had only the ruin of her shattered castles, and the misery, a thousandfold greater, of having lost her own dignity, and stooped to abasement and dishonor!

And Tricotrin, who would have gone half across the world, and given a kingdom if he had had one, to avoid the sight of anything feminine in sorrow, found himself, all philosopher that he was, compelled to look on what he hated, and keep by him, for a minute or two at least, a cucumber that was very acid.

For he loved the girl with all the warmth of his generous and ardent nature; and he was obliged to deal her something of this sense of pain and of humiliation, lest a worse thing should come unto her, and the wood-dove fall a prey to some other tercel's beak.

"Oh, Mistigri, Mistigri!" murmured he to that inseparable confidante, with pathetic regret. "How impossible it is for a philosopher to remain perfectly philosophical when he has once given way to such a miserable weakness as to take an interest in anything that is feminine!"

Viva lay on the grass in an abandonment of shame and sorrow, not for the golden toys, still less for their donor, but for those glorious castles in the air, that were all hurled down and had vanished like a dream of the night, and far more for the terrible sense that filled her of guiltiness and shame.

The forbidden Fruit that had looked so fair had changed to the darkest and bitterest of ashes in the lips of this proud young daughter of Eve.

Tricotrin let the emotion have its way; and his own thoughts wandered, in a fiery wrath, from the child to her tempter, and from him to many things and many memories that were dark and heavy, and rarely allowed to cloud a mind which best loved the light of the sun, and the noonday of clear philosophies, and the rich colors of wine-cups, and the aerial hues of a poet's fancies.

Then—when it had nearly spent itself—he stooped and laid his hand on her bowed head.

"Viva mind, keep thy tears back: life may want them, thou art a woman! Do not weep till thou hast erred, and that most surely thou hast not done now. Let none shame thee, save thyself; and let that never be. Thou art a child, and hast a child's love of pretty toys; that is all; no harm is done. And remember—if thou grievest I am grieved. It is I who have disappointed thee; and each sigh thou shalt give for thy lost bagatelles and thy banished castles, will be a reproach to me."

He had judged rightly the chord to touch. Viva could be led thus, though driven never.

She lifted her head, and smiled at him through her sorrows, a smile very loving, very wistful, and very proud.

"Then—I will not give them one regret!"

And he knew that the word she gave she would keep.

CHAPTER XII.

"MISTIGRI! Can a man be ever certain of his philosophy? Brutus had served her faithfully all his life, and broke down in his very last hour!" said Tricotrin, plaintively, as he stood smoking under the starlight in the porch, when Viva had sobbed herself to sleep under the eaves, with the tears still glistening on her closed lashes. "You and I were wretched sentimentalists in saving the Waif, and I suppose we shall be so to the end, having once concerned ourselves with anything so irrational as the upsetting of her most far-sighted and excellently judicious mother's plans. I have been shockingly weak and unphilosophic to-day;—contemptible! Sentiment the second; and quite as bad as the first. I have interfered between her and the most lucrative trade of all for women who cannot be duchesses. My young lord's introduction would have been an admirable one, and he was right that diamonds would have fallen in her lap by thousands;—

she would have ruined her hundreds and tens of hundreds before two years, I dare say. The world would have raved of her, and she would have had a woman's most delicious empire,—the Power of Destruction. That young man was wise and practical, and I—I was unworldly, unphilosophic, everything that is contemptible, Mistigri! What business had I to put my oar in the boat, instead of letting her drift down the stream to the wine-washed roses and Messieurs les Grands Seigneurs? Ah, grand'mère, hark a moment!"

The little old brown woman, looking like a figure out of one of Ostade's pictures, as she moved across the broad swathes of moonlight that checkered her kitchen, came toward him, trembling somewhat, for she had a horrible doubt that something had gone wrong about the Prince Fainéant, and that she had acted with an infamous want of discretion and judgment.

"Grand'mère, why did you let that young wolf in lamb's clothing get the ear of the Waif?"

Grand'mère began to tremble more and more, and broke into a stream of self-excuses and of protestation. Tricotrin cut them short.

"I know, friend Virelois, I know. You are a woman, and he was comely to look at, and you fancied you heard the chimes of bridal bells, and you thought he was a noble prince in disguise!"

"Oh, mon Dieu, Tricotrin! How do you know all you do?"

"Little birds tell me," responded Tricotrin promptly. "Silly woman! What do you suppose the swallows fly in and out of the ivy all the day long for, if it be not on messages?"

Grand'mère paid no attention; her eyes were sad and anxious.

"Is there anything wrong with the young man?" she asked. "I had my fears; I did what I could. But you see——"

"It was the old story. Love laughing at locksmiths; and the locksmiths do not exist who can shut in such a thing as the Waif. Well, the young man will not come here any more; and if you chance to hear he bears a high name, keep the knowledge to yourself, that is all. There are no disguised princes in the world; and as for bridal bells, no man loves them very much, and rich men not at all."

Grand'mère shuddered, lifting her hands.

"Ah—h—h! The nobles are so wicked!"

"Not in the least," Tricotrin contradicted. "They are no more wicked than other men—not so much so indeed, because they are educated. Vice is as ripe in villages as in cities, and to one peasant that 'falls' for a gentleman's wooing there are tenscore that do so at the asking of Pierre, the postillion, or Jacquot, the cowherd. Well, grand'mère, you loved honor and honesty all the days of your life—what have your deities done for you?"

"Kept my pot empty many a time, but my conscience clean, thank God."

Tricotrin looked at her with the smile that was epigram, satire, sunlight, and sadness all in one.

"Grand'mère! You, the disciple of virtue, are the strongest irony upon her that a satirist could paint! Your pot empty?—ah! And if you had been a philosophically wicked woman it would have overflowed with fat fowls and good rice? This Prince Fainéant was the wise man, and I the fool. Jeanne, the honest woman, clicks about in wooden shoes, sleeps on a flock bed, lives on black crusts and onion soups, gets withered and crippled and weather-stained before she is at middle age, toils in the snow and the sun to keep body and soul together, and dies in the workhouse to be buried as a pauper. Euphrasie, the bad woman, has pretty, warm, broidered slippers, sleeps between cambric sheets, lies in cachemires as her carriage rolls along, eats and drinks the best of all lands, laughs through life to a gay opera air, has a happy paganism that makes her quite untroubled with her future, and when she retires on her pirated gains, can buy absolution from any church extant, die in the odor of sanctity, and have her noble qualities blazoned on a marble tomb. That is what virtue and vice are, grand'mère, and how they pay their servitors."

Grand'mère stood in the strip of moonlight, her head pensively on one side, her little brown face sad and bewildered. Then suddenly the old woman raised herself erect, and her still bright eyes took a resolute light.

"That is true, Tricotrin—that is terribly true. There is not a word of it but is fearfully, horribly, shamefully true. But see here, Tricotrin, though I am old and poor, and but for you most like should be now dead of want, there is something I would not part with for all that gilded shame; it is this—just this: to know, all my life through, that no man ever had the right to scorn me; to know, all my life through, that they were bound to say, 'that woman is miserably poor, but she cannot be bought.' There is something sweet in that—a sweetness that does not perish. Yet I had my tempters too. I was fair to look on when I was young. And I had wealth offered to me if I would have taken shame. But it was just this which saved me, Tricotrin—not religion, perhaps, and not pride of a surety, but just this: that no man should ever feel the sex of his mother was outraged in me, that no man should ever say, 'I can despise you, for have I not bought you?'"

Tricotrin's eyes grew very soft as he heard her. When her words were ended he bent low with a tender reverence to the little, old, wrinkled, white-haired peasant.

"Grand'mère, you are a good woman! If that temper were more taught to girlhood there would be little vice for which to rail against men."

"And that is true, too!" sighed grand'mère as she went back to the fire to boil a pot of chocolate for him.

Tricotrin stood long in the moonlit doorway alone, while Mistigri swung herself in the ivy after the moths, and the quiet night lay soft and dark upon the country, while now and then the lowing of cattle, the bark of a dog, the chimes of a belfry, broke faintly on the stillness.

CHAPTER XIII.

When Viva awoke in the morning with the birds, it was, for the first time in her life, with a certain dull pain at her heart, with a certain dreamy sense of some loss and some sorrow. She sat up in her little bed, and looked at her gold toys where they stood, placed close to rejoice her waking vision, on an oak chest under her casement; and as she looked the tears swam in her eyes, her pretty white chest heaved with a quick sob. It was not altogether alone for the things; she had dreamed such dreams through her Prince Fainéant, and those dreams were all dead forever!

Moreover, her first disenchantment, her first sense of shame, were bitter to bear, and though she had cared nothing at all for her handsome young wooer, she had cared very much for all that he had offered her: so much so that she might have taken that desire for change to have been love for him, as many girls do, had not her own true and strong affection for Tricotrin preserved her from the error. The homage, the flattery, the sense of her power, the belief in his submission to it, had been so delightful to her; all the native coquetry in her had so exulted in its first exercise, all the imperious vanity in her had found such charm in its victory, that Viva mourned the loss of her Faust with a poignant regret, which though only egotism made her almost think it was tenderness. It was not: any other would have done equally well in his place, and with her fancies equally flattered, Viva would have been equally happy. But as it was, there was no one to substitute for him, and therefore she gave him a generous regret that would have looked very much like love to him had he seen her half risen on the little white couch, with her hair falling over her bare shoulders, with her great eyes swimming, and her lovely mouth swollen with tears.

But Viva was brave and was true to her word. She had many faults and more foibles; but she had the one supreme excellence of unerring courage. She had said she would give all her bagatelles up; and she did not once waver. When she had flung the cold bright water over her face and form, and dressed, and knelt awhile under the wooden cross which grand'mère had placed in her chamber, Viva was nerved to sacrifice; and in one sense she hated the things,—they had wounded her pride,—she had no wish to keep them.

Yet her tears fell on them one by one as she looked at each for the last time of all, and put them by, one by one, in a basket. Though she did not know it, she had cause to weep,—it was her first faith broken, her first illusion faded, her first trust betrayed. Youth is wise in its prescience when it recoils from betrayal as the deadliest thing that awaits it in life.

When they were all placed in their basket, Viva looked at her face in her own tiny mirror: "I promised him I would not have one regret," she thought; and she knew her face looked very tell-tale of regret indeed.

The child was frank and honest as the day; she had not learned yet even to dream of concealing what she felt. But she was courageous and she was proud; above all she was resolute not to give pain to Tricotrin. And she dashed her tears away, and leant out into the fresh morning air, and tried to sing one of her river-songs with her old gayety; then ran swiftly down the stairs, and placed the jewels in his hands where he stood smoking, and rushed away without a word into the sunlight. Those pretty bijoux!—and it was not those alone for which she sorrowed—it was for all the dreams that were gone with them!

Tricotrin did not seek to follow her; he comprehended her wish for solitude; he stood looking at the toys with a curious conflict of emotions on his face. If he had obeyed his impulse, he could have crushed them all into atoms beneath his heel.

"Pretty things with which to chaffer and barter away a life!" he said in his teeth, as he folded them aside in a packet and addressed it to the young man's name. Then with it thrust into his pocket he went across the fields toward Villiers.

As he went he softly took from the breast of his blouse, and touched with loving fingers, the Attavante's Dante.

"I did not think to part ever with you," he said gently to the book as though it were a loving thing. "But faith must be kept with the Waif; she must have her toys back; and there is no other way. Since you must go you shall go to him."

He looked long and wistfully at the book's familiar face; then put it into his breast more tenderly than he would have done had it been a roll of banker's notes for thousands. He loved the thing; it had been his from his childhood, and had accompanied him through so many changeful years; the only relic he had kept of a long-perished life forever lost.

But he had promised Viva the equals of her golden toys: wealth he had none: the book must go. He would have worked willingly for the jewels' worth; but that must have been slow purchase of them, and he would not have the child mourn her playthings for an hour more than was inevitable. The leagues brought him to Villiers; the same route which he had traversed the day after he had first found her among the clematis. He paused at the little picturesque building that stood in English fashion beside the huge entrance gates. A comely brown-eyed, laughing woman, with children clinging to her skirt, greeted him with delighted welcome as he appeared; it was Ninette, who had long been Valentin's wife, and who was happy in the tender, sunny, graceful fashion with which the French peasant will so often attain happiness even in the midst of poverty: a dragon, however, that never visited the home of the little quondam fruit-seller.

"Is the young lord at the château, Ninette?" he asked, after submitting to all the greetings of the little brunette, who loved him well as the founder of all her wedded peace by his timely counsel to the over-humble Valentin. Ninette shook her head: the young lord had left Villiers last evening.

Tricotrin put the packet into her hands.

"Give that to his servant, Ninette; and say nothing of who brought it."

Ninette's eyes grew grave and anxious a moment.

"Surely I will; and be silent as the dead. But—is it true, Tricotrin?—I heard the other day that Milord was seen very often with the little angel at grand'mère's?"

"It is true," said Tricotrin, curtly. "But he will be seen no more, I promise you."

"That is well, I am glad you are come," murmured Madame Valentin. "I got a little anxious; I remembered what you told me once about those people's love. And the little one is so young, and so proud!"

Tricotrin nodded; he did not care to pursue the subject; and after a few kindly questions concerning her family and their welfare, he passed onward into the park up the wooded terraces. Ninette knew him too well of old to ask him whither he went.

But as she turned into her cottage her face was grave, and she stood pensively before her old mother, who was sitting by the sunshiny casement, shelling peas and washing cabbages.

"Mother! I hope the pretty child will never bring woe to Tricotrin?"

The old woman cracked a pea-pod sharply.

"Viva?" she murmured. "She owes him everything. I dare say she will break his heart some day. That is the way of them all."

Such was the experience of her own life of eighty and two years!

Meanwhile Tricotrin went up toward the castle. There was a graver and more careworn thought upon him than was usual there. There was something of impatience and of pain. He had resolved to keep faith with the young man, as the young man had chosen exile in lieu of exposure; and the former served Viva by far the best, insomuch as it kept the offense against her untold; and a girl's name is like a peach:

—the down once brushed off the fruit bears the trace of the rough handling forever. Still, though he did not go to expose Estmere's son, it was Estmere whom he sought. He had heard yester-eve, as he had come through the country, that the noble had returned for a brief time to his pleasure-home.

He soon found himself in the gardens; the same gardens where he had spoken to Valentin among the azaleas. Years made no difference here; the turf only grew smoother, the flowers only more abundant, under the culture that wealth commanded. All the old beauty that the place had known in the days of the Regency bloomed afresh over it as though it had never been destroyed under the neglect of long years and an impoverished race: it had looked to Viva like some marvelous chateau of the Rénaissance times, fit for the splendid prison of the Sleeping Beauty, and for once her extravagant fancy had not led her astray.

Tricotrin knew that the English earl rose early; and that most early mornings brought him out on the terraces of Villiers before the more indolent throng of his guests had awakened. Though the name of the foreign race never by choice passed his lips, there was little concerning their life with which he was not acquainted, down even to the trifling details of their daily habits; and here his knowledge proved aright. While still far off himself among the labyrinths of roses he saw Estmere; walking slowly before the chateau with one companion only, and followed step for step, by a great Russian boarhound.

The sun shone full upon the terrace, and on the tall form of the English nobleman; it looked taller still beside the diminutive person of the foreign statesman with him, and his face had the same beauty, scarcely aged since Tricotrin had looked in on him in his banqueting-room: the fair, delicate, grave beauty of one in whom pride was stronger than passion, and the intellect dominated the senses. The face was calm, cold, full of thought; the lines of the mouth were musing and somewhat disdainful, the eyes were blue, luminous, penetrating, revealing nothing, save when, in very rare moments of

10*

pleasure, a smile would gleam in them that women valued as they did not value the less hardly-won smiles of men more easily amused and more rapidly interested.

There was no smile in them now, but a displeased surprise as they glanced over the gardens and saw an intruder there.

"A man in a blouse!—a man with a monkey! Come to beg, I presume," murmured the earl. "What can the gardeners and the park-rangers be about?"

His companion looked where he looked; but with a different expression.

"Why! That is Tricotrin!"

"And who is Tricotrin?"

"A folio could not tell!"

"I imagine one word could!"

"And what word would that be?"

"A scamp," said Estmere, with his eyes still on the man with a monkey.

"Oh, no!" cried the foreigner, eagerly. "You mistake; indeed you mistake. Tricotrin has the most marvelous talents, the most marvelous influence over the populace; he might be anything if he chose, and there is nothing he does not manage to know. He is a character;—quite a character!"

"I do not like characters," said Estmere, chillily. "A man has lost the fact before he acquires the title. 'A great character,' says the world when it means 'a great rogue!'"

"Tricotrin is no rogue——"

"No? Then if he be your visitor, allow me to leave you to him."

"He is not my visitor," muttered the French statesman hurriedly, embarrassed between his desire to speak to the new-comer and his fear of his host's courtly contempt. "I am not aware how he comes in your gardens, but indeed—. Tricotrin is so well with the people, it does not do to incense him. No government dare touch him, though any other man would be proscribed for one-half what he utters. He is a rank democrat; but——"

"A democrat!" echoed the cold musical tones of the owner of Villiers. "With advanced views of 'Progress' that shall turn the lowest strata topmost! With too noble a spirit to be restricted by the petty laws of Meum and Tuum! With a passion for liberty conceived in a wine-shop and nursed at the galleys! Thanks, I have no desire for his presence in my grounds. Since you know him, will you be kind enough to order him away?"

Tricotrin had drawn near enough by this time to hear the concluding phrases, but he had looked so earnestly at Estmere, and as he had looked had been so thoroughly occupied with his own thoughts, that he had not noted the first words; at the last all his archest laughter gleamed radiantly in his eyes:

"Order me away? Ah, M. Pharamonde, what do you say to that? You know I could bring all my Loirais back with me to sack this dainty place!"

"Threats?" said Estmere with cold disdain;—and he glanced at his French friend to see how the insolent challenge was received and resented.

Pharamonde, a minister of timorous policies,—who caressed the people because he feared them, as the hand of a coward caresses the head of a mastiff;—tried to laugh off the embarrassment he felt between his desire to propitiate the Bohemian, and yet hold his dignity with the Noble. But the jest he essayed fell dead. Tricotrin stood unmoved, in merciless amusement at his difficulty; Estmere turned away in a scorn he scarcely endeavored to conceal.

"I will leave you, Pharamonde, to converse with—your friend!"

The minister winced and reddened; Tricotrin laughed outright.

"Nay, I claim no friendship with M. Pharamonde; and my business lies with you, my Lord Earl."

Estmere surveyed him with the amazement of a great man whom no familiarities ever approach.

"I never have business with strangers; and—by what right do you intrude in my gardens?"

"Bah! The right that I found a door ready open: do you statesmen want any other excuse for intruding into a neighbor's empire? Only you go farther;—you rifle his treasuries—I do not touch even one of your rosebuds. A stranger, am I? Ah! Well, M. Pharamonde here will vouch for me; vouch at any rate that I did not come out of the galleys; and that I will not dance the carmagnole yet on your terraces."

Estmere's eyes rested on him as he spoke; eyes well used to read character keenly, well able to penetrate through the surface of all things. He had never seen any one like the man who thus addressed him,—a man of the people, in a blue blouse, and with a little black monkey peering over his shoulder, yet a man with the head of a sun-god and the rich ringing voice of a gentleman.

"Come, M. Pharamonde!" cried Tricotrin. "Stand my sponsor for once! Assure Lord Estmere that the impertinence in me of being original has not as yet led to the addendum of being criminal; which he appears to consider is its natural and due development!"

"Indeed, Tricotrin," murmured the minister, not knowing very well how to reply. "You mistake entirely; I was about to assure my lord how invariably for good is the singular influence you exercise over the people!"

"I doubt if 'my lord' will believe that; he has no love for democrats. Still it may suffice to make him do what I want—buy this book of me."

Estmere—who had paused in some interest, and in more distaste, at the interruption which aroused sufficient surprise in him to make him remain a listener and a spectator of the unknown intruder on his privacy—glanced at the volume and thought to himself that the eccentricity of this new-comer was little short of insanity. Yet that mere glance told him, a famed connoisseur in such matters, that the book was a most rare one: was it possible that the man had stolen it?

Tricotrin, with his swift intuition, read the doubt of him; and the humorous laughter glittered more archly and ironically in his eyes.

"Look at it, monseigneur!" he said, holding it out. "No thief's hands have soiled it. Will you put it among your treasures at Beaumanoir?"

"Beaumanoir!"

Lord Estmere echoed in some involuntary surprise the name of his old native home: what could a French wanderer, he wondered, know of it and his world-famous library? But he took the volume and turned its leaves over in all a connoisseur's interest.

"A genuine Attavante!" he murmured, "and in perfect condition."

The minister beside him glanced over his arm at it:

"The Attavante's Dante!" he cried. "Why, Tricotrin, that is the very book for which you refused untold gold from the Cardinal last year at Nice!"

Tricotrin shrugged his shoulders.

"I did not want the money then: I do now. Besides, I have no affection for Monsignori. I have brought Earl Eustace the book because he has a love of such things, a love more genuine than the mere collector's pride of accumulation and possession."

Estmere's eyes were lifted to look at him for one moment as the words "Earl Eustace" were spoken:—to be called by his baptismal name! No such familiarity had ever been taken in his life with him. He said nothing, however; but continued his examination of the literary treasure.

"You need the money?" he asked at length.

Tricotrin gave a gesture of half haughty impatience.

"My lord, all the questions *you* need concern yourself with are,—what is it worth, and whether you wish for it. There are hundreds in Europe who will buy it if you do not."

Estmere was silent: he felt himself to be justly rebuked, and proud as he was, he liked the rebuke, and liked the speaker better for it.

"It is a perfect copy," he said, turning to the French minister. "What did the Cardinal you allude to offer for it?"

His friend named the price.

"Too much by one-half," struck in Tricotrin. "I have no patience for those fools' prices;—after all, what is an 'antique?' Only something grown mouldy by age and disuse! And with a book, like a man, the lack of pedigree matters nothing, if the pages within be writ fair."

The sentiment was too democratic for the person it was addressed to, and he made no reply: but with another look at the miniatures of the Dante he determined to give it a home in his library.

"If you will accept the Cardinal's very fair price, the book is mine," he said. "It is fully worth it as bibliopoles' treasures go."

Tricotrin bowed his head: and Estmere thought as he saw the gesture, "that man bows like my equal;—and with infinite grace. What can he possibly be? Surely no common vagrant."

He paused a moment, strongly inclined to enter into more converse with this stranger, whose frankness, and whose singularity attracted him: but old habit, natural reserve, and an aristocrat's detestation of democracy and its professors made him resist the impulse: he gave the Attavante back to Tricotrin.

"I will send you the gold, and be good enough to return the book to the bearer. If you will go within, my people will give you some breakfast."

Tricotrin's forehead flushed red.

"I remain here," he said, curtly. "And I do not require your hospitality."

"Ah, Estmere! that man is so proud," whispered Pharamonde. Estmere took no notice, but passed into the house, through an open window; he half repented that he had bought the Attavante; still,—the man must have wanted the money, or he would not have offered it for sale; and it was of genuine worth and authenticity.

Tricotrin paced up and down the terrace with restless uneven steps; the French statesman approached him.

"Tricotrin! if you needed gold why not have asked me?"

Tricotrin's eagle glance flashed on him.

"Gifts to men of my station are bribes: and, if they are not that, they are alms. I take neither!"

"But a wage for a fair service? Look you, what service you might render the government——"

"By making the flocks submit still more passively to be shorn, and the droves to be driven out still more docilely to perish in the war-tracks? It is not my work."

"Nay, nay!" murmured the facile and courteous statesman. "Not that. But by the use of your influence over the people at the elections——"

"I never interfere in such matters."

"Why so?"

"Why? Because if I did I must show them the naked truth as I see it, and if the nations once saw that of those whom they call rulers, the world would be red with a sea of blood. For the people are long submissive as the camel; but when once they rise they are tigers. We, who know that, tremble to bid them to throw off their overladen burdens, lest the patient beast that has knelt in pain for so long should rise, transformed, with talon and fang, to destroy both his kind and his drivers."

He spoke with passion, with more bitterness too than was common with him: Pharamonde looked at him almost with fear, and was silent:

"That is not the usual hesitation of the demagogue," he thought.

"I am no demagogue," said Tricotrin, with rapid divination of his musing. "Do you know what the demagogue is?

The man who rouses the camels into impatience of their burdens, that he may rifle the baggage as it falls to the ground in the strife."

"Milord sends you this," interrupted a servant, approaching him with the gold for the Dante.

Tricotrin took it, and gave the book in its stead, without a word: Pharamonde eyed him curiously, as though he were some natural phenomenon.

"You are a strange man! When you might pick up wealth by the handsful!"

"I do not care to soil my fingers," he answered, curtly, as he made a gesture of adieu to the statesman, and went down the steps of the terrace. He had not been wholly at ease in the interview: it had galled him, and caused him a certain pain. The Waif's pretty toys were purchased, like many another luxury, at the price of a pang to a human heart. He loved the book well: also in one sense he loved the man to whom he had bartered it.

Pharamonde went within and joined his host, who was standing in the library of the château, turning over the leaves of his purchase.

"You do not understand Tricotrin," said the French minister. "He is as proud, in his own fashion, as you can be in yours. Charity, patronage, hospitality even, if it be such as he cannot return,—pshaw! Tricotrin will suffer them no more than he would suffer the lash."

"Well—a good spirit that. But who is he?"

"Tricotrin!"

"That is not a name?"

"It is his name; and no name since Mirabeau's has had more charm for the people. He could have been a second Mirabeau had he cared to be so."

"And why did he not care?"

Pharamonde shrugged his shoulders.

"He loves his liberty; and he has no ambition. I have seen much of him at divers times; he has no love for me, but he is a curious study. He is a ripe scholar; he has marvelous eloquence when he will; he has the genius of command in him if ever he choose to exert it; and—he never troubles himself to do anything except to play at a peasant's bridal feast, or a village wine-shop's carousal, with the talent of Paganini and Bamboche!"

"A bohemian!" said Estmere, with a slight gesture of comprehension and disgust. "He is not the first by many who has wasted a genius that might have ruled an empire, in reigning over a pot-house revelry!"

The conclusion was unjust, but it pleased Pharamondo: it was a little revenge for the rebuff that the bohemian had given him.

"A scholar, you say?" continued Estmere, still looking over the Dante. "Pray what were his antecedents then: he must have had other domiciles than wine-shops?"

"Ah, that I cannot tell you," said the statesman very truthfully. "I do not think there is a living soul that knows where he came from. Antecedents! he would not acknowledge anything so aristocratic. On my honor I think he sprang out of the earth!"

"Full-armed, I suppose!" said Estmere, with a satirical inflection in his voice that his guest did not relish. Pharamonde felt that his English friend had a polite contempt for both him and his bohemian.

He changed the subject, and Estmere put the book aside in a cabinet.

It was late in the evening when Tricotrin returned to his Waif; he had been to Blois, which was many miles distant, and a full day's journey from the little lonely vineyard-shrouded village which lay hidden under greenery by the waterside, like a lark's nest among the grasses.

Viva was sitting on the stone stile of the doorway, with the white cat Bébé in her lap: the sun had gone down, but there was just ruddy glow enough left to warm to rich hues her pretty drooped head, and the soft grace of her shoulders and bosom, as she sat with her arms crossed, inclosing Bébé in their clasp, while the quick heave of her chest was shown by the open square-cut bodice she wore:—a dress half like a peasant's, half like an old picture, in which the provincialism of grand'mère and the fantastic fancy of the child had been blended.

Something in the shadows, or something in the attitude, made her look less childlike and more womanlike to Tricotrin than she had ever done. Perhaps it might be because one man had sought her as woman, not child, that the fact of her childhood having well-nigh passed away struck on him for the first time.

He paused a moment unseen, looking at her; and for the first time also a dreaming conjecture came over him: he thrust it away with half a smile, half a sigh:

"Pshaw!" he thought to himself. "She is a child to me, though not to that youth. What should I get but the fate of Bruno?"

He looked no longer, but softly approached her and dropped the packet he bore into her lap: she started to her feet, upsetting the luckless Bébé, and gave a cry of delight. As the string of the packet had broken, into her hands had fallen the fac-similes of her lost bijoux, with something still costlier and prettier added; golden toys, that glittered with rainbow hues in their gems, under the flamelike reflections that still came from the west.

She threw her arms about him and thanked him with all the vivacity and the frank abandonment of her nature:—and he was repaid for the sale of the Attavante.

"Will they do as well, little one?" he asked her.

"As well! A thousand times better! For you know how dearly I love *you*, and—" she hesitated a moment, then leaned a little nearer to him, with the most charming confidential and penitent grace in the world, "it was very wrong, perhaps, for he meant to be kind, and he begged me so often to love him,—but I never could care for him as much as I wished to do. He was only a Prince Fainéant after all!"

Tricotrin's face lightened with a brighter gleam than it had worn all the day through.

"A Prince Fainéant,—true! And his offered crowns would have been only of brass, and very heavy on your brows, if you had worn them."

"Ah?" Viva looked up into his face with a touch of awe on her; she had some vague impression that some evil of unknown magnitude would have befallen her if she had been enticed into following her fairy prince. "But—Paris would have been real, would it not? I do so want to see Paris!"

"The heaven and the hell of women? Oh, child, you are better here."

"But just to see it?" pleaded Viva. "Just to see those wonderful summer nights he told me of, with the streets like streams of living fire, and the avenues all glittering with lights like a million of stars among a million leaves! As I grow older, you will take me with you, will you not?—take me with you everywhere?"

A radiance shone in his eyes as he looked down on her and laughed.

"We will see;—when you are older!"

The evening seemed very fair to him, as he played her favorite airs of Lulli and of Grétry in the moonlit porch, and the girl listened in thoughtful pleasure, thrown down in her young careless grace at his feet.

The Prince Fainéant was well-nigh forgotten; and Tricotrin was repaid for the loss of his long-treasured Dante.

CHAPTER XIV.

The next day the vintage began.

All through the grape country there were mirth and work, and rejoicing and abundance. Grapes on the laden trailing bough; grapes on the heavy oxen wagons; grapes piled high in the winepresses under the shade; grapes on the braided hair of girls where they laughed in the sun; grapes in the rosy hands of children where they lay asleep, flushed with their feasting; grapes everywhere in lavish plenty, for the summer had been splendid, and the harvest was fine in due sequence.

Tricotrin loved the vintage month.

It had been vintage time when he had first come among his Loirois, and laughed and danced, and been crowned like a young Bacchus in the years of his boyhood. It was rarely that he was away from central France in the wine season; and the good people averred that in his presence the harvest was always more profuse than it was in the autumns he was absent. It was without doubt more gay; for they never worked so joyously, they never danced so heedlessly, as when he was among them. He would work himself, giving the wage that he gained to the oldest woman in the district, or to some fatherless child. He would make the young girls laugh from sunrise to sunset; he would lighten the oxen's toil by bringing them great cool juicy leaves and grasses where they stood in the hot noonday. He would play to the young of the villages half through the sultry starry nights, while their feet flew to the most intoxicating dance melodies that ever were heard even under the skies of France. And of all those whose labor he thus lightened with jest and with raillery, and with a sunny mellow laughter, fit for the lips of a Dionysus, there was not one who was happier than he.

From the first years of her remembrance his Waif had learned to look for him at the vine-gatherings. Wherever he might wander during the three other seasons—and he wandered very far and wide with ceaseless, restless pleasure in the mere sense of motion—he was almost certain to enter France at the late summer-time, to be among the pleasant voices and the brown, bright eyes of the people he loved best.

The vintage had long been the child's festal month, for there were none for leagues around her but welcomed the stray thing whose history they all knew, and who was hallowed and endeared to them by the fact that he had taken pity on her destitution and abandonment. Among the peasantry the singularity and mystery of the child's appearance in their presence had something of the same enchantment

that it possessed for herself. Nothing was too wonderful for
them to believe of any creature whom Tricotrin protected;
and Viva's own views as to her elfin origin were not so wholly
unshared by the country people as might be imagined by
those who are ignorant of how deeply struck are the roots of
superstition in the primitive places of all countries.

She unconsciously had fostered the impression by her
dainty tastes, her proud ways, her haughty young waywardness, to which they cheerfully submitted because she belonged to Tricotrin; and Viva held an undisputed sovereignty
over the whole riverside, in which her fair face was ever seen.
And now, in the gladness and the gayety of the vintage, she
swiftly forgot the love passages of her fairy prince. Her heart
had not been touched, and her admiration had not been
excited. She now possessed as pretty things as those he had
given her, and she enjoyed them more because she enjoyed
them openly, without the latent fear that she was doing wrong,
which had poisoned her pleasure in the young lord's gifts.
Beyond a certain gratification, unconscious, but born of the
innate coquetry in her, that she had been the object of such
an episode, little remained with her of the poison he had
sown—nothing sufficient to spoil her enjoyment of the harvest
time, save that she would now and then think that to ride on
a bullock-drawn wagon, or to dance on the top of a wine-
press, was hardly amusement regal enough for such a princess as he had told her that she was. But the amusement
was too attractive to be relinquished for that consideration,
and she consoled herself by thinking that, at any rate, he was
not there to see.

Tricotrin, moreover, was with her, and Viva, in his presence, was always her brightest, her gentlest, her best; she
felt "good" with him, as she never did with any other. He
knew the way to the hidden gold in this capricious and
thoughtless nature—a way which others continually missed.

Vineyards lay all about the old place where she dwelt, on
either side of the flashing river, and stretching far away into
the interior, broken here and there by path or road, by wood

or hamlet, but extending widely round on every side, and rich, at this period of the vine's life, with the fruit all ripened and glowing to purple or to gold. Viva wandered in them in joyful idleness all the livelong day; and he himself asked no better life than this out-of-door life, stripping the laden branches, laughing with the handsome brown women, aiding the aged who could not work for themselves, and taking the oxen homeward through the cool shaded bridle-lanes.

"The possessor of an Attavante's Dante should not be a laborer in a vineyard," said a slow, melodious voice behind him one morning as he worked—worked in earnest, for he wanted a day's wage to make up the loss of a poor old woman whose hen-house had been pillaged of all its fowls in the night.

Tricotrin looked up and saw the purchaser of the Dante, who, riding by a narrow pathway through the vines, had checked his horse for an instant.

"Good day, Lord Estmere. Why not?" he returned. "Another poet, Virgil, loved the fields right well. Besides, 'to be a husbandman is but to retreat from the city—from the world as it is man's, to the world as it is God's.'"

Estmere regarded him earnestly. Here was a French bohemian quoting Cowley in the purest English.

"You are a scholar and a poet yourself?" he asked.

Tricotrin laughed:

> "'Niemand will ein Schuster sein
> Jedermann ein Dichter.'

"Though it may well be doubted if he who mends other people's shoes is not of more use than he who only tinkers his own sonnets."

Estmere's meditative eyes dwelt on those that the rich Aristophanic humors, the brilliant Swift-like irony, the Burgundian Piron-wit of many nationalities, seemed to lighten to their Hudibrastic laughter.

"You speak three languages with equal purity of accent. Of what country are you, may I ask?" he said, at length.

"I will speak twenty if you like; and I am a Cosmopolitan."

"A 'citizen of the world' then. You have traveled greatly?"

"I have lived all over the world," said Tricotrin, with a shrug of his shoulders; "it is not big enough to make that much of a boast."

"And the result of all these experiences is to bring you back to a vine-field?"

"Well,—Diocletian went back to a cabbage garden. A vine-field is more poetic."

"But Diocletian had been sated with empire?"

"Well; and if the result of empire and satiety be to conclude that there is nothing equal to cabbages for comfort, is it not better to take the vegetables at first and eschew the travail altogether?"

Estmere smiled: despite his prejudices against the class of men to which he believed Tricotrin to belong, and his dislike to anything that approached to lawlessness or democratic sentiment, he could not help feeling a certain attraction toward the speaker. His intuition told him that he addressed no common man, though he spoke with one working like a day laborer among the vines.

"I imagine," he answered, "that Diocletian's was an affectation of philosophy and renunciation rather than a genuine tribute to the charms of cabbages. Moreover, talent is rare; it is always a pity that it should be wasted while its possessor does hand-work that any boor could equally well execute."

"Pardie! May not talent be equally wasted in organizing wholesale murders by shot or steel, or wholesale political chicaneries of the people? yet those are what you statesmen call 'glory' and 'state craft.' Zoroaster says that he who sows the ground with diligence acquires more religious merit than he who repeats ten thousand prayers: and I believe he is right."

"That may be; yet the sowing is only for the body, the

meditations may well enrich the mind, or as men call it, the soul."

"That is true. And a great thought makes the world richer than ten shipments of gold. But, believe me, Earl Eustace, because the hands labor, it does not follow that the soul lies barren of tillage. Goethe knew what beautiful things the vines can utter; he need not have heard those less in working, than in strolling, among them."

Estmere looked at him curiously, and his voice had a certain haughty cadence in it that it had lost in exchanging these phrases.

"Why do you change my title thus?" he asked. "It is a singular mode of address."

Tricotrin's eyes laughed with the same ironic mirth that had been in them before, when he had heard himself arraigned for entering the rose gardens.

"Why so? You are Earl Eustace, are you not? There have been Earl John, and Earl Philip, and Earl Louis, and many more—the Blind Earl, and the Mad Earl, and the Child Earl, and some others, in the chronicles of your race. Why should not you be distinctive, too, by your name?"

"You know much of my family?" asked Estmere, in more surprise than he chose to display.

"Oh-hè!" said Tricotrin, carelessly. "I know most things; and the Estmeres are not lights hidden under a bushel. Your people have never loved obscurity, beau Sire."

"We have done our best not to deserve it," said Estmere, coldly. "Good day to you."

He rode onward through the vine-fields, astonished, perplexed, a little annoyed; he did not feel pleasured by the familiarity of this bohemian, and the off-hand allusions to his great race went against all his taste, his pride, and his caste; and yet,—the man interested him!

And interest was a thing to which he was very rarely stirred.

Tricotrin looked after him with a shade of thoughtfulness on his features; then went on again with his work, laughing with his next neighbor, a noble Murillo-like woman, with all the rich old Gaulois blood in her clear olive cheek.

"That is a very singular person—your friend, what is he called, 'Tricotrin?'" said Estmere that evening to the French statesman Pharamonde. "A most striking-looking man,— the head of a poet, a marvelous head for beauty and power. What a wasted and misguided life must his be that he should be content thus with an errant bohemianism!"

"Humph!" said Pharamonde, who did not forgive the wanderer, being accredited to him as his friend. "I am not sure he is not the wisest man in his generation: I am quite sure he is the happiest."

"Is it possible for a wise man to be happy?" said Estmere, with a smile that was not ironical, but weary.

Some days later, he and some of his guests rode by the same route through the vineyards below Villiers, at evensong. It was the close of the vintage, and they reined up and drew aside, some four leagues from the château, where they encountered the procession of Bacchus borne along, in its relic of pagan worship, with all the old accustomed honors.

Patriarchal as the days of Palestine, classic as the worship of Dionysus, with a thousand memories of old Gaul, and a thousand traces of the cultus of Greece and of Rome, the crowning feast of the grape-harvest came. The meek-eyed oxen, with their horns wreathed with flowers, dragged wagons that were laden high with the yellow and violet clusters, while before them, around them, behind them, crowded the laughing throng of girls and youths and little children, reeling under the burden of the fruit, shouting under their chaplets of late roses. It was like some Merovingian or Carlovingian triumph, when the kings of Gaul celebrated harvest, or victory in war; and the pageant moved to the divinest vintage ode that was ever breathed over the fruitful fields of France— music mellow as wine, full of intoxicating joy that the people caught in echoing chorus, and deepening now and then into the grandeur of a Te Deum, as though in thanksgiving to God who made the earth increase.

Involuntarily the riders paused and listened spellbound to that harvest chant. It was played by Tricotrin where he walked in front of the oxen, in front of the foremost wagon.

On that wagon all eyes turned, and in its decoration all the choice blossoms and the gayest ribbons had been employed. For, throned high among the grapes, with a green crown of vine leaves on her head, and half-covered with autumn flowers, sat Viva—gloriously happy and triumphant, the universally-elected queen of beauty and of the grape festival; all her love of light and mirth and music and homage gratified; all her childlike adoration of display fed to its utmost will.

Estmere looked at her as the bullocks, nodding their heads under their garlands, drew her slowly past him.

"What an exquisite face!" he murmured. "That child cannot belong to the peasantry."

She heard and looked down from beneath her vine-canopy, a deep delight beaming in her eyes, an exultant pride laughing on her lips; then a blush of shame replaced the glow of ecstasy, her head drooped as if her vine-crown were a circlet of lead, her pleasure in the vintage feast was gone;—she had been seen by a great man among the people!

"More poison for her from them!" muttered Tricotrin, as he saw and heard; and for an instant there were discord and a break in the delicious melody he gave the villagers. In another instant the music broke forth again in all its silvery sweetness, but to Viva's heart the harmony was not so easily restored.

Estmere rode on, unconscious of the evil that he had done; and the procession moved away along the line of the river, while the glad tumult of the multitude echoed down the evening air.

"What an exquisite face!" thought the earl once more; and he sighed—a short, quick sigh. The fairness of women had been poisoned to him.

"Will you not dance, Viva?" Tricotrin asked her that night, when the vintage ball followed the vintage feast on the green of her little hamlet, and he played for the dancers in airs so bewitching that the stout-built, white-haired old priest could scarcely refrain from joining in the rounds and measures.

"No!" said Viva shyly and petulantly, with the color hot on her cheeks. She usually danced with all the grace of a fairy and the abandonment of French blood;—would have so danced all night, all by herself, if she had had the chance; but this evening the young boatmen and vintagers vainly pressed and entreated her. She was obstinate: she would not join them—nothing could make her; and the vine-garland pressed almost as heavily on her brows as real crows on those of real sovereigns. Tricotrin looked at here earnestly several times, but he let her do as she would, and did not seek to persuade her.

When the innocent mirth of the young and the old—of the lovers who danced on the star-lighted turf, and the children who played at their mothers' knees, and the aged who looked on amused, and recalling the days of their youth—was over, and the planets were growing large in the blue sultry skies, he approached her where she sat listlessly under one of the lime-trees.

"Viva, what ailed you to-night?"

She lifted her head, and he saw tears swimming full in her eyes.

"He said I could not be of the peasantry! And I am *not!* —yet I live with them as if I were, and I have no name and no heritage!"

The words were violently uttered. As he heard them a look of pain went over his face.

"I have done all I could that you should not feel your loss; but that 'all' is little," he murmured. "Why should a stranger's idle speech move you thus?"

"Because he is so great! And I want to be great too. And he saw me riding among the villagers—among the common people!—as if I were some farm girl, some dairy servant!"

And Viva, a child still, though something more than childhood had begun to wake in her, pulled the beautiful grape garland off her hair and threw it on the turf, and stamped on it with her feet, as though it were the badge of ignominy, servitude, and opprobrium.

Tricotrin caught her arm.

"Viva, Viva, for shame! The people whom you scorn strove their best to pleasure you, and the peasant girls you despise yielded place to you without jealousy, and wove you that wreath in simple love and good will; and at the first light word from a great man you turn against them, and are ungrateful thus!"

The grave gentle rebuke sunk into the child's heart; her chest heaved with a sob, her face grew crimson with shame.

"I know! I know it is wicked; but I cannot help it. He thought I was beautiful; he said so; and he saw me among all the peasantry; he can think me no better than they!"

"If you be as good as they, as single-hearted, as patient, as brave under burdens—you will be nobler than you promise to be now!"

There was the first scorn and the first severity he had ever shown to her in the words.

Viva's fiery spirit flashed up under the lash.

"They are good as the mules are good! Just so stupid, just so plodding; only content because they know of nothing better than their yoke, and their pack-saddles, and their straw-yards!" she cried, vehemently. "I cannot be of them—I know I cannot,—and that English lord said so. And if he meets me again he will never speak to me because he will always remember me on that grape-wagon!"

And her tears fell in swift tempestuous emotion as though foreboding some hour when that memory would rise up between her and the aristocrat whose notice had spoilt all the innocent joy of her vintage-feast.

Tricotrin listened with his face growing darker and more impatient.

"You are ungrateful! Ungrateful as a woman; who can say more?" he said, bitterly. "Why has he bewitched you?

He is a cold man,—he is not even young,—he will never think twice of you!"

"But he looks so *great!*" cried Viva, unconscious or unheeding of the irritated pain in his voice. "And he is beautiful too, like that Arthur of England you have told me the legends of, with his blue grave eyes and his air like a king's!"

Tricotrin left her side and paced to and fro the grass under the limes; he was deeply wounded, passionately angered; but he would show neither wound nor anger to her. The creature that was wholly dependent on him, whom, were it his wish, he could cast back destitute upon the world, should never hear a harsh word from him.

Viva watched him one moment, pride and rebellion still strong in her: then all the child's better nature conquered them, she sprang to him and wound her arms about him in caressing penitence.

"Oh forgive me! I was so wrong—so ungrateful. Do pardon me,—do smile at me. I care for nothing else if you love me!"

He gently unloosed her arms from him.

"I forgive; I am not angered, only regretful—for your future?"

"And why for that?"

Were there ever young eyes that saw clouds on the Future?

"Because you know you are beautiful and have no mother; because you are proud yet are nameless; because you are among the peasantry and pine for a palace; because you are divinely natured in much, but have faults that may make your misery and your sin. Waif of mine! better I fear that you had died among the clematis!"

The words were infinitely tender and solemn in their sadness; Viva was stilled and awed by their grave sweetness.

"I know I am wicked," she murmured at last. "The people were so good to crown me; and you,—oh! how can

I ever love you enough? But—but—was it indeed so wrong to be glad because I had beauty in that great lord's sight?"

"Oh! true to your sex!" cried Tricotrin, impatiently. "The dearest praise comes from the highest lips! Estmere will never think once of you; why waste thought on him?"

"I cannot help it," pleaded Viva, musingly. "He looks like a monarch; I do not know what it is, but his face has a charm——"

"Because you know him to be a great man!—if he were a vintager, Viva, you would never glance twice at him! I would have never believed, till I heard you to-night, that the first vain word that a stranger could speak would turn you against all the friends of your childhood. His one light compliment was ill worth your poor vine-garland. Though your future were to crown you as it crowned the slave Catherine, and the Creole Joséphine, you would look wearily back from your state as an empress to the time when that village chaplet was worn on your innocent forehead!"

Viva's tears fell fast, in remorse and in penitence now.

"My beautiful vine-crown! I was cruel—I was mad," she murmured, brokenly, as she lifted up the wreath in contrite tenderness, and touched fondly and regretfully the drooped tendrils, the faded leaves, the crushed freshness of the fair green diadem.

Tricotrin smiled mournfully:

"Yes, you were mad as those ever are who yield to the tempters of vanity and ambition. Your remorse can avail nothing. You cannot mend what you have destroyed, or recall what you have crushed. The bloom will not come back to your grape-garland, nor your childhood come back to you!"

Viva lifted her heavy eyes to him; lusterless and brimming still with tears, yet sweeter in their grief than in their radiance.

"Ah, I hate myself!" she whispered. "I scorn myself more than you can ever scorn me! I am so happy, and you are so good, and all I do is to repay you with wicked words."

He passed his hand gently over her brow:

"Say no more! All my fear is, your future. The world will not forgive so easily as I. And now—talk no longer, little one. Good night!"

And he left her, and though the day had been long both in mirth and in labor, walked away into the dusky midnight rapidly and alone.

CHAPTER XV.

"Viva, will you come to Paris?"

He spoke very quietly behind her the next morning where she stood feeding Roi Doré and all his feathered serail.

All the barley dropped down in a heap to the hens and chickens:

"To Paris!"—the ecstasy of her face said the rest.

He smiled, a little sadly.

"Well, for a few days. The good woman Blaze Mévert goes up to see her son in hospital; you can go too if grand'-mère can spare you. Ask her!"

The child flew off on her errand: Tricotrin looked after her with a musing doubt in his eyes.

"It may be for the best," he thought; "here she will only dwell on the boy's memory. There,—well! God knows what will happen. It will be a present pleasure at least for her; and a week can do her no harm."

The future was a thing with which he had never burdened himself: he concerned himself with the present. If the fruit in his hand were rich and sweet he never troubled himself with fears as to whether next year's orchards would bring equal blossom. It was only now for the first time as the Waif grew nearer womanhood that the question grew perplexing to him:—for it was the question now, not of his future, but of hers. The future of a girl, nameless, motherless, but for him homeless, proud as though she were the daughter of kings, and passionate in her desire for greatness! What could its portion be except the darkness of disappointed desire, or the false brilliancy of evil attainment? That either should become, hereafter, the share of the creature that he loved and sheltered was a cruel thought to him: yet he could not see how to avert both.

While she had been happy in his country life; while she had been a child to find her pleasures in a play among new-mown hay, in a sail in a cumbrous barge, in a gift of grapes from the vine, or of a fairy-story from a peddler's wallet, to make her happy had been very easy. Even now, if she had clung by preference to the freshness, simplicity, and freedom of rural life; if like himself all her sympathies and attachments had been among the people; if she had been satisfied with the warm and loyal liking of the peasantry who had been about her from her infancy, and—without her vain desire for alien things, for worlds which she had never entered—had found content in her own heart, and in his care of her, it would have been possible to have carried into her future years the sunshine he had shed on her early ones. But he knew well that an unfulfilled aspiration, a strangled ambition, an ever-struggling, ever-repressed longing, are as poison to the soul in which their stifled fire burns: he knew that to such a woman as Viva would become such poison is worse than death, such fire is an ever-devouring flame of hell.

Tricotrin, who had led so careless and so rich a life of laughter, meditation, indolence, labor, love, and wisdom intertwined to one harmonious whole, had never had in the whole course of that life a pain so keen, a fear so intangible, as faced him now in the future of what, on the pure instinct of pity, he had rescued and succored without thought of the burden it might become to him in an after-time.

It was possible that some man might behold her who would be won by her beauty to lift her into that blaze of worldly power which she coveted. But he knew that it is not to the foundlings of bastardy, that love which is honor also is offered: and—even love with honor—if ever it were given to her, seemed to him a robber that would steal from him that to which he had the natural right. A right precious to him, though for so long he had only thought of her as a pet thing like a spaniel or a bird.

He started as the old woman approached him through the yellow leaves of the autumnal gourds.

"Is it true the dear child is to go to Paris?" she asked.

Tricotrin looked down on her with compassionate kind eyes: he knew the pang that it dealt to this aged soul.

"Well, grand'mère," he said gently. "Is it not best? Only for a week or two?—and a week or two will chase away this young hero from her memories. Now he is nothing to her:—but if she have naught else to think of he will gather, from absence, beauty and stature not his own. Tell me, does not your experience of your sex suggest the truth of that?"

Grand'mère sighed, and shook her white head.

"I dare say, Tricotrin;—you know in my girlhood, among my people, if one had a dream in the head, or a pang at the heart, there was the baking, or the washing, or the beetroot-hoeing, or the grass carrying, or the cow that was sick, or the calf that was hand-reared, always to occupy one, and thrust one's self out of the way,—see you? With the little darling —it is different of course. She has nothing to do but to dream."

"And such dreams are the highways to sin! It would have been better,—ten thousand times better,—if she had had the beetroot-hoeing and the farm-house cares. But between us we have spoilt the child."

"Tricotrin! She is a little born princess!"

"Born princesses without palaces ready for them are in a sorry plight. Viva is only—vain, ambitious, and thoroughly feminine. Those qualities are not confined to palaces."

"You always jest," murmured grand'mère. "But will you really take her to that terrible city?"

"That city is more terrible while it is seen through the mists of her unsatisfied longing. And she shall come back in a fortnight, at the farthest."

The still bright black eyes of the old woman clouded with the slow painful tears of age.

"Come back?" she echoed, as she turned away. "Never the same, Tricotrin, never the same!"

And on her there weighed a bitter foreboding:—she had seen three fearless hopeful young lives pass from her into that furnace of Paris, never again to sit in the light of her lonely hearth.

"Never the same!" thought Tricotrin. "She will never be the same, though she stay here for year after year. The aged will never remember that the youth which they love will escape from them,—will die out of their sight into its own all-absorbed ego."

Meantime the Waif herself grew wild with rapture: Paris suggested to her a beatitude that Paradise entirely failed to do. All her elastic and vivacious nature was loosened to ecstatic joy, in which both her young Faust and her King Arthur were alike forgotten.

True, she was going in a manner very different from her ambition: she was going with the homely wife of the miller, whose mission was nothing more elevated than to seek a sick son, a private soldier, in hospital: she was "going like a peasant" she thought wistfully, into that great blazing whirlpool of sovereignties and splendors. But the delight of it far outbalanced the minor drawback; and moreover her love for Tricotrin was so much stronger than even her ambition as yet, that when she was with him, no want or wish remained upon her. His influence was great on her; greater because rather suggested than ever forced; and in his presence all that was nobler in her awoke, all that was baser waned.

Besides, she was but a child, a child who had seen nothing, and to whom all the earth was glorious. Paris was the golden land: once permitted entrance to it all things seemed possible to happen to her:—even to its people finding in her the daughter of the old dead races of the throne of Gaul! To be claimed and crowned in Paris would not have been too wonderful an apotheosis to her triumphs,—as she dreamed of them.

It is said that earliest youth is so happy because its present is sufficient to it: is it not rather because the future is still an empire as yet uninherited, in whose uncentered domain all glories and all ecstasies are possible?

It went to her heart, warm though wayward, to give pain to the old woman she loved; to bid adieu to the poultry and the doves, and the pigeons that plumed themselves all day long on the thatch of the shed, and knew her voice and their own names so well; to kiss the white cat for the last time, and know that for fourteen long days it must miss her when it mewed for its milk and its bread. But the joy of her departure outweighed her regret; and though she felt all that clinging to the only home she had known, which every young thing does when it first goes forth into its new and separate existence, the magnificence of the possibilities that she saw before her in that one word "Paris," stifled the emotion as fast as it rose.

She went, with scarce a sigh, with scarce a backward glance, away from the home of her childhood. Away—for aught she knew—forever.

The slow sail, miles down the river, in the early dawn to the landing-place nearest the town whence the diligence started. The posting-inn, with its busy noise and movement, its ponderous gilded sign swinging against the wooden grape-wreathed balcony, its chatter of many tongues. The dashing of the cumbrous vehicle along the sunny road, with the incessant flack-crack of the leathern whips, and the jingling chimes of the galloping horses' harness-bells. The stoppages by picturesque wayside cabarets, bowered in pear-trees golden with fruit, or chestnuts full of their spike-armored nuts, where the timbers were old as the days of crusades, and the lichens all gray from six centuries' growth.

The night's sleep in an antique town, where a cathedral

that was a Kyrie Eleison in stone uprose in the midst, with
the low-peaked crowded roofs lying far down about its
feet, as the worlds lie around the feet of God. The next
day's repetition of the joys of the day past, while the varied
scenes flew by like magic, and woods and streams, hamlets
and convents, church spires and river bridges, were all left behind in the sunlight. The approach to Paris in the mellow
evening time, through the beautiful broad road of Versailles,
down the stony slopes of Sèvres and Billancourt, past the
noble wooded heights of St. Cloud, and so into the city in its
gorgeous night-beauty:—all that was tedious or irksome to
others to her was one perpetual panorama of delight.

Viva was in enchantment.

In that warm, ruddy, luscious autumn, when summer heats
stretched over the vintage-month, there were high festivals
in the City of the World. Even as Rome before her, she,
with her vast proletariate and her vast armies, lulled the
hungry cry of the one with the feast and spectacle in which
she celebrated the victories of the other.

There had been war, and successful war. The blood and
the treasure of the people had been poured out on the African
sands, and the tricolor had been borne aloft over thousands
of quivering bodies. France had conquered, and was
rapturous in pride: for the vulture of Greed and the skeleton
of Debt were her trophies, and they wore to her eyes the
shapes of the archangels of Patriotism and Honor.

There was a week-long rejoicing and ceasing from labor.
The dumb brutes travailed in agony; the women went down
into the depths of bestial vice to find their daily bread; the
patriots and the thinkers were forced into silence in prison or
in exile; the future was pawned to the Gold Devil, that he
might gild with its happiness the present. But the song, and
the dance, and the laugh, and the trumpet were all that were
heard on the air.

In the first of those nights, when the populace was mad
with delight, when the long avenues shone with a million of
lights, when the red white and blue banners tossed in the

golden gas-glare, when the wings of the glittering eagles glowed in the ruby torch flame, when the air was alive with wild melody, and music burst from every nook of the city—in the first of these nights the Waif first beheld Paris.

She forgot all her woes and all her ambitions; she cared nothing whether she came as princess or peasant; she was in a delirium of delight, a trance of magic—this was the world! Oh, how rapturous a thing was the mere sense of living!—how endless a pageant the mere succession of years! So the child thought, wafted into the victory-drunk, flower-crowned joy of the city, and gazing over the throngs with her eyes like two stars, and her cheeks burning scarlet, and the breathless laughter on her happy parted lips.

CHAPTER XVI.

LIFE had no terrors, no darkness, no sadness, no peril in the sight of Viva; it was only one moving picture of changeless color and endless charm. There was nothing in her of the poet's melancholy, of the visionary's instinctive sigh for woes that are old as the world, and that keep their cruel time with every pulse that beats. Paris and she were like one another—gay, beautiful, volatile, vivacious, inconstant, ardent, glittering things, full of fond enthusiasm, yet full of fickle caprice, always willing to smile, never willing to weep, ardent in instantaneous worship, cruel from pure thoughtlessness. The city caressed the child, the child loved the city.

Her fair bright face, with its great dark radiant eyes, and the yellow hair pushed back under her little scarlet hood, drew every glance after it, in the crowds of the theaters, in the little wooden booths of the fairs, under the trees of the public gardens, or beneath the lamps of the boulevards at evening. He was with her, she was sacred to the people; and all the flowers and flags and wreaths and toys that form the current of merchandise of such festal times were rained upon her.

But that which Viva loved the best was to see the throng in a street turn by one impulse to gaze at her. What made her pulse throb highest was to hear the men who looked noble murmur after her, "Is it a child or woman?—what a perfect face!"

The air was rife with adulation for her, but it was less dangerous than one voice whispering it in solitude; even as poisons that neutralize each other injure less than one drop poured alone. She lived with the good woman Mévert, high in a quaint old wooden house on the border-line of the Pays Latin; but she was with Tricotrin all the day, and all the long lustrous evenings. She was ecstatically happy, and he imagined her content; so she was, because, wandering through the palaces, or watching the grand people in their carriages, Viva already mused, "I have power because I have beauty. I will be great, too, some day."

He thought her satisfied with the lot he gave her, as she laughed on her buoyant way beside him; she was only so because, without reasoning why, she felt she should ere long escape from it.

Tricotrin, for once, was blind, and believed that which he wished to believe. Living in a poor little room with the miller's wife, she was happy, he believed, in the people's pleasures, in the luxurious sense of young life, in such music, such mirth, such festal sights as he could give her by merely bringing her through streets and gardens. There had been nothing inordinate in her desires; they were gratified by such mere change of place as this. Why should she not always be happy thus?

The man's own intellect, so richly stored, and his own soul, so catholic in sympathy, made him contented in the simplest form of life, so long as he had liberty, and health, and the beauties of the earth. Forgetful of the difference between a life that draws its pleasure from the mind within and the life that needs to have them supplied by the world without, he saw no reason why she should not be happy thus also.

But Viva was dreaming a different dream. When she had been six nights in Paris, and three of them had been spent at theaters thrown open to the public in the Parisian holiday, a new and strong passion took possession of her. It was the passion for the stage. Nothing of all she saw, save the splendid pomp in the courts of the Tuileries, charmed her like the stage.

Her vine-harvest feast that she had scorned was a million times more poetic, more picturesque, more classic, more full of peace, and mirth, and beauty than aught she saw in the theaters. But to the child, the artificial brilliancy, the mock sovereignties of the drama were far more attractive; partly because they were novel, chiefly because they represented that phase of life which had a fatal charm for her, and gained that visible and public applause which seemed to her the choicest and the sweetest of rewards.

She was all in the wrong. Her imagination, although so fanciful, was barbaric, in its passion for show and for triumph; but her nature had been created thus, and nothing could have eradicated that one evil instinct from it.

The chief thing that enchanted her with the stage was this: she heard that actors and actresses were people whose origin was either totally obscured or confessedly very low; she saw them intoxicating a multitude, and receiving a public homage of whose real character she was wholly ignorant. She, who began to suspect that her fairy progenitors would never do very much for her, did not see why to her also this golden path should not open. She would glance at herself in the mirrors she passed, and would think, "If even I had not genius, I should have beauty!"

And her feminine instinct told her that the latter was the greater and more potent influence of the two.

There was one actress who especially influenced her—an actress who looked almost as young as herself on the stage, with a gay, innocent face like a cherub's, and the most graceful caprices that ever adorned the coquettish parts that she played. She was a very great actress, very famous, very full of riches, very widely worshiped—one who ruined every fool that loved her with a laugh as light as a lark's song, and who triumphed in the height of her reckless vice as a conqueror in the altitude of his power. Of that Viva knew nothing whatsoever, but she heard the thunder of applause with which the public greeted her; she saw the crowns, the wreaths, the jewels that were flung in profusion at her; she thought nothing on earth could be so glorious as to be this enchantress whom they called Coriolis.

Coriolis's eyes—acute, swift-seeing eyes, though so lambent and so blue with their sunny laughter—caught the look of rapt adoration on the handsome young face under its scarlet-hood among the close-packed audience, and, well used as she was to homage, was amused and pleased with the child's rapture at her. She knew that it was the most sincere she could have, and she gave Viva one night a smile across the house that made its recipient as proud as though an empress had caressed her.

One day the child—wandering under the boulevard trees with her old friend Mévert, in a morning when Tricotrin had not as yet joined her—was touched lightly by the long white wand of a lacquey glistening in gold.

"Come to the carriage; Madame wishes to see you," said the servant.

Viva turned, and saw, looking out at her, the lovely cherubic head of her stage-sovereign. Viva—restlessly uneasy because Mère Mévert wore the quaint costume and white cap of her province, and she herself was dressed half like a gipsy and half like a girl of the old ages—went up to the equipage, breathless with wonder at seeing her deity in mere mortal guise and out in the daylight. She felt giddy, and incredulous of her own fortune. Could it be that this potentate, whom all Paris adored, would prove after all Queen Titania?

Coriolis leaned over the low door of her carriage.

"Child! You are an adorer of mine, are you not? Where did you come from with your picture of a face?"

"The Loire, Madame."

Viva, for the only time in her life, was shy; she was absorbed in gazing at the matchless tints and graces of her idol.

"Sprung out of the river?—a second Venus!" laughed Coriolis. "Do you know what a fortune you have in your face, little one? Here, take these; you are young enough still to care for them."

She put into Viva's hand some silvered, painted, glittering bonbon boxes, that were among the many purchases piled in her elegant carriage.

"Would you not like to come on the stage?" she went on, as the child tried to thank her as well as she could in her amazed entrancement. "You have got it in your face, in your limbs, in your smile. It is a fair life enough."

And the actress laughed. She—a lovely, soulless, sensual, airy thing, with a cherub's face and a kitten's folly—had found it so. She did not mean evil; she meant kindness in her way, in inciting the girl to follow her choice of it.

Viva flushed crimson to her temples.

"Oh, Madame! you think that I could?"

"Of course you could. Why not? With a face like yours you may have no more brains than a wooden Punch; you need act no more than a stick; they will run after you. Look! You are poor, I suppose?"

"I suppose so," assented Viva, with a burning sense of shame, and a glance at Mère Mévert's costume.

"Of course you are; you were among the populace. Well, come to me to-morrow, at that address, and I will see what I can do to put you in the way and show you to some impresario."

"Ah, Madame!" cried the child, rapturously. "And I shall have all that applause? I shall have just such homage as yours? I shall become like you, shall I?"

"Become like me? Oh yes!" laughed Coriolis; but for

the moment a shade of irritation clouded her gay forget-me-not eyes.

"If I thought so I would kill her where she stands."

Viva and the actress both started at the sound of the voice near them. Tricotrin had drawn near as the last words were uttered. He put one hand on his Waif's shoulder, and with the other tossed the costly sweetmeat boxes back into the carriage. The eyes of Coriolis glittered with astonishment and wrath; she was a sovereign in her way, and a pampered one.

"Monsieur! who are you that dare——"

Tricotrin turned his flashing glance on her.

"A year ago I saw Jean Bruno—a maniac."

And without another word he forced Viva away;—far away down under the trees of the street.

She looked up at him piteously.

"Was *that* wrong too?"

His mouth quivered with rage.

"My darling, my darling! not wrong in *you*. Ah, God! why cannot they let you be?"

"But you said you would rather kill me than let me grow like her? What is she?"

"Woe to those who teach you what sin means," he muttered in his beard. "Viva—that woman broke the heart of an honest man. Would you not rather die, in poverty and obscurity, than do that?"

Viva hung her head in silence; she knew in her own heart that she would not.

"But she is so lovely," she murmured, "and such an exquisite life she must lead; and—and—I do so want to be an actress!"

"What!"—he moved from her as if he were stung; he seemed to see a bottomless abyss yawn beneath the light-dancing feet of the child that he loved.

"I do!" murmured Viva. "All those brilliant nights, those beautiful dresses, those jewels that they toss her. Oh! I should be so happy on the stage!"

His face darkened with hot wrath, with bitter disappointment; he had fancied her happy because she was with him!

"I have said;—I would rather see you in your grave!" he answered her.

"Why?" asked Viva, awed but undeterred.

How could he tell her?

"I thought you were proud, Viva," he said bitterly. "Fine pride! To desire to show yourself nightly for gold! to lay bare your beauty to the populace! to be one living lie from the hue on your cheek to the passions you simulate! to be a thing whose graces, and features, and limbs, and laughter, the lowest cur of the people can gaze at or enjoy if he pay a few coins to your master! Noble pride truly!"

Viva, who had never heard from him that scathing irony of word and tone, was rather terrified than convinced. Her head dropped; she kept silence.

"But that exquisite woman!" she whispered at last. "*She is happy?*"

"'That exquisite woman!" he echoed, with acrid contempt. "Happy? Oh yes! Possibly she is happy. Without soul, without pity, without honor, as mindless as any flower that blows in the breeze, but a flower that poisons all who breathe near it,—she is happy doubtless, because things without conscience or brain cannot suffer, because gold makes the paradise of such creatures as she! 'Exquisite?' Pshaw! have you lived amid nature not to be able to know what is false when you see it? The red of her lips, the flush on her cheeks, the white of her bosom, the tears and the laughter you by turns deem so divine—they are all lies! Lies like the life she has chosen to lead. Think of that woman's old age, think of her future; child though you be, cannot you feel *some* of their horror?"

He spoke with the more vehement bitterness of the things he could speak of to her, because he could not taint her young mind by all the truth of this lamia whom she took for an angel. It awed her, it frightened her; but it utterly failed to convince her. The actress, and the triumphs of the actress, had taken too deep a root into her fancy.

"Ah!" said Tricotrin, half fiercely, half tenderly, "you prefer a painted lie to an undecked truth? That is ever your sex's choice!"

He walked on in a silence which the child did not break; she was puzzled and keenly disappointed; he was wounded and roused to hot wrath with this traitress who must needs seek to taint and allure what he cherished.

Viva took courage at last to speak, though she felt the only fear of him that she had ever known.

"But the Coriolis asked me to go and see her to-morrow," she whispered, "at the place on this card, in the day-time, you know. May I not even do that?"

Tricotrin stopped in his rapid stride, and looked straight in her uplifted eyes.

"Yes, Viva. Go if you choose. I coerce no one's liberty. But—I do not share your life with that wanton. If you go to Coriolis you will be dead to me."

The girl's head dropped again; she was struck with the sharpest terror her fair caressed life had ever known. He waited vainly some moments for answer; then he asked her,—

"Which do you choose?"

She lifted her face eagerly, and he saw her lashes all wet with unshed tears.

"Oh you,—you! What should I do without you?"

His face cleared like a landscape from which the sun sweeps away all the storm-mists.

"That is well," he said simply. "And now,—let us go and look for some bonbons as handsome as those I threw away from you just now!"

Viva shook her head with a sigh.

"I am not a baby!" she said, impatiently, and a grave shadow was over her face, that no pageant of the streets, no passage of the troops, no Polinchinelle chattering his fun, no Dulcamara vaunting his wares at beat of drum, nothing of all the frolic and the glitter of the holiday-noon availed to chase away. In the audaciousness of her supreme ignorance she disbelieved that this woman could be aught save what the fair cherubic face of her avouched; and she looked back with passionate vexed longing to those golden gates that he had closed upon herself—the gates of an actress's career!

She is not the first, who, saved from hell, have thought that they lost heaven.

"Is this all that Paris has done?" thought Tricotrin. "To exchange her young Faust for the stage of Paris is a poor mending of evils!"

His spirit chafed within him; all his happy philosophies, which loathed anxiety, and sought mirth and serenity as the essence of existence, were jarred and dethroned by this feminine incarnation of Caprice which he harbored.

He felt a sort of despair before her future; he to whose strong and sunny nature despair had been unknown. Rich he could never make her; give her the life she coveted he never could; how then could he make her content, or even perhaps keep her from destruction? For Tricotrin knew her sex well; and knew that these passionate propulsions, such as hers, to wealth, and glitter, and luxury, are a hundredfold more likely to be the cause of a woman's fall, than the softer and more generous emotions to which their dishonor is sentimentally attributed.

He had answered her with a bitterness and a sternness wholly unnatural to him, because his powerlessness in this one thing stung him so keenly. For one solution only of the problem rose before him. She loved him with a genuine ardent love, if it were only the love of a child; she had grown infinitely dear to him in the past year—her loveliness beguiled his eyes, her grace bewitched his senses; and all his heart and his soul had kept so full of youth still through the warmth of his sympathies and the healthfulness of his life, that he, so young still in all the best things of youth, forgot he was not so in her eyes. Forgot it at times when the thought swept by him,—why should it not be possible for this bright bird to find its best-loved nest in his own bosom, there to be safe-harbored ever from the beat of the storm-wind and the swoop of the hawk? He never drew the thought out into full light from the golden haze of immature resolve and resisted desire in which it lay; but it abode with him, and grew daily stronger than he knew. It had moved him to the vehement and caustic satire with which he had retorted on her allurement to the pollution of the stage:—he had indeed scorned the traitress of Bruno, but it was as the temptress of his Waif that he abhorred Coriolis.

He had been unable to foresee, when he took the child to the gay follies of the gayest theater, that this woman, whose triumphs were more than half due to her sins, would exercise so instantaneous and fatal a sorcery over the mind of a creature whom he would have thought far too proud to care for the tinsel luster and the false glamour of a dramatic career. To him, knowing the vain, cruel, criminal, sensual life of the lost wife of Bruno, the actress was no more than a marionette set in play to provoke a crowd's laughter: that she could be, by virtue of her smiling eyes and her enchanting grace, an angel in Viva's sight, was incomprehensible to him. Long doubtful whether or no to darken the sunny horizon of her thoughts by the knowledge of evil and misery, he was stung at last, by her persistent regret for her lost deity, to tell her the story that the Marseillais sailor had told him. He did not show her the guilt to which Bruno's wife had fled, but he showed her the heartlessness of that flight, he sketched to her the awful wreck of the man's mind, and the pathetic fidelity of his wronged love. Viva was volatile, careless, selfish, though in a soft bewitching fashion: he fancied almost, at times, that she needed to be scourged with pain to become, like Undine, a human creature to feel.

She listened, where they had stopped by a bench under the great Luxembourg trees, with her eyes full of earnestness, her face full of wondering regret. It touched her, this tragedy —if it did not penetrate very deeply.

"The poor Bruno!" she said softly, with a sigh of pity:

she was always pitiful, when—she paused to see pity was needed.

"Well?" said Tricotrin gently, when the tale had been told. "Well!—which are your sympathies with now, your goddess Coriolis, or the sailor whom she wronged and forsook?"

Viva meditated wistfully, her head sinking down like a flower with dew in its bells.

"Of course she was cruel—she was wrong," she murmured. "But then,—how could they be happy? He was content with the life, and she was not!"

Even while the swift instinct of the child fixed with accurate aim on the one secret of the misery of so many wedded lives, she stabbed, in her innocent unconsciousness, to its core the generous and noble heart that gave her such unrequited tenderness.

Tricotrin rose quickly from their seat under the chestnut-tree.

"So! Discontent is pretext enough for disloyalty!" he said bitterly. "Well—what we allow to nations we must accord to women, I suppose!"

And he took her home in silence to her little city-nest, high in air, in the Pays Latin.

She knew that in some way she had vexed him, but she did not seek to find out why, with her customary caressing penitence: she, in her turn, was aggrieved because her fair idol had been cast down from her altar, and proved no longer of soilless ivory and of pure silver, but of common dark-stained clay. The actress had brought the first severance and difference between them; because, by the lips of the actress the voices of the world, the voices of sins that are sweet, had spoken to Viva.

Meantime, Circumstance fashioned her fate as it commonly fashions the fates of all, let prescience, and sagacity, and skill, and care strive how they may to shape them so that no chance or accident should ever have power adversely to affect them.

That night Tricotrin's heart smote him; he thought he had been harsh to the "little one." He rebuked himself for having so roughly brushed away her happy ideals; for having so ruthlessly shown her the corruption of what looked to her innocent eyes so divine. He had spoken on the spur of an acute pain, and of the fear that had filled him lest she should fall into the pleasure and passion-baited snares of a courtesan's career. He fancied he had been cruel to her, as he watched her sitting in the attic window, looking out over the sunset-tinged roofs of Paris with a troubled shade on her face and her hands lying listlessly in her lap.

Yet—if she deemed him cruel because he would not launch her on that life, he knew that she must continue so to think him. He would as soon—or sooner—have aided her to throw herself into the black Seine, flowing yonder under the old walls of the Palace of Justice.

He went up to her and laid his hand on her shoulder.

"Well, Viva!—what good was it for you to set your heart on roaming with me, if the first yellow-haired woman you meet makes you dissatisfied thus?"

"It is not that," the girl answered slowly. "It is——"

"It is what?"

"Well—I was thinking if one would be like *her* through being wicked, it must be very hard work to keep good!"

Tricotrin smiled, a little sadly.

"You have found out that common-place? I do not dispute it. Evil thrives; and honor will not be wooed because she brings plenteousness. It is just this which corrupts the world, Viva,—evil pays well, honor will not be followed by mercenaries."

She gave a deep sigh.

"But *she* looks so happy?"—the question could not be general to her, she argued only from the personality.

"Happy! As a mollusc is happy so long as the sea sweeps prey into its jaws; what does the mollusc care how many lives have been shipwrecked so long as the tide wafts its worms? She has killed her conscience, Viva; there is no murder more awful. It is to slay what touch of God we have in us!"

Viva was awed, and was silent.

"Why does God let such things live then?" she asked, at the last.

"Ah, child! Why does God let the dumb beasts be born only to perish after lives of long torture? The marvel of creation is one we shall never solve on earth. But come! Those problems are too deep for your age. Let us go and see the last fireworks!"

The fireworks made her a child again; they were the end and crown of the long week of festivity, and they fell in golden showers and leapt in fires of every hue, till they were seen by those far away on the distant terraces of Saint-Germain.

The young uplifted head, with that glow and conflict of color reflected on it, as the sparkling rain of flame sprang upward and descended from the summit of the Arch, attracted many a glance near her far more than did the fire-play. With the lofty stature and the leonine head of Tricotrin behind her, as he guarded her from the pressure of the crowds, she was a picture;—even to the picture-sated eyes of worn Parisians.

Among those who thus saw her were two whose gaze never left her face, so unconscious of their study of it, as her eyes followed the gay magnificence of the fireworks' display.

One of them was a man jammed in the dense press, into which he had accidentally been entangled—the man to whom Tricotrin had given his "chance." And he read her face with a hard eager intentness, as one who reads the lines of a book that he must commit to memory and use at need.

The other was a person looking wearily out from where his carriage was blocked, in a by-street, refused entrance into the Champs Elysées that was consecrated to foot passengers. He was an invalid, a scholar, a nobleman, a recluse of middle age; and the face of the girl with its brilliant tint, its careless happiness, its marvelous perfection of beauty, youth, and health, stirred him to a strong emotion, half pain, half pleasure.

The carriage was close to the corner of the street; its object had been to cross the road, but the mounted gendarmes had interposed. Tricotrin was scarcely a yard from it; its occupant leaned slightly forward and spoke to him.

"Tricotrin! Let your young companion come hither; she is not safe in that throng."

Tricotrin looked round, and smiled.

"Thank you;—you are very kind."

The offer had been frankly made; he accepted it as frankly, knowing well the speaker. Viva was lifted in an instant upon the seat of the equipage; and, as she thought to herself, if she had only not had that scarlet cloak on, with its hood half over her curls, who could have known she was not a young duchess? Her vexation about the cloak slightly spoiled her pleasure in the fireworks; she had not thought of it on foot, but in a carriage—it was so different. She would not have been much consoled if she had known how exquisitely picturesque that costume made her look. Viva, like many of her sex, well as she loved her loveliness, would rather have looked greater than have looked beautiful.

She was occupied, too, in glancing at the owner of the vehicle; he was worn, pale, attenuated, plain of feature, though his countenance was one of great intelligence; he did not at all look like the knight-errant who was to take a dispossessed princess back to her rightful heritage, but he had an attraction for her because he was visibly of some high rank by his attendants, and because his weary melancholy eyes dwelt on her with so unmistakable an admiration.

She talked to him, in answer to his questions, with vivacious volubility; she was happy, elated, excited, and had an intense enjoyment in being so prominent in that grand carriage—an enjoyment only damped by the hapless scarlet cloak.

Tricotrin leaned against the door, and listened to her mirthful chatter—in silence.

"May I not drive you home?" asked the owner of the carriage, when the last of the fire-show was over. Tricotrin lifted the girl down on to the ground.

"No—those born to walk had best not learn the ease of equipages. Many thanks for your kindness and your courtesies."

The Duc de Lirà smiled wearily.

"That man is a character," he thought, as Estmere had done before him; "and the child—the child is like a summer-day in one's youth."

The next afternoon the same elegant equipage entered the Pays Latin, and its master ascended the five flights of rickety stairs to the chamber where Viva, after a long morning out of doors, sat on the boarded floor, cracking nuts, and tossing them uncracked to her old friend Mistigri, singing to herself a gay opera air of Ricci's, caught up from the streets. Mère Mévert was with her sick son; Tricotrin, on a smooth-planed plank of deal, was painting with that rare happy skill he possessed, smoking the while, and thrusting out of sight for the moment that vexed question, "what would become of her?"

He rose, and welcomed the new comer cordially, though with surprise. Viva dropped her nuts, and sprang to her feet—to be caught sitting on the floor was worse than to have been seen in a scarlet cloak! But, his carriage apart, this stranger had so little of grandeur about him, was so grave, so unassuming, so dumb, as it were, before the dauntlessness and the pretty insolence of her own air, that Viva concluded he could have been nobody very great, after all, and heeded his presence but little.

Tricotrin, on the contrary, treated him with a regard he rarely showed to men of rank; he knew the worth of character when he met it, and this character was of pure gold.

Years before, in the wild, hot days of a midsummer revolution, he had seen it tested. The mob had thundered at the

gates of a great hotel, and forced the bronze and brazen
scroll-work in. On to the flight of steps that led to the
entrance-door, when the court was filled with seething human
life, there had come one weak and slender form, inspired
with all the fire and the dignity of a great race in that one
moment. The sickly and suffering Duc de Lira had looked
quietly down on the infuriated people with a look half contempt and half compassion. "You intend to pass my
threshold?" he had said. "Very well. But it will be over
my dead body. Now—advance!"

And Tricotrin, whose pulse never beat so high as under
the wine-draught of revolution, and whose voice the in-
surgents followed as chargers the trumpet-call, hearing that
quiet and gallant defiance, had turned on his own people,
and forced them back at risk of his own life and limb, and
scourged them with fiery words as pillagers and thieves.

The nobleman and the revolutionist had rarely crossed
each other's paths since then. The career of the ailing,
learned, secluded gentleman, and that of the adventurous,
erratic, sunny-tempered bohemian, could have few points of
meeting; but there had been ever since esteem between them,
though the enormous divergence of their lives kept them far
asunder.

The Duc de Lira—last of a mighty race—oftentimes
envied with a sigh the superb health, the careless joyousness,
the liberty, and the wanderings of the man who owned naught
but his Mistigri and his Straduarius. He himself had been
delicate of frame from his birth upward; and—for this
solitary representative of his old legitimate line—there was
but one creed, one king, one flag, possible; and he had no
place nor part in the France of the present. Lonely are the
men who are before their own time; but doubly isolated are
the men who are behind it.

Restrained by a fancied honor from departing ever from
the political traditions of his house, he spent his years in
charity, in study, in travel, mingling little in the pleasures
of his rank, not at all in their ambitions. He had never

married; he had shunned the society of women; he was of
a nervous and sensitive temperament, and now, even the
presence of the gay and haughty child—foundling though
she was—kept the great nobleman almost silent and almost
embarrassed. For so long a period he had never heeded the
fairness of woman; her beauty, her youth, her pretty au-
dacities were like some startling revelation to him of all that
he had missed and lost.

He stayed an hour or more, watching the progress of the
painting, talking with Tricotrin as scholar with scholar,
glancing always at the child. Her history he learned in a
few words; and he wondered to himself what lordly or
princely stock had given to this nameless Waif her royal air
and her imperial grace. He offered her many pleasures;
among them he invited her to go and see his house, a palace
filled with the treasures of art that Tricotrin had saved from
the mob's destruction. But Tricotrin gently declined all his
proposals; he followed his visitor out down the staircase, and
spoke what he would not speak before Viva.

"See here, M. de Lirà," he said, as they stood in the
doorway. "You have just heard the little one's history. I
have no riches; she can have none. What avail to give her
tastes that cannot be gratified, desires that can only be
wormwood? I let you come near her because you are a man
of pure honor—she is safe with you; but I would scarce do
so with any one else. Viva is a foundling; Viva must be of
the people. She is ready enough now to rebel at her lot;
ready enough in her innocence to throw herself into misery,
if the misery have gilded gates that she fancies are the por-
tals of power. We must teach her content as best we can,
or her future will be one of absolute wretchedness—if not of
disgrace. I know well that you would be the last to push her
one step nearer that; so,—understand my sole motive when
I say, 'be merciful to the child, and do not suggest to her
brilliancies she can never justly enjoy.'"

The Duc de Lirà listened and bent his head.

"God forbid she should be harmed; but—such a creature

as that—Tricotrin, believe me it will not be possible to teach her contentment in poverty."

Tricotrin's eyes darkened with impatience.

"I saved her life for wretchedness then, or for shame. How can riches come with honor to a nameless, ownerless thing? You forget; men have hard enough work to emerge from the prejudices of your legitimate world, women are crushed to pieces under them!"

"That is true," said the nobleman, simply, and he went away without more words.

Tricotrin stood looking out down the narrow street, with its peaked roofs, and the sunset glimmering ruddily in the casement-glass. A band of blue-bloused workmen were coming along it singing cheerily; some boy-painters were laughing and talking over their thin red wine in the little cabaret opposite; in a window high above sat a pretty black-eyed girl stitching away at the rose-colored skirt in which she would dance at a barrière ball that night: it was all of the "people," but it was all bright and contented.

He crushed, ere they rose, both a sigh and an oath.

Ninety-nine out of a hundred would have been happy in Viva's place: why must she alone have this restless, ambitious, incessantly-aspiring, unconsciously-disdainful nature, which made her so ill at ease, so petulantly impatient of the life into which accident had thrown her?

Was it the irrepressible natural instinct of some patrician blood in her that thus worked in her soul and corroded her present peace by its desire for unattainable power? It might be:—who could tell whence she came, this child who thought herself born from the fairies? Be that as it might, it was true that she would never be satisfied as she was. And his heart was heavy within him, for his love for her grew very great.

After a while he turned and went within; he ascended the stairs and called to her: she came thrusting her head out of the gloom like some Old Master's Angel out of a background of bistre shadow.

"My child," he said gently, "you have seen some of the sights of Paris; but there are some still that you have not. Come and look at those now."

She came: he was more silent than his wont, and she wondered where he was going. He did not tell her; but he went first to a building, where within the entrance-way was a little iron cradle that swung on a pivot: just placed in it was a year-old child, naked and crying piteously; the cradle was just turning for the infant to be taken within. "That boy is a foundling, as you were, my Waif," he said softly.

Some streets farther on he paused again; a group of young students were reading what was written on the door of a hospital. "They are looking what operations take place to-morrow," he said, in the same tone. "There are six: six lives then that will suffer the torment of the knife, suffer it that they may still drag on existence, sweet to them, though they are poor and of no account."

Viva did not answer; the unusual seriousness of his voice awed and stilled her. He led her next to a long low shed around which a silent crowd was pressing.

"A dead body lies in there," he said to her. "A young girl not much older than you; who drowned herself last night in the Mare d'Auteuil. People have come all day to see if they could recognize her; no one has done so yet. There are lives that are quite lonely upon earth."

The child's face was grave and pale; she still answered nothing, but he heard her breath come and go quickly. He passed onward to a great dark melancholy pile, where the high casements were barred with iron: he motioned to her to look up at it.

"That is a madhouse for the poor. Among them is an actress, once as brilliant as your Coriolis. Can you guess what made her a maniac? she had an accident that spoiled her beauty, and when she first appeared after it the cruel people hissed as loudly as they had adored her. She stood a moment under the storm of execration, then burst into frantic laughter. Her brain was gone from that night. She had been extravagant and vicious. Such women have many lovers and no friends. There was only the public asylum for her. Yet Coriolis now is not so great as this maniac once was."

Still, Viva said not a word: but her hands twined on his arm, and clung there closely in the fading evening light. He led her onward in silence through dark, crooked, wretched streets that she had never dreamed of; she had seen the Paris of pleasure, the Paris that was full of light, of wealth, of merciless gayety, of boundless recklessness; this was the Paris of crime, of misery, of famine.

Fetid odors met her like the blasts of poisonous furnaces; hideous outcries filled the air; ghastly shapes flitted through the gloom, of raving women and of starving men, and of creatures all unsexed by drink or guilt, who had nor womanhood nor manhood left: standing at the entrance of that Gehenna, where the love of that brutalized populace made him sacred, he felt the child, brave though she was, trembling through all her delicate limbs. He passed his arm around her.

"Viva, look well. Take that picture with you on your memory. This is how the mass of human lives in every city lives; they who of their own will sink to it may merit their hell, but thousands on thousands are *born* in such a pit of crime, of infamy, of agony as this, breathing its poisons as their first and only breath of life—and then the world can wonder that it reeks with sin!"

She shuddered, and clung closer to him, and hid her face upon his breast.

"Take me away! Oh, take me away!" she whispered. "How wicked I was to ever complain or repine!"

He led her home in the same silence; and up the stairs to where a wood fire burned cheerily in the little chamber: in its light he saw that she was very pale, her hair was heavy with night dew, her limbs shook still. He drew her to the warmth, and looked down in her eyes.

"Have I been cruel, my child? Your fever of discontent needed a sharp cure. Life lies before you, Viva, and you alone can mould it for yourself. Sin and anguish fill nine-tenths of the world: to one soul that basks in light a thousand perish in darkness; I dare not let you go on longer in your dangerous belief that the world is one wide paradise, and that the highroad of its joys is the path of reckless selfishness. Can you not think that there are lots worse than that of a guiltless child who is well-loved and well-guarded, and has all her future still before her?"

Ere his words were done she had thrown herself into his arms, in an abandonment of emotion,—the loosened tide of all her pent-up wonder, grief, and fear. It was the terror of every young life that sees for the first time the hopeless and unnumbered miseries that fill the world.

"Oh! how wicked I was!" she murmured, again lifting her tear-laden eyes to the face that ever for her had the compassion and benignity of a god. "I—who am so happy! I—who have you to care for me!"

A beautiful light shone in his own gaze as it dwelt on her; he answered nothing in words, but he stooped his head and kissed her. To her it was only the old familiar tenderness of pardon and of sympathy; but for him it had a new sweetness —the sweetness of a new love.

As children dream by firelight, so he dreamt too in the warmth of the burning logs.

Her love for him was deep and true; the unrest of her very early youth would pass away; her fanciful desires were the caprices of an imaginative and but half-dawned intelligence; was it not possible that his pity on her when she had been naught to him might be rewarded now that she had grown dear to him?

Feminine natures were things so mutable; the fanciful ambitions of women faded so often and so happily in the dawn of their affections;—could she not find her pleasure as he did, in wandering over fresh lands, keeping ever in eternal summer? —could she not, as others of her sex had done, forget the desires of pomp and of power, in the sunny eyes and the murmuring lips of offspring that should spring up in her youth, like the white blossoms that encircle the scarce-opened blush-flower?

It was only a dream; but dreams, only, are fair,—till the dreamer awakes.

CHAPTER XVII.

The dream remained with him all the following day; a day spent at Great and Little Trianon, where every graceful tree that grew tall and beautiful above the mossy sward, and every water-bird that splashed and floated in the weed-choked pools, whispered to Viva's fancy some mournful warning of the instability of power. She was in the mood to listen to the warning. The Trianon made her very thoughtful; she did not know much history, but she knew that one history which looks from the blue eyes of the portrait on the wall, and speaks in the yellow leaves of the old music, and steals down the gentle winds that stir the same boughs which once screened sun and heat from the white Austrian brow.

It made her thoughtful; but she was very happy lying under the odorous pines, and listening to Tricotrin's stories of that old dead time.

The thoughtfulness passed; the happiness remained when she was back again in the Pays Latin, in the little high cosy chamber, watching the simmering of a wonderful sweet soup she had concocted in Spanish fashion, after his directions, of potatoes, and wine, and fruit, and spices, bubbling altogether in a brazen jar.

"Shall we go to the theater, Viva, when we have tasted that olla podrida?" he asked;—they had gone to the theater each night that she had been in Paris.

Viva shook her head.

"And why? Theaters were your Elysium."

"They are nothing to me since *she* is not true!" murmured the child. "I could not bear to see her act again!"

"Chut! How can actresses be true, little one? They are always representing what they do not feel."

Viva shook her head again.

"I *thought* it was all true," she said softly. "Else I should not have cared."

She had been wounded in her tenderest point—her good faith. She had believed in this woman with all her soul; she had identified herself with all that the actress had portrayed; that all this which had so moved her should have been false, made her feel cheated and despoiled; that the sweetness of that angel-face should have been only a painted mask, made her resent the theft, on false pretenses, of her sympathy and love.

At that moment, happily for the distraction of her thoughts, the soup boiled over; Viva was at once absorbed in its rescue. It was hot, sweet, strong, delicious, and, better than all, of her own preparation. She was just pouring it out when the door opened, and the Duc de Lira entered in the twilight. Viva was incensed beyond measure!—ah! how mean a thing of the people she must look, she thought, her cheeks scarlet with the fire, her hands filled with a brass pipkin, her laugh ringing loud and long because the little round apples, stuck all over with cloves, bobbed so drolly up and down in the fragrant mixture! So she fancied;—little dreaming that the stranger was musing what a picture for Hebe she looked, and thinking that he would have given all he owned to be able to find mirth and pleasure in apples dancing on a frothy lake of wine as she did, and as Ben Jonson had done before her.

She did not attach any importance to the new-comer; she did not know his rank; she thought him cold, gray, silent, uninteresting,—not the least like King Arthur, or even the Prince Fainéant; but he had given her a seat in a carriage, and Viva was of the temper that made her always want to look her very best, even in the eyes of an organ-grinder that she listened to in the streets. Moreover, she saw that he admired her and studied her, though he said little to her, but conversed almost entirely with Tricotrin or Mère Mévert; and she had that thorough coquetry by nature which made her love homage, whether or no she cared two straws for the one who rendered it. To some, admiration is valueless, unless from those who in turn they also admire: but Viva was not so fastidious. She delighted in even the stupid open-mouthed stare of amazement at her loveliness, that a despised cow-boy would give as she passed the place where he lay among his grazing herds.

For she was feminine to her heart's core.

The Duke's advent spoilt her soup, and also spoilt her content.

Tricotrin saw that,—impatiently. Himself, he had both regard and respect for the grave, gentle, melancholy person whose dignities brought so little joy with them; but he wished the nobleman had not found his way to this attic, and he was perplexed as to his meaning in coming there. With less than his usual courtesy he cut the visit shorter than it would have been by bidding his caller farewell, and taking Viva with him to a Café Chantant.

The girl heartily enjoyed these things, and he loved to see her among them, since they were what he could easily bestow.

The music enchanted her; and the coarser meanings of some popular songs could not harm her, since she was in absolute ignorance of the construction put upon the phrases that evoked such laughter around her. She laughed, too, because the melodies were so mirth provoking in their airy and droll cadences, because the gas-lit scene was so pretty and exciting, because all those students and grisettes about her laughed so riotously; but the songs might have been in Greek for aught that she understood of them.

Then, when they were over, she sat at a little round table and ate her ices, and tasted her first champagne, and amused herself with the eternal stream of picturesque gas-lit life that passed before her, and went to bed just tired enough to fall asleep at once and dreamlessly. He had made her forget her own discontent: she was happy, and found that it was after all possible to enjoy one's self among "the people."

But fate undid all that he had done. The next day, in the dusky hour, Viva, left alone for a little while, sat in the window-seat reading by the lingering light a historical romance that delighted her—a romance wherein a herdsman's adopted daughter, after many vicissitudes, was proved to be sole heiress of the mighty castle that had frowned upon her from her birth. She was absorbed in it when the door was thrown open by some personage in a glimmer of green and gold, and into the chamber, thus ushered but unannounced, came the most exquisite little figure she had ever beheld. The figure of a very small, very old lady, with the most delicate features conceivable, white hair, black eyes that still shone like stars, a profusion of laces, a gold-headed stick, and red, high-heeled shoes that clicked a musical patter over the bare floor.

A fairy at last! Viva rose, transfixed. "It must be Cinderella's godmother herself!" she thought; "there could not be *two* fairies like that!" And in an instant her imagination leapt back to her home by the Loire, and she saw Roi Doré changed into a beautiful prince, and Bébé into four white horses, and the pumpkins into gilded carriages, and the chestnuts into diamonds, and herself into——but her dreams were broken by the fairy's voice, imperious but kindly:

"Do you know who I am, my child?"

"Yes," murmured Viva, awed by this immortal visitant as she would have been by no mortal empress.

"Indeed! Who, then?"

Viva's answer was hushed and reverential.

"A Fairy! And I have hoped for you so long."

The lady looked at her in astonishment, then fairly laughed outright. She was not displeased; her old age being very lovely and delicate, it was neither distasteful nor inappropriate to be taken for a fairy.

"No, my dear, you mistake," she said, seating herself on one of the hard chairs. "I am no fairy, though I may do as well as one perhaps. I am the Duchess de Lirà."

Viva said nothing; she felt perfectly certain that she was right, that nothing mortal could be so exquisite, so small, yet so awe-inspiring as her visitant; but she knew how dangerous it was to contradict fairies when they wished to suppress their identity, and remained discreetly silent accordingly.

"Come here and let me look at you," said her visitant.

Viva obeyed, a little anxiously; how did she know but what her guest might change the brass pipkin into a chariot, and whisk her off through the open lattice?

Madame de Lirà turned her gently to the fading light, and looked her all over with inexorable scrutiny. Not a single flaw could have escaped those ruthless and piercing eyes; but they failed to find one, and softened their gaze ere their inspection was done.

"Very well, very indeed," she muttered, as she loosened her hold on the child. "Of an exquisite grace, as he said; and surely not of the people."

Viva colored hotly as she heard.

"You are very pretty—nay, you are very beautiful," pursued the old lady, calmly and critically. "With another year or two, when your form shall have fully developed, you will be magnificent,—with culture and dress. I have heard all about you. You call yourself Viva?"

"Yes, Madame;" she was still thinking of all that she would get this fairy to do: first and foremost, Tricotrin must be made King of the World, and grand'mère must be given new youth.

"Viva! It means nothing, but it is not ugly. You could not have been baptized in a Catholic country, for there is no such name in the Saints' Calendar. Well, you are a handsome child; and I pity you, my dear. I will take you home to stay with me."

"To stay with you!" echoed Viva, in amazement. She had been a little bewildered as to why a fairy godmother

should allude to the matter of a baptism at which she must
have been the principal person present, and she did not think
it according to elfin creeds to be very particular about the
saints or their calendar either. But to go and stay with her,
in her palace of cloud or of sea-cavern, was an instantaneous
transformation about which there could be no doubt. Did
she not know what Cinderella had gone to! "But I cannot.
I dare not!" she murmured, in sudden remembrance. "I must
hear first what he says. He was so angry about the young
Prince; and I cannot vex him again!——"

"I thank you, my Waif!" said a voice from the doorway.
"You have been faithful under trial, which Peter, whom men
call Saint, was not."

The Duchess de Lirà put up her gold glasses at the figure
she beheld—a figure very strange to her, with his linen
blouse, and his great meerschaum, and his little black Mistigri,
who spoke in this careless fashion, and blasphemed the rock
of the Church!

"Madame la Duchesse," he said, as he approached her
with that courteousness which, frank to all men, was graceful
to all women, "you are come to see my Waif? Nay, that is
kind and generous. May I ask to what you were tempting
her?"

The old Duchess gazed at him in silence; she had heard
of him, but she had never seen him. She had expected a man
of the "*bas peuple*," with whom she could have dealt in
sublime condescension; she saw a man to whom even she felt
condescension was not possible, and who had, even to her
fastidious eyes, an air of race and of breeding undeniable.

Tricotrin turned to the child.

"Go to your room, Viva; Madame and I will talk alone."

Viva obeyed, though very reluctantly, and with many a
glance at her fairy.

"There was no need to send her away," said the old lady,
coldly. "My son is interested in her; he begged me to show
her some kindness. It is to be regretted that a child of so

much promise should be lost in such a life as this. I am willing that she should come and stay awhile in my household, that I may see if anything can be made of her——."

"Made of her!" echoed Tricotrin bitterly. "You mean, Madame, that you would amuse yourself with her while she is fresh to you, as with some new bird from the tropics; and then, when you have tired of her, have her trained for the opera, or cast off for the theater, as the bird might be given to sing in a public show, no matter whether its first notes were its death-knell?"

He spoke with unconsidered irony, on the sting of the impatient wrath that he felt that these aristocrats could never leave her in peace, but must ever try to turn her away from him at the very moment her heart seemed knit closest to his.

Madame de Lirà rose with that dignity which, in so fragile a form, had so awed the Waif.

"Whether it be ignorance or ingratitude on your part," she said, icily, "I do not attempt to decide. Your insolence is sufficient to frustrate all my efforts for the young girl's welfare."

Tricotrin's forehead flushed; he saw that he had been rude to an aged woman.

"I was wrong, Madame," he said, quickly. "Pardon me. It stings me to hear her spoken of as a thing to be bartered in, that is all."

"There is no question of barter," said the slow, gentle voice of the Duc de Lirà behind him.

His mother interrupted his words:

"My son, to comply with your wishes, I have done what has been exceedingly distasteful to me. The matter has concluded as I foresaw; take me to my carriage."

"Stay, Madame," entreated her son, reverentially. "The matter is but commenced. What has Viva herself said? The Duchess," he continued to Tricotrin, hurriedly, "came to invite the child for a month's stay with her, at my wish. Surely you cannot refuse such a——"

"I leave you to make your entreaty to your—friend!" said the Duchess, with her delicate, glacial sneer, that she did not spare even to her son. "The girl can accept or can refuse. But I must beg you to take me down stairs. Whether it be ignorance or insolence in this person I do not seek to inquire, at all events it is ingratitude, and strange neglect of that young creature's interests."

The last sentence struck Tricotrin with a pang. Was his love growing brutal in selfishness?

"Forgive me, Madame!" he said, rapidly; "I was rude to you. It stings me to have her spoken of as a thing to be traded in; but what is it you mean to her?"

The old aristocrat was softened from her wrath.

"A fine man, and gracefully mannered," she mused, as she answered, still coldly. "I mean well, as you may imagine. M. de Lirà interests himself in this child. She is beautiful; she is unfortunate; she occupies a terrible position in having no friend but yourself. I would rescue her from it if it be possible. M. de Lirà affirms that he himself answers for the truth of your story concerning her,—he has perfect faith in your integrity; and it seems to us——"

Tricotrin's eyes blazed like a lion's.

"Madame! I can hear no more words in that tone. Do you speak of us like paupers? 'A terrible position!' Why does Viva occupy a terrible position? She has been reared according to nature, and not according to art. Is that terrible? It is rare."

"It is impossible to converse with any one who demeans himself thus," observed the Duchess, frigidly. "I say 'terrible' advisedly. The position of any female child just growing to womanhood must be so with no friend but a man who states that he is not her father, and does not purpose to become her husband."

Tricotrin started, and the blood flushed his forehead as he heard; he paused a moment ere he replied.

"I am old enough to be the one, too old to be the other,"

he answered, at length. "But—I thank you for having shown me a danger for her that I had overlooked."

The old woman glanced at him with her piercing eyes, which had lost little of the keenness of their youth.

"The girl is beautiful," she said curtly, taking a sweetmeat from a silver box. He felt all that she intended to convey under that simple observation.

"Madame, I thank you," he said hurriedly. "You have recalled to me the world's skepticism of all innocence or honesty, and its ready credulity of all vileness! Forgive my late roughness; what is it you would offer to the child?"

Madame de Lirà coughed a little: she was hardly prepared for so direct a question, so she parried it.

"I offer her—my countenance. If she come under my roof for a few weeks I can better determine what will be for her real good hereafter. In any case you may be certain that I should do whatever was just, and give whatever social advantages she might prove herself to deserve."

He repressed a passionate oath at the insolence of patronage that ran through all the words: they were meant in kindliness, and out of justice toward Viva it was not his right to cast them back with all the contempt and impatience that rose at them in his soul.

"Do you mean," he said at length, and his voice was hoarse and hard, "that you will play with Viva for awhile as with some new lapdog, or rare piece of faïence, and when you have wearied of her, cast her aside as you cast the dog and the china to the pages or the cabinets? Or,—do you mean a noble and humane benevolence, which will honor you more than all your charities and bequests to all the churches in the world? Do you mean——"

Madame de Lirà's sparkling eyes were gathering fierce fire, and she would have answered the audacity of such an arraignment by withdrawing, once and for all, her unappreciated condescension, had not the gentle voice of her son interposed.

"Tricotrin, you misapprehend us, I fear. It is at my entreaty that my mother has come hither to see what it may possibly be in our power to do for your Waif. Will you come aside with me, and let Viva return to the Duchess?"

Tricotrin shook himself with a gesture of intolerable impatience.

"For what? That she may be made more ill-content still with the life that is simplest, truest, and most innocent for her?"

Madame de Lira rose from her seat.

"My son, oblige me by taking me to my carriage. You will be so good as to acknowledge that I was in the right when I predicted the outrage I should receive as my reward for gratifying your wishes against my own judgment."

"Outrage! By heaven!" cried Tricotrin, with all the headlong impulse of pain. "Would you admit the title of a stranger to claim one of your lapdogs? Viva has as much interest for me as your greyhounds for you!"

But the old Duchess had passed beyond the reach of his words, and was descending the crooked stairs to her equipage. A few moments later, her son re-entered the room. Tricotrin stood silent on the hearth, with the red blaze of the stormily setting sun shed full across him. He did not look up; he did not speak: the other hesitated a minute, then approached him.

"Tricotrin, you were surely discourteous to my mother?"

"Possibly."

"And you totally misapprehended her."

"That I doubt."

"The fault of her visit, if fault it be, lies with me. I have endeavored to interest her in Viva; I have succeeded in doing so. You must know that she can be a valuable friend if she pleases; and in this instance I believe she would so please. Are you justified in depriving the child of all the benefits she would derive from such friendship?"

"Benefits! What benefits? To be subject to the cold winds of caprice? To be the plaything of a fine lady's vagaries? To see the smile of to-day become the sneer of to-morrow? To be a patronized thing, on whom great people can vent at their will their variations of ennui and spleen? I perceive nothing in such 'benefits' deserving either of my acceptance or of her gratitude."

"You are unjust. We are not the heartless and frivolous creatures you would make us to be. If Viva——"

Tricotrin was not softened by the gentle words; they tenfold increased the unreasoning, vehement rage that possessed him; the rage born of pain like that of some gallant animal under a shot-wound.

"Viva! what of Viva? What has any living creature to do with Viva save myself? Because I cannot keep her in the luxurious wastefulness of a palace, can I lay no claim to a life that I saved? Because I found her nameless, penniless, ownerless, is that any reason why the first stranger that fancies her has stronger claim on her existence than I? Because a child's heated imaginations, and the poisonous whispers of fools, for awhile make her ingrate enough to despise the life that has sheltered her body, and kept stainless her soul, is that plea enough for me to surrender every right to protect, and every title to guide, her? 'She is ill-content,' say you! Good God! Was there ever a fondled thing that did not bite through the hand that caresses it? Was there ever a plant reared with care and with tenderness that an alien hand did not break off the flowering-crown when it blossomed? 'Ill-content!' A fine plea! Would she have been more content, pray you, reared in the public nurseries, where the children of bastardy are cursed from their infancy up, for the crime of having come to the birth undesired and unwelcomed?"

The fiery torrent of words rushed headlong from his lips; the claims he never breathed to her, he flung out in the face of those who desired to rob him of her; the passion of his temperament, that slept under the sunny vivacity of his habitual nature, broke loose under the unbearable pang that it was to him, to have her thus sought and thus bribed. His impulses were hot and swift as volcanic fire, and he stayed neither to consider nor restrain them.

The Duc de Lirà listened with regret, but not in anger, for he knew the provocation that he gave; and he knew the justice of the resentment it awakened.

"Will you forgive me if I speak quite plainly?" he said at last. "Of course you have indisputable claim to all her love and fealty; indisputable title to defend and shape her life, howsoever may seem best to you. But what is it that does seem so? What is it you intend to do with her?"

Tricotrin's eyes fired like an angered hawk's.

"I deny the right of any one to ask the question!"

"Perhaps I have no right," answered his hearer, patiently. "Nevertheless, I do so. Listen, Tricotrin: if you project to make this girl anything more to you than she is now, say so, and I will not press a single word more on you. She *is* yours by right in that case: and none of a surety have weightier or nobler claim upon her heart or her future than you, who stand in the stead to her of every tie. But, if you have no such intent, and all you have hitherto said implies that you have not, you will scarcely be enabled much longer to continue your present relationship to her? Reflect, you have no parentage to her; can you be the sole companion and protector of her life without exposing her to injurious suspicion? Will the world give you credit for your disinterestedness, or her for her innocence? It has too little of either, itself, to do so."

"Pshaw!" broke in Tricotrin, with imperious scorn. "Have I ever lived for the world? That bugbear and scarecrow of the millions of fools, the breath of whose lungs is the lies off other men's lips? The world! What have Viva and I to do with the world? We forget it; it can afford to forget us—a bohemian and a foundling."

"You can forget it: she cannot, she will not. For it will not forget her. Hear me out: you are just, you are true.

You will admit a truth even when it militates against your desire. If Viva be not your wife, not your daughter, how shall you persuade others that she is not your mistress? If her love for you be not such as would make her happy in union with you, how shall you render her future content? You said yourself, a few nights ago, that, if ill-content, she must become of all women the most miserable. It is certain she will do so. You will attempt impossibilities if you seek to keep her womanhood in the same solitude that has made her childhood so joyful. She is ambitious, proud, quick to resent, eager to enjoy—is it for the child whom you regard so tenderly that you can determine to prepare a future in which all the darkness of an imputed shame, and none of the solace of an indulged love, will be her portion?"

"Oh God!"—the words escaped him with the stifled cry of a fierce suffering. He swung round and flashed his eyes over the speaker.

"You find strange eloquence! Are *you* her lover too?"

"You know me better than that," said the other, simply, with a gentle dignity that bore an unspoken rebuke in it. "A lover!—I! My years may be no more than your own; but I have none of your youth left in me. Left, do I say? I never knew it. No; I speak as I do merely from such interest in her as any one—not a brute or a libertine—must feel for a young creature of such promise. What I say sounds harsh and insolent doubtless;—but your justice will acknowledge the singleness of my motive. I have no title to dictate to you, no excuse perhaps for interference with you, but I do repeat this:—you, who are so anxious to guard her from every evil breath, you who have acted with so much nobility toward her in her defenselessness, must, for your own conscience' sake and the sake of her future, choose between one of two things. Take the right of marriage over her life, or do not stand between her and my mother's protection of her. You alone can know which of the two will best advance her happiness and yours. Whichever you decide on, tell me;— and in either case believe me my friendship is yours if you will have it. A Lirà does not soon forget; I have not forgotten the July night in my Cour d'Honneur."

He passed quickly through the evening gloom, and out from the little chamber as the words left his lips; he was generous, sensitive, sympathetic, it had not been without fear and hesitation that he had spoken them.

Tricotrin, in his solitude, never stirred from where he stood before the wood-fire, whose flames were now the only light left in the darkened room. The chimes of a neighboring clock told off two quarters, with the strokes echoing through the open casement, but he did not hear them. He was lost in thought.

The mercy he had shown was bringing its reward—in bitterness.

"To have the fate of Bruno!" he muttered, dashing the falling hair from his eyes that looked gloomily down into the leaping flames.

To take from gratitude what would not come from love; —to gain through innocent tenderness what would not be given through riper passion;—to bind to him in its wax-like malleability what, when it changed shape with older years, would recoil perchance from his clasp;—to claim the sweetness of kisses by the plea that the lips which he sought had been fed by his bread,—these were what he would do if he chose the first of the alternatives presented to him, if he cheated her and himself into the faith that a child's affection was a woman's love. And these done, what would be their end, their sequel?

The freshness of winds and waters, the changes of motion and rest, the sound of a song on the air, the glow of an alp in a sunrise, the tire of toil among vine or olive or millet, the play and the pleasure of sinew and muscle, the bright shock of sea-water in a leap from the rocks, the careless zest of free days untroubled with thought for the morrow, the frankness of welcome from the grasp of the mountaineer or the eyes of the girl-gipsy,—all these made his life rich, made it happy, because with them also he had the heart of a poet, the liberty

of a man. But she,—her fancy panted for power; her scorn
recoiled from this simplicity of joy which, being far above
her, she deemed lay far beneath her; the frail strength, and
the languid senses, of a girl's youth could not grasp the
warmth, and the force, and the rapture which he could feel
from the mere life within him, and the mere life around him.
The happiness he had he could not transfer to her. She would
lie in his bosom, restless as a bird restrained by a captive
hand; she would ache and sigh and grow weary for the things
of wealth and of pomp that he could not bestow; and then
—and then—to those sighs some other would answer; and
across his life would be the blackness of dishonor and
desolation.

He beheld her future and his own as in some mirror of
prophecy. He could make her his own—yes; as the hand
that has fed and fondled the tame hare can stay the trustful
creature as a captive when it comes for a caress. But scarce
at less cost than the fate of Bruno for him,—of Coriolis
for her.

And yet—he loved her with all the power of his tropical
nature; loved her with a new and sudden love, since the day
that he had flung her young Faust from him. To let her go
from him, to let her drift to others, was torture to him.

With unconscious violence he struck his clinched hand on
the iron of the stove by which he stood.

"My God! For the first time in all my life I wish——"

The wish died unuttered in his throat. For the first
time in all his laughter-lightened years he wished that a
thing done, that a choice made, in his earliest youth could
be undone, and be reversed. These were the rewards that
his tenderness to a foundling brought him,—futile regret, and
vain desire!

CHAPTER XVIII.

He stood there still, in the darkness, with his clinched hand resting on the iron; a light swift movement came near him, a gay laugh echoed through the silence.

"I could not stay in the dark any longer. Have you sent my fairy away?"

The thoughtless words thrilled through his soul as Viva came to him: was the jest symbolical of a terrible truth? Was he, in his own selfish covetousness of her, driving away the influence by which all the colors of glory that she dreamed of might bathe her life in their radiance?

She, all unconscious, came nearer still, and put her hands upon his arm.

"Was she a fairy? I have been thinking since it might be foolish of me to fancy her so; and yet,—she looked so exactly like one, and nothing but a fairy could have promised me all she did!"

"What a child you are!" he said impatiently, with an accent in his voice that she had never heard before. "Fairy? No! Do you suppose fairies are real things?"

"Grand'mère does," said Viva, gravely. "But do tell me, why did you send her away? May I go and see her? If she be not a fairy she must be something very great; and—oh, those diamonds on her fingers when she uncovered her hand to feel my hair!"

He shook her clasp off him and walked to the window:—his heart was full of tenderness, anxiety, yearning, pain, and contest for her sake;—and she thought of the glitter of jewels on a stranger's hands!

Viva looked at him with a little sense of fear; then glided down on to the floor, and leant there in front of the stove, with the light from its open door playing fitfully all over her picturesque limbs.

She began to think he was unkind;—he had sent away her Faust, her Coriolis, and now her Fairy.

It was some time before he spoke to her; then it was gravely but very gently.

"You thought me harsh to your actress, Viva?" It seemed an irrelevant question, but it sprang from his own train of thought. Viva looked into the embers.

"Yes," she said truthfully at last: she wondered how he knew that she was thinking of Coriolis.

"Do you deem her justified then in the blow she dealt to her husband?"

He stood behind her; and she could not see the intense anxiety that was in his eyes as they were fastened on her.

She took thought a moment,—then she answered him with her golden head dropped on one side in meditation.

"Justified? No. You say nothing wrong is that; and it was wrong in her of course. But,—you see I can fancy what she felt. He had the sea, and the storms, and the boats, and the other fishermen,—and he was born for it too, and chose it himself. But she,—she might love him all the same, you know, and yet she might hate the life, might she not?—feel the cabin stifle her, and the days go slowly, and the great waters look dreary, and so, grow half mad, never seeing the world that she wanted to see. It was wrong, because he loved her you say, and did all he could, and could not help being poor. But still for her;—ah, it is so hard never to do what you want to do! It made her wicked I fancy; and then she grew cruel; and forgot that he would suffer, because she went to enjoy!"

He heard in silence, then moved from her back to the open casement: he was answered; and each word had gone through his heart like the thrust of a knife.

Her very ignorance of the extent of the sin made her pleading for its excuse more pregnant with meaning to his ear. Unconsciously to her, her sympathy with the actress was prescience for herself.

Viva sat silent some moments gazing into the fire, too absorbed in her own thoughts to note that he had not replied to her. She started as his voice, after awhile, came again through the gloom from where he leaned by the little lattice.

"You justify infidelity and ingratitude! Well, they are accursed sins in my sight, but it may be I am too harsh to them; it may be they grow ingrained in women!"

"Oh, no! I do not justify them!" cried the child, as she sprang to her feet, frightened and grieved. "What do you mean? What can you think? I tried to say—only I say it so ill—that what she did was heartless and guilty, but yet she could not help doing it as it were, because the weariness in her life drove her to it. Now look!—how I love grand'-mère, how I long to see the little kitchen again, how fond I am of Roi Doré, and Bébé, and the pigeons, and all. And yet!—so wicked I am, so shameful I am!—that I *know* if you take me back and leave me there month after month, year after year, I shall grow so impatient of them every one, I shall so long for excitement, and light, and music, and applause, and all that one hears and sees here in Paris, I shall so hate that still even life with no change in it save the change of the leaves from green into yellow, that—let me try how I may—I shall long for that glitter and renown on the stage as she did. Do not be angry with me; it is better to tell you the truth; and how can I help what I feel?"

He gave a sharp quick sigh as he heard the words poured out in half-penitent vehemence:—how was he to hope to keep happy and innocent, since he could not keep it in riches, this nature that panted so wistfully for forbidden and unattainable things?

"I am not angered," he said wearily, "and God forbid I should blame you for truthfulness. But, I see plainly your danger and my duty. You must tread a path, high and bright in the sun of the world's smile; or,—or—my child, you will live to curse me that my feet did not stamp the life out of you when that life was scarce more than a butterfly's among the flowers!"

Then he stooped, and touched her lips with hot swift kisses, and put her gently from him, and went out alone into the shades of the autumn night.

She, awed and contrite, stood bewildered in the glow of the burning wood, with a vexed impatience on her beautiful quivering mouth.

"What could he mean? He grows so strange!" she thought, restlessly beating her foot upon the boards. "And he never told me now of the Fairy!"

"Viva!" said Mère Mévert from the doorway. "Viva, here are some chestnuts the greengrocer below us has just sent you. Look what fine ones!"

Viva took them without attention, but they were so large and so tempting that she interested herself in setting them on the embers to roast, and as she watched them in their cooking laughed and talked with the good woman, and had forgotten all her wrongs and her woes, as she peeled off the shining brown skins from the white fruit within, and dipped it down into the salt.

She had no care but what the chestnuts consoled: what did she know of the great soul that suffered for her sake?

CHAPTER XIX.

He did not return all the following day.

Viva, accustomed to look to him for all her amusements, and impatient to hear more of her Fairy, grew restless, peevish, wayward, and full of impatience.

It was a glorious sunshiny autumnal day, and she had to spend it all in-doors. The woman Mévert was with her sick son, Mère Rose busied with a full household. Viva tried all her occupations, to fling each away in discontent, and spent the chief of her hours beating her rosy fingers on the lattice in petulant wrath at her detested detention. As the day wore on into evening she grew very angry, like the spoilt child that she was; and deeming herself injured by such unwonted neglect, worked herself into a chafing rage at her captivity; which at sunset she varied by gliding unperceived down the stairway, and seating herself on the wooden step of the door,—a forbidden seat that she was resolute to occupy since she had been kept imprisoned from sunrise.

Some momentary anxiety touched her as to what could have kept him away; but she believed devoutly in his omnipotence, and her chief sensation was fiery anger at her own disappointment.

"He is cruel—cruel!" she said feverishly to herself. "He will not let me go to Coriolis, and he sends even that lovely old fairy away! He is cruel!"

And she felt that for once she could rebel against him without scruple.

A caged linnet sang above her, shaded by a lime-bough: a pot of autumn roses shed their fragrance near her: the sunshine was playing brightly through the picturesque old alley —but she found no pleasure in anything. She was restlessly flinging away the gold treasures of her childhood in reckless eagerness for the mirage of her womanhood.

"If only he would let me go to the stage!" she thought, with wistful vehement longing. "He says I must tread a high path, why will he not let me make one for myself there?"

The words that he had spoken had made a deep impression on her capricious mind: they had startled, touched, and moved her; but she was capable rather of feeling vividly and passionately, than of feeling for any very long duration. She was at once intensely childlike and intensely woman-like; and she had all the fervor of the first, with all the changeability of the latter, temper.

"Souvent femme varie, fol à que se fie," was never truer in its unmerciful statement than it was of this bright changeling; but with her as with most of her sex, though the needle of her fancy veered round so many times and with such swift alternations, it never long ceased to point to the one pole star of her own vanity.

The pageant of the stage had allured her with fatal power: the blaze of a public recognition wore to her all the luminance of a heavenly apotheosis; she panted to be great: —as a young leopard, captive since it was a cub, pants for the freedom of the forest and the riot of the chase:—and she could see no other way to greatness. He told her that the way was thorn-set, and ended in a Lake Avernus; but she disbelieved him with all the assured audacious obstinacy of young ignorance, and she thought,—if only she could find it out, and pass upward by it, and smile at him from the eminence to which it led!

The poison had entered her soul: and although he had thought that he had drawn out all its virus, it had sunk too deeply for any antidote wholly to act against it. Moreover, the face and the grace of Coriolis had seduced her imagination; and no warning, no counsel, no statement of fact could dethrone this sovereign of her fancy. Through Coriolis she had had a glimpse into the one world that attracted her; the one life that to her looked well worth the living: her thoughts recurred to her lost paradise again and again and again. But now with more dangerous force: for they were nursed in silence. She had learned not to speak of the thing that lay nearest her heart:—there is no surer sign with any youthful thing that its consciousness has come, and that its innocence is in peril.

A few noons before she had sat on the sill of the little window, impatient to go out into the sunny noisy street below. She had wondered why the grisette, who a few days before had been sewing so merrily that rose-colored skirt, now worked without song and with her head drooped so low.

"What ails thee, Therèse?" She had heard the girl who leaned out beside her: and the dark-eyed worker had dropped her head lower over her labor.

"Lulu is gone to study in Rome!"

"Ah, bah!" the consoler had cried. "There are plenty more students as good as Lulu: and besides— he will come back."

The grisette had shaken her glossy head with a smile as sad as tears.

"They come back from Rome—yes: but back to what they left—never."

And Viva, with a dim perception of what her meaning had been, felt her heart ache for the speaker, and had watched her with a dreamy interest, half sympathy, half scorn.

"Why care for a student?—if it were a king now!" thought the patrician foundling. "Still—it must be very sad to love like that, a creature who does not care, but only goes away, gayly, to his Rome and to his pleasures!"

She was being quite as cruel as the painter Lulu: but she did not dream of applying the lesson to herself.

As she sat there, fretting at her durance, doing nothing, thinking herself cruelly used because she had missed one day of sunlight in the streets and gardens of Paris, she looked now and then up at the opposite window, where the grisette sat at work. She saw how tearfully the stitcher's eyes drooped over the heavy work; how wearily yet how tenderly the sewing-girl stooped ever and again to a little wooden cradle at her feet; how listless and full of pain was the wan faded look of the face that the sunset light only lit to make paler still: and she felt vaguely sorry for the sorrow that never had touched herself. Yet she thought, half in contempt, half in compassion:

"I would not sit weeping there;—I would go to a Rome of my own, and make myself happy with somebody else!"

Of the love that sees all the world centered in one single life, Viva had no conception. It looked as foolish to her as a bee would have looked, which, finding one flower yield it no fragrance, yet should have clung persistently to the one cruel and sterile blossom, rejecting all the thousand odors of the thousand other roses round it.

Instinctive egotism is ever instinctively philosophical.

As she sat there in the sun, with the striped awning over her head, and the carol of the linnet on her ear, there came to her a dainty little page, all scarlet and gold, like a little gallant from the galleries of Versailles, with his hat in his hand, and a profound obeisance that would have done honor to a prince. Viva started and colored at the sight of him: then, mindful of her dignity, sat still and regarded him with a mingling of curiosity and command,—her memory went to her lost Faust: this dazzling baby-servitor looked just like such an emissary as he would have sent.

He bowed again, very low to her.

"Mademoiselle, my mistress entreats to see you once more."

"Your mistress!"

Viva's heart beat loud; her cheeks flushed crimson, her thoughts sprang instantly to the truth:—earth held for her but one woman.

"Madame Coriolis,—she begs to speak to you," continued the little page. "Her carriage waits—at the end of this passage-way,—she trusts you will do her this honor?"

Viva pressed her hands to her heart, to still the choking sob that rose in her throat at the recollection that she must refuse this by every law of duty, of love, and of obedience.

"I cannot, I must not!" she murmured. "It would be so wicked!"

The page, regardless of her words, pressed his message on her: his mistress only craved a word, his mistress never was answered by a refusal, his mistress was accustomed to have her own way and will at all times.

"I cannot, I dare not!" pleaded Viva, losing all the memory of her own dignity, and ready at every word to burst into tears. "He has forbidden me: he will never speak to me again if I go to her. I long to come,—I do indeed,—but how can I disobey him? He is all I have in the world,—he is so good, so noble, so generous;—it would be so hideously wicked to rebel against him!"

The baby in scarlet and gold suppressed the immeasurable scorn that he felt, and proved himself a delicate tactician. To live in the service of the actress was to live to do her desire, by fair means or by foul. He entreated, he beguiled, he argued, he begged for his own sake, and he counseled for her own, in language so well chosen, that, when backed by the seduction of her own wishes, it proved only too powerful with Viva.

"It is only to speak to me, it cannot be much harm?" she pleaded with her conscience, as she cast a hasty glance back into the house. The two women were not there to see; Tricotrin was away, there was no fear of detection; and,—who knew what she might miss forever if she flung this chance away untried, if she threw this offer away untested?

"I will go!" she said breathlessly, casting her red cloak that lay behind her over her head, and fleeing fast down the street, as fast as though she fled from temptation.

She knew that she was committing a great sin; she knew that she was doing what was base, disloyal, and cowardly, since she would not have disobeyed him thus, save in his absence; she knew that she was false to every better thing within her. But the temptation was too strong, the allurement was too glorious in hue to be rejected; she felt vile in her own sight, yet, nevertheless, she went.

It was the transgression of every law of love, and honor, and duty, and pure faith, that bound her life: it was the casting away by deliberate act of all the sweetness and the safety of the guardianship which environed her; it was the oblivion of his gravest counsel, and the defiance of his tenderest desire: but the passion for glory that possessed her, for the glory that to her was embodied in the form of Coriolis, was stronger than every other feeling in her. She blindly followed where that ignis fatuus led.

Panting, trembling, growing pale and scarlet by turns, with expectation and her own consciousness of evil doing, she stood by the closed carriage from which the face of her angel looked out, in the little antique darkened street, through which the evening light was wandering in rich, deep rays of blended color.

"You sent for me?" she asked tremulously; and looking

up in this woman's sweet azure eyes, she thought with all the noble, senseless, vain, generous obstinacy of youth that her intuition must be more true than all the experience of others, that with this fair bright face no sin could go!

"You little fool!" said Coriolis with a smile. "Why did you let that man take you away from me the other day?"

Viva grew very pale; but she gave an honest answer.

"He says you are very wicked, and he would rather see me dead than like you!"

Coriolis laughed aloud; a silvery musical laughter, happy as a child's.

"He is complimentary—your friend! Well! do you believe him?"

"I ought," murmured Viva, wistfully and piteously. "But I cannot! I think you are an angel."

Coriolis laughed afresh: the ingenuous simplicity of reply did not touch her to pity, merely to amusement.

"Think so if you like," she said, "and I will be your good angel. See here, little one, I was in earnest when I offered to help you to a career. I can make you the fashion in a night, and I will do it if you have any sense, and are any way tractable. You have a splendid head—I tell you so—I was not handsomer myself, I verily believe. A creature with a face like yours can always have the world at her feet. But not if she be shut up in a garret where no eyes see her. One may as well be a sparrow as a kingfisher, if one never glitters in the sun under men's sight. You are a kingfisher. Well, come and fly in the light, do not mope in a wicker cage. I will take you with me, and show you my world,—come!"

Viva, white to her lips, and trembling sorely, looked up with appealing eyes.

"Do not ask me, do not ask me!" she cried, piteously. "He says he will never share me with you, that he will never look on me again if I go with you! I would give all the world if I had it, to come—but I dare not grieve him; I dare not!"

"Pooh!" cried the comedian. "What are women made

for but to plague the souls of men? It is our empire, that—of course he likes to keep you in prison, all jailers love power."

Viva shook her head.

"Oh no, no! You do not know him; he is so good, so generous, so gentle. He would never tell me anything but for my happiness. He fears you because he thinks you are so wicked, and he says that you broke that poor sailor's heart with your cruelty."

Coriolis set her delicate teeth, and a slight flush heightened the bloom of art on her cheeks; but she smiled with amused negligence, and took the means which she saw would be the surest to blind the child's instinct of right.

"Your friend calumniates me: a very general crime. It is the penalty we pay for our eminence," she answered. "Sailors! have I aught to do with common seamen? He errs strangely: but we will show him his error. Come you only with me,—just for these next few hours,—and I will make a princess of you. He shall see you on the throne of the world; for is not the applause of all Paris that? and he will thank me, and worship me as your best friend. Look you, little lady;—he is poor, this Tricotrin of yours; you are a great tax upon him, you are a burden that serves him in nothing. Have you ever thought of that?"

"Never!"—her head drooped, the remembrance was a deadly blow to her pride.

"But it is the truth nevertheless. Now, if you will trust me, I will make you great, applauded, courted, powerful, above all, independent. And what is there so sweet as independence? To go where one will, to do as one chooses, to have to ask naught except one's own fancy, to scatter money where and when and how one pleases! Ah, try that! you will never endure dependence after it. You have a proud face: how can you bear to eat the bread of charity?"

The child was stung to the quick; the merciful hand that had saved and sheltered and succored her, looked now like a glove of iron, whose clasp froze her blood.

Coriolis saw the pain that she inflicted, but she was pitiless to it.

"You are nothing but a young pariah, a young pauper now," she continued. "If you will come with me we will change all that. You will leap at a bound into your proper sphere; you will become rich as well as famous; think then how you can repay this man whom you love, whereas now you are only a care, a weight, an expense, an onus upon him. Have you remembered all this? Come!—just to see for two hours what my empire, what my world, are like. You shall return at nightfall: I will send you home; and I will take care that he hears at once that you are with me,—I know where he is,—and he will be too just, I trust, when he sees my desire to serve you, to continue to think such false and such evil things of me."

"Oh, yes! I know well that he would, if he would but believe!" sighed Viva; and a beautiful vision arose before her, of her idol purified in the sight of her friend, cleansed of calumny, and beloved by him as well as by herself, in all the radiance of that new world for which she pined. It was a child's vision, all glorious with colors never seen upon earth, generous with all the fanaticism and chivalry of youth, vain and self-confident with all youth's headstrong bigotry and ignorance. Every warning had died out from her remembrance. Coriolis was in her belief at once the noblest empress, and the noblest martyr, that the world could hold.

"You shall make him believe," said her temptress, indifferent what she averred, so that she became successful in her caprice of divorcing from the man who had offended her, and aroused her hatred, the only creature that was dear to him. "Come with me,—at least for an hour or so? You are no baby, that you must have no will of your own. You are old enough to act for yourself; and you must act if ever you desire to be great. The years are few that a woman reigns: she cannot afford to waste one. Come with me; and you shall see what my life is like. I will give you a glimpse of it tonight. I will metamorphose you into a young sovereign,—

you are nothing now but a little peasant. You want costume, jewels, lace, trailing skirts, everything! All those embellishments are to a creature like you, as its gold setting is to an emerald. Without them you may be a gem indeed, but you are unpolished, and will glitter in no regalia. Come! you cannot be afraid? You look brave enough to take your own way, and adhere to it. If you listen to him you will pass your whole life in an attic like the one that imprisons you now; you will never be seen except by some clowns on a farm, or some boors in a tavern; you will never wear anything better than linen and serge; you will always go on foot and have others splash you with the mud of their chariot wheels; you will always sit at your lattice window to see the world's processions pass by without you; you will always be obscure, obscure like a wretched mole under a tree, when with one effort of will, one touch of sense, you might have changed all that, and been as great as I am. Only think, little fool,—only think what it is that you do!"

Viva's color had changed many times during the utterance of the actress's conjuration; her breath came and went rapidly; her whole form was tremulous with emotion and desire. "To be obscure!" It was the one hell that she dreaded. "To be great!" it was the one heaven that she craved. To be one of those who "sat at their lattices" in the quietude of an humble home, while the great pageantry of life swept on below her window with no place in its carnival crowds for her, no voice of hers in its laughter, no banner amid its proud standards upheld by her hand, was the future that she feared with a passionate terror—the terror of inborn ambition, of predominant vanity.

With a single bound her foot was on the carriage steps, her hand upon the carriage cushions.

"I will come!" she cried, breathlessly; shame was on her, and all the consciousness of sin against the one to whom her lifelong allegiance, and her uttermost sacrifice were due. She felt the burning horror of some great wickedness consume her, she knew that she wronged him in his absence—a crime

nd a cowardice in one. But the temptress prevailed with
her; the desire for the unknown conquered her; her idolatry
of this one forbidden thing was stronger with her than all
ties of gratitude.

"I will come!" she cried; while in her ear there seemed
to sound the words that he had spoken: "Share your life with
that wanton, I will not."

"That is right, that is wise," said Coriolis, with a smile,
as she drew her up into the carriage. "You are a baby no
longer; you have a woman's divine right—Self-Will."

Viva did not hear; her eyes felt blind, her senses grew
dizzy, her ears had a singing sound in them. She could have
sobbed aloud with remorse, and fear, and contrition; but the
guilty joy of victorious rebellion, the guilty sweetness of un-
lawful longing near to its fruition, the guilty liberty of self-
emancipation, were in her veins, and there was too much in
her of the leaven of Eve for her not to deliver herself up to
their usurpation. She knew herself treacherous, faithless,
cowardly; but curiosity, vanity, and the desire of pleasure
conquered her conscience. She elected, as millions wiser
have chosen, to turn her face aside from duty, and follow
where her sorceress led.

The equipage dashed off with her; and if conscience
spoke, it could not be heard in the noise of the flashing,
whirling, azure wheels that swept her down white roads and
under green avenues through the gold and bronze gates of
the actress's villa.

Coriolis was not without her kind impulses; she was of a
sunny temper, and could be generous when to be so did not
interfere with her own supreme selfishness. The rapt adoring face of the child had attracted her, and she had felt a
fancy to see it closer. But beside these she had motives less
innocent: one, on whom her own charms had palled, but
whose contentment and patronage were essential to her, had
also seen that "flower-like face" under its scarlet hood, and
had bade her let him see it once more, and more closely. And

Coriolis was one of those women who own but one cultus and one passion—those of gold.

Viva's heart was beating at fever heat as she followed her enchantress through the exquisite miniature palace, in which the stage-sovereign reigned. The knowledge of her own sin in coming thither, her terror for the rebuke her flight would draw down on her head, the sharp stinging sense of a criminal action that seemed to prick her like an iron goad, served yet, in some fashion, to render her ecstacy in her own transgression wilder, and sweeter, and stronger. She had done very wrong, she knew that; but she had rushed forth into perilous liberty; she had seized the forbidden fruit; she had entered into the unknown land; she had too much of the spirit of Eve in her not to take delight in her daring deed. Moreover, glancing around on all the luxurious beauty that blinded her, she thought: "She was unknown and penniless once, they say; why should I not become like her, too?"

In this lay Coriolis's charm for her:—that the actress was to her the incarnation of all that may be accomplished by the force of beauty alone, against every antagonism of origin and of circumstance. And of the price at which such accomplishment was attained, Viva knew nothing.

"Come in hither," said Coriolis, leading her into the daintiest of dressing-chambers, that made the child think of an empty bird's-nest she had once seen in an elder bush, all silvered over with glistening hoar-frost inside and out.

"Let us look at you," pursued her hostess; and she remorselessly pulled off the red cloak, and shook down all Viva's hair, talking in a pleasant little murmur like a singing-mouse all the while herself. Coriolis was a woman without any sort of mind; she was almost as absolutely brainless as any parroquet; but she knew human weaknesses well, and she knew how to flatter them; and those two forms of knowledge suffice to conquer a child. They suffice, many times, to vanquish a man.

"Have you sent to tell him, madame?" asked Viva, a

pang of conscience stirring amid the bliss of her intoxicated vanity.

"Your friend! oh yes," said Coriolis; and Viva did not know that the daily bread of such women as this lies in falsehood.

Coriolis asked her all her history, and Viva told it; the sense of shame at her costume, and her homely dwelling, striving with her own conviction that she belonged to some lineage of special though hidden splendor.

Coriolis heard and laughed.

"Ah, ha! It is always out of such as you that women like me are made."

"Is it?" asked the child, breathless with hope and joy, unwitting the frightful truth that lay in the words.

"Is it? Of course it is!" cried her temptress. "The world is against us as we start, and we have our revenge; we trap it, and strip it, and make it our laughing-stock and our golden-granary both in one. You do not understand? Pooh, little one! You will learn all this fast enough. Oh, life is a pleasant thing! you may believe that. Look here! since I—since I came on the stage, have I not lived like an empress, and eaten like a Strasburg duck, and dressed like a fashion-plate, and had jewels that outshone the duchess's diamonds, and seen all the world turn after me as I drove or as I walked? To be sure! It is hard work at first, perhaps;—but not for a beautiful woman. I am beautiful; you will be so. When a woman can look at her face in the mirror, and say honestly, 'I am handsomer than one in a million,' it is as good for her as if she said, 'I am born to a crown.' Better, indeed —because it is a much gayer time that waits for her. Do you see?"

"Yes," said Viva, drinking the poison in as though it were the water of life.

Coriolis believed what she said. To a creature without soul and brain, the lusts of the flesh, and the joys of the palate, and of the vanity, are all in all.

Coriolis was honest;—she enjoyed.

"Stay an instant, and you shall behold yourself as you will be," she pursued, as she threw open the door of one of her cabinets, and pulled out laces, and silks, and velvets, and gems, till the girl's eyes were dazzled.

Viva felt none of the prescience which usually awakes in innocence that is brought into the presence of vice. There was nothing of warning mingled with the allurements exercised over her. She had no idea of aught of evil or of danger in her sorceress; she saw an exquisite thing with a cherub's face, and the power, it seemed to her, of a magician; and every one of Coriolis's movements fascinated her with a sense of wonder, attraction, and delight.

"As this woman was, she might herself be one day!"—this was the one thought that enchained her.

Laughing, and keeping up her silvery, mirthful babble that was like the ring of sleigh-bells over snow, Coriolis, who had much of the infant in her and much of the fool, and who had as many caprices as a spoiled marmoset, loosened and tossed aside with disdain Viva's white linen dress, and threw over her one of her own costly trailing robes, and all the fantasy of a jeweled court costume. Her hands were quick and agile at such transformation; and she changed her in fifty seconds from a little picturesque bohemian, to a magnificent young beauty; while gazing at the alteration in the long mirrors that fronted her, touched herself to know if she were awake, and gazed, with parted lips and throbbing temples, at her own apparition.

"There!" cried Coriolis, laughing more and more. "Look there! See what Dress—the god and the devil of women—can do for you. Dress—dress! Why, child, your beauty, without the aid of costume, is nothing better than the pearl before it leaves the oyster-shell. Will you go back to your shell, you pretty pearl? Not if I know aught of your heart."

Viva made her no answer. All the self-love of Narcissus held her entranced.

"I am as beautiful as you!" she cried, at last, aloud, in ecstasy, throwing her arms above her head.

Coriolis turned away, with a cloud for once over her smiling azure eyes.

"More so!" she said, shortly, with the impulses of frankness at times natural to her. "More so! You have what I have lost!"

Viva did not ask what this was;—she did not inquire at the price of what loss this celebrity, and this wealth that she coveted, had been acquired. She was absorbed in contemplation of herself. The actress looked at her, and smiled; her own passing emotions had swiftly vanished.

"How it runs through us all!" she cried. "With all the love one has, one never loves anything like one's self! What a supreme joy it is—that knowing one's self fair! But there is a still greater joy than that: it is to hear the world say so. Do you see, you charming bagatelle, how happy you are?—you are beautiful! You can scoff at all the Cæsars; their power is nothing to yours. To be handsome while one lives, and to die before any of *that* fades: if one can do this, one can laugh at all the priests and all the sages!"

And she laughed yet again, and Viva joined in her laugh. The airy paganism suited the child's temper, and Coriolis was that most persuasive of proselytizers—a disciple who believed implicitly in the doctrines she inculcated. To be fair all her years through, and to die before any of "*that*" waned and withered, was to Coriolis the perfection of human existence; and the only form of dread that ever weighed on this careless, thoughtless, mindless, shameless thing, was the terror that the day should ever come when she should dash her hand through her mirror in despair at the lusterless eyes, and the lined brow, and the dulled tresses it should give back to her vision.

Viva gave a deep sigh as she heard.

"Ah!" she murmured, "if I could only have ten years of a life like yours I should be content!"

"'To resign it? Not you. Little one,—when we have tasted triumph we have fed on a fruit of Olympus, that makes all mortal food flavorless, and leaves us with a cruel craving appetite, never still!"

Coriolis had heard a poet say this: and used the answer, as one picturesque and likely to be persuasive to this young listener and tyro.

"What matter!" cried Viva, in the magnificent recklessness of ignorance. "I would rather taste it once and hunger forever, than never know its flavor all the days of my life!"

Coriolis, with a curious fancy for this daring, vain, lovely creature, who made her think of her own childhood, laid both hands on Viva's shoulder, and looked at her with a gaze that was more earnest than her volatile, sparkling, wandering eyes had ever given.

"Are you too good for it?" she murmured to herself. "No. Not a whit. You are just what I was;—cleverer perhaps, and of more wit, but just like me. You would only break an honest man's heart, if you were to begin with one: it is better to commence as you will end, with pillaging fools and knaves. Pooh! you don't understand," she cried aloud, with all her gayety. "You are a little simpleton. Listen; I will put you on the stage. You will have talent, I can see. If you have not, it will matter nothing. Walk well, dress superbly, do strange things—the odder the better, and with your features you can make your fortune, though you can say no more than a squeaking doll at a fair."

"But I want to be *great!*" cried Viva, dissatisfied with her future prospects.

"Nonsense! When a woman passes down through a crowd, and the people look back after her and call out, 'that is *she!*' has she not greatness, the best greatness? Some Latin idiot says, they have told me, that the 'pointing finger' is no sure sign we are great—Ridiculous! When it points *our* way we may be pretty sure we are on the highroad to fame. Besides 'great, great, great!' What does that matter? What matters in this world is to eat and drink well, and dance, and play, and laugh, and see others perish in envy of us, and have more gold than we can take up in both our hands, and enjoy ourselves while we are living. That is what matters. And no one can do all those better than a beautiful woman. Now go you in there, and wait till I come to you. I will not be long."

She pushed Viva gently through a door that opened into a small cabinet, and closed the door upon her. It had been very late in the day when she had met the actress; it was now evening; the little chamber was softly lit, and full of the perfume of flowers and the luxuries of wealth. Viva dropped down on a couch, and wondered whether she were awake or dreaming; a sense of fear and a great remorse stole on her; she knew she had done wickedly, and a vague, indefinable dread of some unknown evil came over her. She began to grieve for her disobedience, and to long to be safe in the little attic with Tricotrin. What would he say! what would he think!

Her throat swelled; she felt as if she must scream out loud; even the elegance and the fragrance of the place added to its strangeness and her own fears:—instinctively her hand wandered over the rich silk of her robe, and her eyes watched the glisten of its gold embroideries, seeking consolation in these. They brought a certain solace.

"If I could only wear them always!" she thought: and the vision of herself upon the stage, before the world, covered with flowers, welcomed with tumults of applause, intoxicating multitudes with her grace and her glance in all the triumph that she had seen attained by Coriolis, arose before her, and numbed all her repentance.

The desire to be "great" possessed her: when that insatiate passion enters a living soul, be it the soul of a woman-child dreaming of a coquette's conquests, or a crowned hero craving for a new world, it becomes blind to all else. Moral death falls on it; and any sin looks sweet that takes it nearer to its goal. It is a passion that generates at once all the loftiest and all the vilest things, which, between them, ennoble and corrupt the world; even as heat generates at once the harvest and the maggot, the purpling vine and the lice that devour it. It is a passion without which the world would decay in darkness, as it would do without heat; yet to which, as to heat, all its filthiest corruption is due.

"I shall be great!" thought Viva, to whom the greatness of the stage looked as the greatness of an empire: and remorse ceased to touch her. They must suffer that she might ascend:—this was the reckless reasoning of the human and female egotism within her.

A flood of light startled her as the door was flung open and Coriolis entered; freshly arrayed, and with her fair feathery hair lying lightly on her shoulders, diademed with flowers and with gems. She floated to the child with her soft swift undulating movement—the movement of the born *almàh*, in whom motion is poetry, and in whose limbs lies eloquence.

"Thou art in the twilight, little one!" she cried, using the familiar and caressing "thou" for the first time. "Come; —I have a better light for thee than that; and one in which there are eager eyes to behold thee. Come!"

"Where?" asked the tempted one, with wistful wonder.

Coriolis smiled a little bitterly.

"Hush! We never ask 'where' in *our* world,

> On va où va toute chose,
> Où va le laurier et la rose!"

And she drew the girl from the chamber, with her soft, white, dimpled hand clasped on Viva as though it were a glove of steel.

The roses had all cankers at their cores, and poisoned the lips that kissed them; the laurels were all twined in with thorns, which drew blood from the brows that they wreathed: —what of that? Cankerless roses die also; and there are no laurels whose fruit is sweet.

She led the child in its ignorance to perdition: but she did not think so: vice was fair in her own sight, and the devil of gold was her god;—a good god who enriched those that served him: she thought she could do no better than bring a neophyte to believe in her cultus, and serve in her temple.

"Enjoy—enjoy—enjoy," her heart had whispered in her own childhood, when she had sat on the lonely seashore and longed for a world that was unknown: and she had enjoyed, and it seemed well to her still, and the sole thing that it was worth while for a mortal to do. In tossing the fruit of desire into the child's young bosom, she only gave that which had been luxuries to her own lips, and which seemed to her still the one apple of life worth the plucking. She was wicked, because things all sense and no soul must be so; but she was honest, and she only led where she herself had ever gone, with tuneful swift feet, rejoicing.

"Evil, be thou my good," she had said, in her fair, wanton, indolent, careless fashion, and evil had been her good; it had served her well, heaped wealth on her, made the air she lived in full of laughter, and the lovers she sought facile to their yoke, and the years that flew over her head, sunlit and short and radiant with mirth. Evil had been prodigal of gifts and graces to her, and had recompensed her as kings recompense; she deemed that there was no better master upon earth. Virtue was a niggard tyrant, who left his servitors to starve: but Evil was a prince, who scattered gold and flowers with both hands.

There be those who in their gilded shame feel the shrinking scornful passion, at their own fall, of the poet's Egyptian harlot,—

"What is Life without Honor?
And what can the life that I live
Give to me I shall care to continue, not caring for aught it can give?
I, despising the fools that despise me,—a plaything not pleasing myself,
Whose life for the pelf that maintains it, must sell what is paid not by pelf!
And the fancies of men change. And bitterly bought is the bread that I eat,
For, though purchased with body and spirit, when purchased 'tis yet all unsweet."

But there be also many others in whom this sting of scorn is dead, this ache of conscience is lulled to rest by the opiates of vanity and of pleasure; there be those to whom the life that they lead looks the best life, and to whom license is precious, to whom enjoyment is the Alpha and Omega of existence, and to whom the chime of golden coinage is the only music of the spheres.

And Coriolis was one of these. She had been very weary, and fretful as a caged bird, in innocence; in vice she rejoiced and was free! A future might come indeed when she would perish of famine on the stones of the streets:—what of that? They must have some soul in them who dread a future; and there was no soul in this gay airy thing, though her dancing feet trod the souls of men down and killed them.

Like Dorat she had gathered every flower except the Immortelle: and the one that she had passed over she never missed.

Immortality!—the world is ridiculous named in the same breath with such things as Coriolis; what has eternity to do with women such as this, too foul for heaven and too frail for hell?

She led the child through dusky fragrant passages, aromatic in odor, with the sheen of silk and satin glimmering in the shadow from their walls.

Then she drew back, and sweeping aside a curtain that hung before an arched and opened door, motioned to Viva to pass within before her.

It was the entrance to a banqueting-room.

Viva, touched for the first time with a chill of timidity, a throb of fear, hung back, wistful yet longing.

Through the arch of the gilded portal there were a blaze of light, a glisten of rose color, a splendor of gold, a wilderness of flowers, an odor of wines and spices and burnt incense, a gay laughter from young men's throats, that all blazed and whirled together upon the girl's wondering eyes and ears.

She paused, hesitating and half frightened before that paradise of forbidden evil.

"Is it a temple?" she murmured breathlessly.

Coriolis laughed; a more cruel laugh than any that had rung from her mocking lips.

"A temple! yes! Go in,—and worship our god."

And she thrust the child through the opening.

CHAPTER XX.

It was toward the close of the day when Tricotrin returned.

He was tired out, heated, exhausted; as his habit was when in pain, he had wandered far, walking on and on through the open country, seeking solitude on the same impulse as the stricken stag. In the red woods of the late autumn, in the wide fields, with their arc of purple angry sky, in the bleak plains swept by equinoctial gales, he could breathe, think, resolve, kill passion in him, and call back his strength. In joy, this Arab little loved the oppression of cities, the pent confines of chambers, the close atmosphere of crowded roofs; in suffering, they maddened him. They were like the bars of his den to a caged lion whom his juilers wound and taunt.

By evening-fall he returned; the linnet had ceased to sing under its plume of lime; the sunbeams had ceased to play through the little brown dusky street; in the doorway stood the woman of the house looking up and down, with her head on one side like a robin's, and the bright dress of her native Basque province glowing in the shade like a poppy growing out of a pile of black timber in a wood-yard.

"Is the child not with you?" she cried, as he drew near.

He lifted his head wearily.

"With me? No. I left her at home."

Mère Rose turned pale under her ruddy southern skin.

"Left her here! Where is she then? She is not gone with the Mévert—that I know—we have not seen her all the last half of the day, and we made certain that you had taken her."

He said nothing, but pushed past her and sprang up the staircase.

He threw door after door open, the house ringing with his voice as he called her name aloud from cellar to attic;—there was no answer. Her books, her bonbons, her knot of autumn daisies, lay on the table in the little chamber; but of Viva there was no trace.

The woman, joined by two or three of her neighbors, stood listening below, frightened and bewildered. They had no love for this fantastic child, "la demoiselle," as they called her ironically, who held herself so haughtily with so much airy scorn above them and theirs; and who either sat aloft in her casement like a framed picture, or glittered out in the sun, with the negligent grace of some elfin thing far too good for the earthly shrine that inclosed her. But they loved Tricotrin with the faithful impassioned love that all the populace gave him; and for his trouble they sorrowed themselves.

They felt a certain fear of the look on his face as he descended the stairs and came to them.

"When saw you her last?" he asked them.

They had seen her at the doorway some hour in the afternoon, they told him; they could not be sure of the time; they were busy people, occupied with their washing, their ironing, their cooking, their flower-making, their sweetmeat-baking; they had had no time to take further note.

The grisette, sewing still by the fast fading light at her lattice, looked down; moved by that sympathy which makes strangers become in a second as friends of a lifetime.

"You ask for the child?" she said to him. "I can tell you,—the little one sat there on the doorstep as four o'clock sounded; a little page, a creature all red and gold, came up to her and took her away. They went together down the passage to that first corner yonder; and after a little while I heard the noise of fast wheels and the trotting of horses. She is gone,—that I know,—for she never came back to the doorway."

Then, without interest to see how her news was taken, she bent again over her work, to save the few precious moments of dying light; rocking the wooden cradle with her foot, and coughing, painfully, a short hard feverish cough. A month before she had sung, as blithely as the linnet under his limebough, the mischievous students' wine-songs that had served her as cradle-ballads.

Tricotrin heard:—and he drew a deep shuddering breath, as a soldier will do when the bullets have struck him.

"It is Coriolis," he said in his throat,—then without another word he swept the eager women aside, and passed down the street with the speed of the wind.

At the turn of the alley into the breadth of the street adjoining there came at a quick pace a string of young horses: they were from Normandy, and were wild and strong, and, being young, fleet of foot.

He knew the man who rode their leader; a sturdy Norman breeder of cattle;—they had been friends for many a year, smoking and sauntering and laughing together, under the spring-blooming apple orchards of the pleasant farm-country.

Tricotrin caught at the rope bridle of one of the foremost colts.

"Will you lend him to me?" he asked, breathlessly. "I am in sore need of haste: he shall be back by dawn."

"Take him!" cried the Norman, startled, like the women, by the look which he saw on a face that he had never beheld before clouded with aught of care. "Take him; and keep him as long as you need;—I am at my old stables; you will bring him there."

"Surely,"—he stayed for no more words, but threw himself across the colt's bare back, and urged it at a stretching gallop through the crooked streets of the quarter.

The young horse, nothing loth to be free of the string, flew fast without urging.

Tricotrin turned its head straight southward, to where the actress rested in her gilded harbor, rich and soft with the plunder of many lofty galleons that had struck flag and foundered under the pirate's prow.

He had spent no time in speech; he had wasted not a single moment in self-abandonment to the anguish that possessed him. But as he rode his heart was a hell within him: he was not alone a man who went to rescue from his spoilers a child that he cherished, he was a lover who went to save from dishonor the creature that he idolized.

And he knew that he might reach—too late.

The Norman colt, with its rough mane flying and its bright eyes full of flame, asked no more welcome task than to be let loose to its fullest speed, as though it were once again at play in its own native pastures. Buildings and throngs, and all the varicolored evening life of the city were passed by as fast as a summer breeze sweeps by over the corn; yet night was down ere he reached the outlying woods and gardens amid which the toy-palace of Coriolis reared its gilded cupolas and shining roofs.

The colt was panting and tired out by the pace at which it had been ridden; it stood passively while he flung himself from its back and tied the halter to the post of an entrance gate. The gates were unfastened; he passed through them, and up the grounds of the villa, strewed with the damp odorous leaves of the late autumn. Lights glistened through the interstices of the shutters all over the frontage of the dainty dwelling, bosomed in its shrubs and trees.

He cursed it as he looked.

Vice lived like this, while innocence died daily in the streets!

As the velvet curtain fell behind her, Viva found herself within the chamber.

The fear died away in her; curiosity, wonder, eagerness, a thrill of triumph and a throe of delight at her own rebellion all conquered it, and were stronger than the instinctive and nameless dread within her a moment earlier.

Six or eight young men all rose and all turned their eyes on her, and all came to her with words of admiring greeting, which fell in a confused but delicious sense of homage on her ear. She shrank back with all a child's innocent shyness; she went forward with all a coquette's innate impulses.

She knew that she looked very lovely; she knew that this exquisite sorceress at her side was content to be eclipsed by herself; all the weakest and the worst things of her nature were appealed to and inflamed. The room whirled round her in a blaze of color; the heavy perfume on its air seemed to float round her in clouds of odor; the dazzle of the jewels and the precious metals on the banqueting table looked to her like the riches of an India—she drew a deep breath, and laughed a little soft quivering wondering laugh, that yet had half a sob in it.

This was the world at last then.

The world!—this paradise of brilliant hues, and priceless gems, and subtle perfumes, and honeyed words, and ardent adoring eyes! The world!—ah! how she marveled that there could be found lives holy enough to sigh for heaven if this elysium were to be found on earth!

She had never a clear memory of all that followed on her entrance into that enchanted room. All distinct remembrance was lost in a chaos of splendid images. For splendid this false glitter, this glory of meretricious color, this joyless joy, this hackneyed revelry, looked to the youthful eyes which only saw its surface. For Viva, reared amid the truth and the beauty of nature in innocent solitude, was too essentially a slave to the feminine soul within her to be poet enough to recoil from the falsehood of pleasure, poet enough to cling to the severity and simplicity of nature. The higher life escaped,—the lower allured her. It was the beaten-out gold of the jeweler's laboratory, which was still far more beautiful in her sight than the sun-fed lilies and lilacs of the spring.

She had a confused knowledge of being led to the first seat at the table under the dome of light, that seemed to her like the noontide sun. Of seeing some handsome courtly faces bent toward her with that delight in their regard which she already knew so well as the tribute to her charms. Of hearing such flattery that her brain grew dizzy with it, and she felt stupefied, like a bee overcloyed with honey. Of catching the vision of herself repeated on every side, in mirrors, till she saw that one best-loved image wherever her eyes turned. Of being moved to her gayest words and brightest laughter, till the audience applauded her idlest phrase as wit, and she felt herself a sovereign, whose words were precious as pearls and diamonds. Of tasting strange fruits, and wondrous confections, and wines that shone like so much sunbeam, till she seemed to float on air and to lose all sense of earth, and to dream that she was among the gods of the Greek fable.

She was drinking in poison—the poison of a hideous evil—with her lips, and ears, and eyes, and thoughts; but she did not know it; she was happy, she was victorious, she was exultant, and she was too innocent to be conscious that sin was encircling her on every side.

They were heedful not to affright her, but only to allure; they wreathed the death's head in summer flowers for her; they drew her to the abyss with sweet careless joyous music; they killed her with a poisoned rose. And she did not know; she was still a child, and still only happy.

As she reigned there proudly and joyously, the actress Coriolis looked at her once with a throb of remorse in her dead conscience; but she hunted it away as it arose.

"Pshaw!" she murmured. "What matter? A little earlier?—a little later? Things like her are made to slaughter and to plunder. She would end like me—it is better to begin so. She will thank me one day that she has wasted none of the years of her youth!"

As she thus thought, a door at the farther end of the chamber opened; through it, facing her and behind the child, came softly the graceful, slender shape of a handsome boy—a boy with dark eyes that gleamed with malice and triumph.

He stole gently across the room and up to Viva, and as gently his arm stole round her fair throat, and his lips brushed her curls.

"Viva!" he whispered, "I have thee at last—oh, my truant! And here are the deathless roses, the fairy pageants, the wines of the gods, that I promised thee!"

With a scream, as though a snake had touched her, she sprang to her feet.

The spell on her was broken; the netted dove soared from the snare.

"Let me go!" she cried aloud, as though by some instinct the full sense of her peril flashed on her. "Let me go! Oh, how vile I have been to come here! It is *you!*— you whom he forbade me ever to see, ever to speak to, ever to think of again; you who gave me your toys, and deemed me some peasant girl you could kiss at your fancy! It is *you!* How could I tell it? How could I dream it? Let me go—let me go! I have sinned once against him; I will not disobey him again—never again, never, never!"

The childlike words rang out loudly through the chamber; she stood with her face flushed, scarlet with rage, and shame, and outraged pride; her eyes flashing with scorn on her boy-lover; her mouth trembling with grief for her own disobedience.

In an instant, by the voice of her young Faust, the full knowledge of her own error had burst on her, piercing through the mists of vanity, and delight, and wonder, and intoxicated triumph.

She stretched her hands out in a piteous appeal to Coriolis.

"Oh, take me back to him; take me back. You said you would; and I feel so frightened!"

Coriolis looked at her, and laughed.

The devil is never so brutal as when he comes into a woman's form.

The cold, cruel, mocking laugh stung all the child's proud spirit into life.

"Oh, I see now!" she cried out, in a mortal anguish that no man there heard unmoved. "I see now how true he was —how wicked you are! You laugh!—you laugh because you have made me disobey him. It is Satan who laughs just so when men disobey God. Oh how mad I was to hearken to you!—oh, take me back, take me back! Has not *one* of you all a heart to pity me? I never meant to grieve him! I only meant to grow great, and to pleasure him, and to be his glory. And I loved her so—that woman!"

Her voice died in a sob. It was a bitter suffering to her, the fall of her sovereign, the death of her ideal.

Her young lover smiled.

"Love her still!" he murmured. "What is her guilt?—to have brought you to *me?*"

He stooped as he spoke, and sought to draw her into his embrace,—the door was burst open, the curtain dashed aside, a strong hand fell on him and forced him from her, and tossed him like a broken bough across the chamber.

With a shriek of joy she threw herself into the arms of her savior.

The voice of Tricotrin rang like a trumpet-call through the silence.

"What!—had men need to dream of a Devil when the world held Woman!"

Holding her to him with both arms he faced the baffled and silence-stricken revelers; and a great awe fell upon them, such as fell on the dissolute patrician mob of Rome before the passion of Virginius.

"One cannot kill such things as you—the vilest things that breathe!" he cried, as his eyes blazed upon Coriolis. "You murder—body and soul!—and yet we must let ye go free because ye are women, because ye can crouch and shelter behind the shield of the sex that ye outrage! God! if I set my heel on your throat I should do no more guilt than if I strangled the life from an adder. Yet I must leave you free because you are 'woman'!—because you are the sole thing living on earth that can slaughter yet break no law; that can slay yet be left to smile on; that can make men curse the mothers that bore them, yet be safe in the safety of feebleness; the only thing living on earth that has the strength of the giant for crime, and the weakness of the coward for shelter. Had Israel no courtesans in her camps, that, in the parables of her Scriptures, she made the chief leader of hell a *male* creature?"

A dead stillness followed on the scathing fury of his words.

The banqueters drew aside, and gathered together, and left the woman alone.

Men feast with Coriolis, but none will fight for her.

They drain her wine-cups, for their own gold fills them; but no sword leaps from its scabbard for her sake.

In pleasure she has many followers; in need she is ever alone.

Then with hands that were, for that one time alone, ungentle to the child he loved, he tore from off her the jewels, the flowers, the laces of her festal robes, and flung them all crushed and torn down at the feet of her temptress.

"Great God!" he cried aloud in the bitterness of his soul. "The tigress and the leopardess are tender beside Woman. Brutes though they be they do not drive the young of their own kind down into the nets and the knives of the slaughter! That work is spared for *her*—Man's helpmeet, God's best work!"

CHAPTER XXI.

What followed she never remembered.

When she recovered consciousness the cool autumn wind was blowing on her, and the starless rainy night skies were above her; she was lying on the turf that edged the highway, under a knot of roadside trees; beside her in the gloom stood the dim shadowy form of a man and of a horse.

The former leaned over her and touched her lips with his hand as she strove to speak.

"Say nothing; there is no need."

The old familiar sweetness of the voice struck through her heart; she raised herself and gazed into his eyes; then trembled and hid her face in her hands, and sobbed bitterly: she felt unutterably ashamed, though the shame on her was vague and without name.

She sank back upon the turf, and turned, and rested her forehead upon the wet short grass, moaning a little like a wounded fawn.

He said no word, and his eyes were dry, as he stood over her in that attitude of abasement and humiliation. But he suffered a greater torture than had ever wrung his bright and happy life.

He had come, indeed, in time to save her from more than a child's broken ideal, a child's sorrowful disenchantment; but nevertheless was she to him as utterly killed as though he stood beside her dead body. His rage had spent itself upon her temptress: he had none for her.

It had an exceeding pathos for him, this frailness that had been seduced by such fictitious greatness, this innocence and folly welded into one, which had been allured by such a painted, worthless, wooden shape, mistaking it for the goddess of loveliness and pleasure.

He saw it with the pitying tenderness with which a gentle shepherd would see his youngest lamb allured by poisonous and gorgeous blossoms, sweet to the taste, and splendid to the eye, on to the edge of a volcanic pit. Anger against her he could not feel; she was too young, too blind, too well-beloved. But the thing that he had cherished seemed forever dead to him; and a great blow smote him in the knowledge that the first hand stretched out to her with the world's golden bribes had been strong enough to lead her away without a thought of him.

He had said that if she forsook him for that wanton he would leave her alone to her choice; but when the test had come he had been governed by no impulse save that of saving her from peril and pollution. Yet the same feeling which had made him say that, were she faithless, he would never seek to coerce her to fidelity, moved him now, and made him hold her forever as utterly lost to him as though her will had had its way, and she had gone to the career which to her ignorance and her credulity looked so fair.

He was struck the deadliest blow that life could have dealt him.

In the same sense that the sailor of the Riviera had been robbed and deserted by the flight of the wife he adored, so was he by the abandonment of the creature that had been made his own by every tie of human gratitude.

He had reached that sublime self-sacrifice which speaks in the words—"If I love thee what is that to thee?" But he knew the bitterness which goes with those words, in the knowledge that the love which is given is counted as naught by the one on whom it is lavished; that it is of so little account that the life which it cherishes passes heedlessly on, with no more thought of it than a laughing child on the first day of spring takes of the shy primrose and the purple bells of thyme, which his foot crushes as he runs.

"If I love thee what is that to thee?"—it is the supreme utterance of the passion which can withstand absence and neglect, and oblivion, and opprobrium, and scorn, and thoughtless cruelty, and still live on, strengthened by every year, and purified by every stroke. But none the less is it the supreme martyrdom of love.

And it was in this wise that his good deed returned to him; and the bread that he had flung upon the waters came back, and was as ashes in his teeth. For of all things that are true upon this earth this is most true,—that the recompense of our holier acts comes not in this world, and is not given by the hands of humanity.

"Rejoice, oh ye faithful servants," is not uttered under the sun; for Life is merciless, and in its many agonies and in its many evils there is not even the wild justice that belongs to vengeance; there is but the sound of a mocking voice through all the desolation, laughing ever at the travail and the cheated hopes of men.

Suddenly she lifted herself, and caught hold of him, and gazed up in his eyes again; she did not ask for pardon with her lips, but her gaze prayed for it with the mute touching prayer of a dog's.

He turned from her with an irresistible shudder; she was a child still; she did not know what she had done; she was conscious of her error, but not of its effect; she knew she had done wrong, but she did not know that she was, in his sight, lost to him forever.

The creature that had forsaken him must go from him; the love that paid its fealty only to coercion, was worse to him than hate.

"Hush!" he said gently, as she strove to speak. "You are not well enough for words. There is no need of them—I know all."

He knew all—without her shedding one ray of light upon the tale; knew all the weakness, the folly, the innocence, the willfulness, the vanity, that had lured her down a flower-sown path, on to the very brink of ruin; knew all the insufficiency of the affection borne to himself, and given by himself, to hold her back from the sweet insidious seductions of riches and of flattery; knew that he had been deserted and betrayed with none the less cruel, the less merciless infidelity, because that infidelity was the fault of a child's selfishness, in lieu of a woman's passion.

Then, still with the same gentleness that had more terror for her than his heaviest anger could have borne, he lifted her into a covered cart that he had summoned, as it rolled slowly toward Paris with a night freight of autumn flowers, and leading the Norman colt by its halter, walked slowly toward the city by the side of the little wagon, in whose shelter Viva crouched, sobbing bitterly, with her rich silk robes covered by a leathern rug, and her face buried in her hands.

For the hour the bitterness of her chastisement equaled the cruelty and the weakness of her fault.

To the child—proudest among the proud—no punishment could have been so great as this intense humiliation, this passionate shame, that seemed to her scorching her very life up with its ignominy.

The way into Paris appeared one endless road of martyrdom; only two brief weeks before she had passed along this self-same highway, in the luster of the illuminated night, dreaming that the city would receive her as some royal creature, some daughter of Carlovingian or Capetian races, born to wear their diadem, and sway their scepter! And this was how she returned from her first flight toward greatness.

No discrowned queen ever went with heavier heart from her palace than she went now, back from the first-fruits of her own will, the first reward of her own ambition.

"Shall I *never* be other than I am?" she thought in desperation; the dread was stronger on her, even in that hour, than any other fear, stronger still than gratitude, or repentance, or love for her redeemer, though these were all startled to vivid existence in her.

He, himself, walked in silence, wearily and slowly through

the dark and chilly night, the tired steps of the colt keeping pace for pace with his own.

Passion had spent its first outburst of mad fury; a dull hopeless anguish remained.

For she was dead to him as utterly as though he had slain her like Virginius, to save her from the arms of her spoilers.

The life that was faithless to him, could stay by his side no longer.

He spoke nothing as the wagon rolled tediously on its way; nothing as it paused before the door of Mère Rose, and he lifted her out from its shelter and led her within the house.

As the women rushed to her, with tearful cries of welcome and of joy, he motioned them away.

"She was lost. Let her be—she is tired."

The mingled love and fear in which they held him subdued their curiosity; they herded together in the passage hushed and afraid; and she,—with her head hung down, and her face hidden from them, crept up the wooden stairs in the dull oil light with slow sad steps, from which all the elastic buoyancy of her youth was banished.

Once within the little attic that served her as her bed-chamber, she thrust the rusted iron bolt within its socket, put out the oil flame with a quick gesture, as though she dreaded still that there were some to look on her, and flinging herself down on her straw pallet, wept with heart-broken self-pity; half like a child from whom his favorite playthings have been taken, half like a woman from whose passions an ever-abiding shame has sprung.

"If I could only be great!" she prayed;—and fell asleep with that prayer on her lips.

Without—through the heavy rains that were falling through the dark and weary streets—he went slowly, leading the colt homeward.

He had received his recompense.

CHAPTER XXII.

At midnight, and till midnight was long past, he waited in the great court-yard of a great building.

The rains beat fiercely on him, but he did not heed them.

It was almost dawn when the lights of a carriage flashed red through the mists; he sprang forward between it and the gateway.

Its occupant alighted, and was stopped by him.

"One word with you?" he asked.

The Duke de Lira started, turned, and paused.

"Now!—yes, if you desire it."

They went within, out of the wet black night, into a great lighted frescoed chamber, like the chambers of the palaces of Rome.

His hair, his garments, his beard were dripping with rain; he was splashed and jaded, and pale with exhaustion and pain; he observed no ceremony, and heeded no form; he stood facing the man he had sought, and spoke without preface or address.

"You were in earnest to-day?"

"I was."

"Then I come to take you at your word. You were right—I was wrong."

The noblest words that can be uttered by human lips cost him a great pang in their utterance.

The other looked quickly at him, and said nothing.

"I was wrong," he pursued, rapidly. "I mistook selfishness for justice, and was led astray by my own desires. I threw aside a great good for another, because I considered and studied myself. I was rough in anger with you, and ungrateful for the benefit that you offered. You stung my pride and my heart, and I was blind—blind to duty and justice. Stay! hear me out—it was so. To-night I have had my punishment."

He paused abruptly. He breathed loud and fast; but his eyes never left their straight and keen regard into his companion's, and his words were spoken unflinchingly.

"You said rightly. No duty can hold a female thing, no tenderness can content her, when once the passion of her vanity has been fired. Look you,— that child is innocent as any lamb in the meadows, any dove in the woods, and yet the leaven of her womanhood is in her, and will urge her on to destruction. I thought, in my folly, that not to sin, not to suffer, not to know the meaning of evil, not to want any more than a bird wants in spring, just to live the free harmless life of a country-born creature, would suffice to make a child's joy, and a woman's content. I erred; many men have erred like me. There is a devil thrice as strong as we are—the devil of Discontent. There is the tempter that lures away from us our wives, and our mistresses, and our daughters,— there is the huckster that buys a soul with a string of seed-pearls, and chaffers away honor for a knot of sapphire stones."

His listener grew paler as he heard.

"What has chanced to the child?" he asked, hurriedly. She had touched his heart more deeply than he knew.

"This has chanced to her,—that the word of a strange woman had more sway with her than mine; that the eyes of men have found out that she has loveliness; that the snares of the city have been spread for her, and have caught her, and have maimed her. Two hours since I brought her out from the house of Coriolis."

"Coriolis!—the actress!"

"Coriolis—the courtesan. Why be choicer in names than she is in her sins? She lured the child thither by specious words and gracious promises. In the eyes of Viva she was an empress—an angel! Coriolis caught her fancy as the light takes a moth's. She led her where she chose, for she promised to give her greatness! She decoyed her there toward evening. I had left her alone. When I returned she was lost: she had been absent some hours. I knew at once where she was sure to have wandered. I forced my entrance into the villa—into the chamber where they sat at their banquet. They had throned the child there as a queen, and a terror of her reign had just commenced to touch her. I was in time to save her. What I said, what I did, I have forgotten."

The broken, abrupt sentences escaped him harshly and in haste; the recital was terrible to him. Honor and honesty demanded it from him; but none the less was it bitter exceedingly.

"Stay! Hear me out," he said, quickly, as his listener interrupted him. "Let me end what I have to say. I rescued her from that accursed place ere she had learned more than a vague fear and a wakening horror of the world into which she was flung. But what use is it to rescue the goat from the pit, if it return again and again to eat the poison-flowers that grow on its sides? And that is what Viva will do. She is innocent—yes; but how long can innocence grow side by side with vanity and ambition? The eyes of libertines have beheld her; the brutality that christens itself love has fastened on her; the powers that lie in wealth are arrayed against her—she is not safe one moment longer. If her own heart were content, indeed, all these could with ease be defied. But against the foe in her own soul I can bring no army. I may restrain her from sin,—she is brave, and proud, and pure of thought—vice once unmasked to her would be loathsome. But I cannot keep her in peace; and—and—I dare not keep her in misery! Now, I have told you this. It was your due to know it. It may well be that you will withdraw the offer you made her two evenings ago. You will be justified in so doing. She does not know the evil she has wrought herself; but I know it, and I know that a woman-child that has been once beneath the roof of Coriolis may well be marked as dishonored forever."

"Hush, hush! Would you deem me so brutal, so harsh? —for a young girl's unthinking rashness, a playful creature's foolish fault?"

"It would be no harshness; it would be justice. A woman's fair repute is like a blue harebell—a touch can wither it. What she did to-day—in rashness, in folly, as you say—may rise up in future years, and bring her bitter chastisement. Yet—it makes no difference with you, this thing that I have told?"

"None. I desire to serve her as greatly as I ever did."

"That is very nobly said. Then I accept your offer. I do not dare to thrust it aside."

He stopped abruptly; his voice was hoarse, and died away in a whisper. The other made no answer; he divined the suffering that accompanied this adhesion to his will.

"Let her come," he said, softly, at length. "For a brief space, at least. At its close—who can tell? Early impressions have great force, and what we are nurtured in we commonly prefer; her absence may show her how strong her love for you is, and how needful to her is the life of which her ignorance now wearies."

"There is no likelihood of that. She is a hawk that once cast down the wind will never come back to the wrist of her keeper."

"Why so? She loves you?"

"Ay, as children love. Where is the child whom some costlier bauble than what you can give will not lure away from your hold soon or late? No—if she come to you once, she goes from me forever. But—there is no need to speak of myself."

"There is great need. Look what an immeasurable debt she owes to you."

"I do not count it. Neither need she nor any one. I desire her to be happy, that is all. There is another matter which concerns her. The youth of whom I spoke to you, that young lordling, was one of the accursed crew to-night. Doubtless it was his gold that bribed Coriolis to the setting of her snare. He has had his punishment; he will not stir his bruised frame for months. When he does arise, shame will tie his tongue, and I can drive him from the country, for a season, by a power I have over him—the power of the knowledge of his own vices. But if you have aught to do with Viva, it is needful that you should be aware of him—he is the son of Estmere. He has broken faith with me; he is traitor as well as tempter; but I care not to wring his father's great heart with the tale of his shame; cowardice and falsehood never before touched his race."

"You spare the child's tempter! You are generous indeed!"

"I spare Estmere—not him."

"Lord Estmere! What is he to you?"

"He is a man who is honored; he is a man who has suffered. They are titles sufficient to forbearance. Beside a girl's innocent name, a girl's stainless youth, they are things that will no more bear men's handling than will a snowflake as it falls! Is there any other thing to be said? Tell your mother what I have told to you; Viva enters no home under the shelter of falsehood. But—do you know that the world will call you a madman?"

"Wherefore?"

"For believing the word, and receiving the Waif and Stray, of—a bohemian!"

"The world can do so. I have attended to it as little in my fashion as you in yours. I know that I have the truth from your lips; I have been, also, at the pains to verify the facts that you have related to me; and I believe that I see my way to rendering another life happy. As for my being deemed a madman,—it is ever the better things in us that the world calls our insanities."

Tricotrin gave no reply; his eyes dwelt on those of the speaker with a long searching, penetrative regard, that seemed to seek to pierce the secret thoughts of his innermost mind. Then, with an abrupt movement, he turned away.

"You have a noble nature, and you do a noble act," he said, briefly. "But—I cannot thank you till, in the years to come, I see how it is with her."

Then, without farewell or obeisance, he quitted the chamber swiftly. He was even as the shepherd who had left the ewe lamb that he had saved through storm and drought, and warmed in his bosom, and fed with his hand, at the threshold of the rich man's palace.

The Duke de Lira started as the door closed, and leant in perplexed meditation against the bronze reading-stand, on which the great volumes that he usually studied lay.

He was a man of pure intent, of gentle heart, of noble nature, untouched by pride, untainted by evil desire. He earnestly desired to benefit this beautiful young thing, whose bright youth fascinated him. He was wholly unconscious that any selfish impulse prompted the determinate effort with which he had vanquished his mother's disinclination to take a foundling beneath her roof. He was incapable of cruelty, incapable of a base egotism; he believed himself only actuated by a genuine compassion; he had in no way awakened to any perception of the attraction that Viva's personal loveliness possessed for him; he had been entirely honest in all that he had said.

Yet, as he leaned there, a certain sense that he, with every sincere and good intent, had still done that which was cruel and unjustified, stole on him. He had considered only her welfare; he had been callous to the pain that her loss might cause to the only one who hitherto had set any value on her undefended and unclaimed life. He had thought only of gratifying the wistful desires that shone in her radiant eyes; he had forgotten that her translation to new spheres might leave a void, never to be filled again, in the heart that had grown to hold her as its treasure.

He had known Tricotrin to be a careless, fearless, high-couraged, laughter-loving wanderer, imprisoned by no ties, bound by no creeds, chained to no home. It had never seemed possible to him that such an one could love as tenderly as he loathed bondage passionately, or that his affections could strike deep root, though his temper flung off all fetters. It was only now, now when to perceive this was useless, that any glimpse of its truth flashed upon him.

"I hoped to do good," he thought wearily. "What if it end in evil?"

CHAPTER XXIII.

VIVA slept all the noon of the next day.

When she awoke, rest and slumber had healed all the harm that the night's terror and fatigue had wrought on her: to the health and the strength of her youth illness was impossible. But the wound to her pride and her conscience had struck more deeply; it was with a dull, heavy sense of pain and of shame that she arose and dressed herself, and went to her accustomed seat in the attic casement. For the first time fear—the sure shadow of all evil doing—possessed her: for the first time, she felt afraid of meeting the eyes of the friend whom she had wronged.

Moreover, there was the old leaven still working in her, despite all her loathing of her tremptress, despite her instinctive consciousness of having escaped some terrible danger. The old desire and discontent still murmured in her soul as she gazed at her white linen dress, and thought of those pearls and sapphires she had worn, as she looked round the wooden walls of her attic, and thought of the soft scarlet hues and silver glisten of the actress's banqueting-chamber.

"Ah! why does wickedness have all the beauty and all the pleasure?" she wondered with an aching heart, perplexed by the question that mocks divines, and scoffs at philosophers, and baffles at every turn the efforts of moralists and teachers.

Virtue gives her children so often but stones when they ask of her for the bread of life: wickedness casts the golden apples by thousands to her followers. And false is the preacher, who, denying this, bribes to the allegiance of the first by promise of her crowns, and seeks to affright from the palaces of the last by oaths that her festivals and banquets are Barmecide feasts held above an oubliette of death.

The poignant grief of the past night had somewhat softened with the waking day; had somewhat changed into the flattered sense that her very error, her very deception, her very peril, were befitting the romance that belonged to such an enchanted princess as herself. Although the natural conscience and impulse of the child had made her recoil from her disobedience, and repel, in an instinct of loathing, the overtures of her young lover, now that she was safe and was alone, a certain sweetness lay for her in the remembrance of such an episode, a certain delight existed in the sense that she had been deemed worth the weaving of such a web to entrap her.

The dominant thing in her was pride, and her pride had been up in arms against her tempters: but the next strongest thing in her was vanity, and vanity found a charm in the remembrance that she had passed through such a proof of her power.

At night she had wept with joy to be given back to the safe, familiar, innocent life of her childhood; but with the morning she grew well-nigh ungrateful for safety, and thought in all the restlessness of nascent ambition: "Shall I always stay thus, like a wood-dove in a wicker-work cage, when the world holds so many palace gardens whence such paradise-birds as I can spread their golden plumes in the sun?"

She had escaped from Coriolis; but she had not escaped from the poison that Coriolis had breathed over her.

It was well, she knew, to be safe in her haven; but it was tedious, it was monotonous, it had no picturesque color in it: and she began to sigh again, though ashamed of her sighs, for those glittering pleasures that she had just tasted, as a humming-bird just tastes the honey in a flower which a cruel wind shatters down into a heap of bruised petals.

The poison had touched her lips; though she had shuddered at its baneful sweetness, yet the thirst for more of its lusciousness had been left awakened and unappeased. She thought, with a sort of despair, of her future: it was the first time that ever she had dreaded this unknown thing, which, ever ere now, had been enfolded in the gold-spangled mask-dress of so mysterious and royal a new-comer; for the first time she now remembered that under its gay domino there might be seen, perchance, a skeleton,—a death's-head. She had no accurate knowledge of what it was that she felt: but she had a vague nameless terror of herself, as though she were conscious that if innocence must be leashed with obscurity, the wild desire for greatness that lay in her would hurl her, sooner or later, into the dominion and the power of evil.

The full noon light was slanting through the lattice when the step which she knew and loved the best came up the wooden stair. She cowered down and buried her face in her hands: she felt heart sick with humiliation, and all the love she bore him smote her with its remorse.

One thing alone had he ever forbidden to her; and that one thing she had seized in all the willfulness of rebellion!

She never looked up as he crossed the chamber; she trembled as she felt that he drew near; she heard him pause beside her, and she shrank farther and farther back—in silence.

He stood near, silent also.

Then by a swift impulse, she caught his hands and gazed up in his face.

"Forgive me! Oh do forgive me!" she cried, while her voice was choked with tears. "I was so wicked! and yet I meant no harm; she said you should know, and that you would learn to see you wronged her, and that I was a burden to you when I might grow great and be your glory! I never knew that young prince would be there—I never did indeed! Believe me—oh pray, believe me!"

"I believe you. If I had thought that you could lie, I would have left you to live and die in that hell you had chosen."

The words were stern and chill, and perfectly calm: she shuddered under them, yet she took courage to look up in his beloved familiar face. And she saw that his eyes were fixed on her with a look that smote her to the heart; the look that tearless eyes will give to some treasured thing that lies cold in death. She gave a cry as of irrepressible pain, and flung herself at his feet, all the force and fervor of her variable nature roused in self-accusation and self-hate.

"Blame me—beat me—kill me! but do not look at me like that! I was wrong—oh, I know it so well! I was vain, and foolish, and mad, and wicked, but throw me out on to the stones of the streets. Do not look at me again like that!"

A great pity changed and softened his gaze as he heard; he stooped and raised her gently.

"I was harsh—forgive me. I forgot how weak and young a thing you are. Hush!—do not sob so bitterly. You were tempted, and you had not strength to resist. Well, it is oftentimes so with all. You are not alone my little one."

There was an intense compassion, a passionless sadness in the words, which awed her as no words of upbraiding could have done.

"But I am vile!" she murmured. "So vile to have ever disbelieved you, and disobeyed you! Let me tell you all, and then——"

He stopped her.

"No. I know all I need to know. Spare me the tale of how much dearer than I, were the world and that wanton to you."

He turned from her, unable to hide the anguish that this one disloyalty had wrought him: the child hung her head and said nothing. She blushed for the thoughts which a moment before had haunted her; she was disloyal to him still, the world still dethroned him.

He paced to and fro the chamber awhile, conquering the fierce longing which possessed him to seize for his own, let it cost what it would, this fair faithless life that already seemed so wholly his own. When he came again to her it was with that tranquillity in his look and in his voice, which he had striven, so many hours through, to attain ere he had come into her presence.

"We will never speak again of this," he said gently. "You disobeyed me, indeed, but you were sorely tempted; you were wooed through your weakest follies; and you were moved by a noble thought even in the midst of your selfishness. I forgive it. I do not say forgive yourself: for you were very wrong, and I would fain have the remembrance of your error wound you sharply awhile, so that the cicatrix it leaves be a warning to you forever. But we will never speak again of your action, or of your tempters. As you grow into womanhood you will see, as you cannot see now, the full extent of their wickedness and of your peril. I have other things to say to you. Listen."

Viva, stilled and vaguely half affrighted, half consoled, raised her tear-laden eyes to his, and held her breath, and waited with an indefinite prescience that the time was near at hand when he and she would be no more as they so long had been in this joyous and unshadowed life, which to her impatient ignorance had grown so wearisome.

"Listen," he went on, speaking still with that calmness which he had taught himself to wear before her. "Your act last night has taught me what I had feared before; that I have not the means nor the power to make you happy any longer. No! hear me out. It is not ingratitude in you; it is your woman's nature. You pine and pant for things that are not in my hands to bestow on you. A female soul that chafes, and longs, and harbors discontent is ever on the balance toward evil: for sin has already its surest forerunner and ally fastened upon the life that is at war with itself. Therefore, since I cannot provide the gratification of your desire, others must do so."

He paused, and his breath came with a short, sharp sigh: she listened, moved with keen repentance, yet also moved to a vague and eager expectancy.

"I should have told you yesterday," he continued, with an effort, "that your fairy was no fairy, as you may be sure; but what is quite as potent in this world, a rich and nobly born person. She is the mother of that gentleman whom you have seen here some few times; the Duchess de Lira. She is very aged, but very powerful, very eminent, very wealthy: and she is filled with excellent intent to you. She invites you to pass a brief season with her, as her guest. Yesterday I refused; perhaps selfishly, but deeming that it was best for you not to enter and enjoy a mode of life that I cannot continue to you. Now, I know that some change must be made for you, and I have accepted this offer: because otherwise much evil will come unto you."

"Oh no, oh no!" she murmured. "I will be good, I will be content, I will try, indeed I will try, never to long for anything save what I have."

"That will be vain," he said bitterly. "The dog that is only held by her chain will be faithless the first instant that she tears her neck from her collar! No, I do not mean to be cruel to you, my child. I mean only, that though you should honestly intend to be contented, and strive to be so, the content which requires to be striven after, is a hollow thing which embitters and deceives alike the one who seeks for it and the one who lives near it. The moment that love or content need an effort to keep, both are valueless; both are dead bodies from which the spirit has flown. I have been your guardian, I will not be your jailer."

He stopped once more; the child said nothing; she could not have promised him honestly a content that should have been spontaneous and shadowless.

After awhile he spoke again.

"The change that your temptress offered you, was to woo you from health and peace to the plague and the horror of a

lazar ward; but the change that this great lady holds out to
you may be, as in all likelihood it will be, splendid. At any
rate it is a chance: a chance for you that I dare not put away
untried, since the past night showed me how easily to be led
into peril you are, and how hard to be weaned from evil. At
your years, Coriolis was no worse than you are now, a young
thing, an innocent thing, a thing gay and careless, and full
of play on a sunny seashore; but vain and restless, and full of
vague ambition and seething discontent, and impatience at her
lot and at her home. Lest the time should ever come when
looking on you I should curse you—as every mouth that is
pure with truth curses hers that is one lie incarnate—I know
that you must go from me, I know that you must pass out of
my life and out of my love, now, and it may be forever."

His voice sank very low, and grew unsteady over the last
words; but there was in his accent that which struck her with
an intense fear, and moved her with a strange dim horror of
the thing she might become—as though in some glass of
sorcery she beheld the fair face of her beaming youth, gray,
and shrunken, and sightless, and ghastly with the corruption
of death, with the ashes of age.

She seemed to behold, as in some vision, the power of evil
that lay slumbering in her: the weakness that would grow to
guilt, the dream that would fructify in sin, the ambition that
reaching up to heaven would recoil and fall to hell; the nascent passions hushed under the calm of youth, like painted
snakes asleep beneath the leaves of roses, that would arise
and coil, and sting, and slaughter, and die at last of their own
poison. She shuddered where she stood, and her lips grew
pale, and she stretched her arms out to him with a blind
piteous gesture.

"She said that such things as I were always born for evil;
it seemed her glory, and she bade me make it mine; ah! why
did you not set your foot on me and crush me when you found
me among the grasses? It had been better so."

He quivered as though she had pierced him with a knife;

the reproach that he had so long foreseen and feared rebuked him; he had his reward at last.

But his thoughts chiefly, even in that moment, were for her. He took her hands, and looked down on her with pitiful gentleness.

"My child, I knew the time would come when you would utter that plaint against me. You are a woman, and born of a woman! But you are, for all that, of a brave spirit; and your reproach to me is the reproach of a coward. It rests with you to live your life nobly or vilely. We have not our choice to be rich or be poor, to be happy or unhappy, to be in health or in sickness; but we have our choice to be worthy or worthless. No antagonist can kill our soul in us; that can perish only from its own suicide. Ever remember that. Indeed, to creatures like you, the way to evil is perilously easy; but none can force you down its incline unless your own vanities and passions first impel you. You have reproached me, for the first time, with having saved you to run your course of life; it is that you may not have to utter that reproach in far more deadly earnestness in years to come, that I shall send you from me now. Frail flowers such as you need fence, and shade, and culture, and training toward the sun. You cannot soar upward and grow straightly in storm, and cold, and drought. I was to blame that I forgot this. But I shall never again forget it. I was unwise enough to dream that I might graft on you some of my philosophy;—I forgot that you were not of my sex! The life that has been so good to me would not suffice to you. I should have known it earlier——"

"Yet my life has been so happy!" she cried, in involuntary self-reproach.

"Ah—so you will remember and realize, years hence, with vain regret, but it is no longer happy to you now. The desire for the unknown has come on you. Let us speak of it no more; I have fair news for you. This great lady seems willing to befriend you; go to her for a short season. It will be something fresh at least."

"But what will grand'mère think?"

"She has not lived through eighty-three years to expect gratitude in the young, or memory in the absent. You were angered with me yesterday that I told you no more of your 'fairy.' I ought to have done so. It might have saved you from one harsh experience. But—I was selfish. I waited on my own wish, and I forgot your welfare."

And to the breadth and the depth of the man's generous nature it seemed, indeed, that he had been guilty of an ungenerous and of an illiberal thing in counting, before the benefit of this foundling whom he had harbored, the wish and the peace of his own future. It seemed to him that to lay a claim to this existence which he had saved *because* it had been thus saved by him, was a meanness and a cowardice that deserved its chastisement.

"I rejected the offer for you," he pursued, with effort. "I did wrong; I see that now. I can only hope my error can be repaired. Last night I sought out the Duke de Lira, I told him this; I told him also what you had done. Nay—do not shrink at that. You might shrink indeed if I let you go under his roof with a lie in your mouth. I told him—all. Of your passion for the stage; of your idolatry of this dazzling sinner; of the scene in which I found you; of the allurements that had tempted you. He knows everything. But your folly does not change his desire to befriend you. I have seen him again this morning. You can go—at once—to the existence he offers you."

Viva drew a deep breath.

"They are great people?" she asked wistfully.

"They are of great rank,—do you mean that? There are great lives spent in garrets, in mines, in beds of agony, in galley slaves' benches. But 'great' in your sense means only affluent and arrogant!"

A feverish bitterness in his tone, altogether foreign to him, arrested her attention.

"You do not wish me to go?" she asked, with the same

wistfulness. "Tell me, you know I will never disobey you again?"

"Disobey! Am I your taskmaster?" he said fiercely, the fierceness that pain arouses in man as in every other animal. "If you loved me, would you talk of obedience? In love, two wills move together, inspired by one soul, as the two wings of a bird move, ever apart yet ever in union. But—that love is not between *us*. Your wings are your own; let them bear you where you will. What pleases you pleases me. Be free as air to follow your fancies. It may be for your good that this thing opens to you; it is not for me to close the door——"

"But what do you *wish?* It is that which I want to know!"

"What you wish is the question here. You wish for riches, rank, luxuries, prominence, all sorts of vanities and indulgences: well—you will see them nearer at least by this visit. That is something. It may be that they will lose their enchantment; and then——"

The sentence broke off abruptly; he could not put into words the hope which rose in him that, closely seen, these things which looked to him so idle and so artificial might lose their glittering bewitchment for her; and that in their hot-pressed atmosphere her young free heart might spring back at a rebound to the liberty, and the freshness, and the sincerity, of the life in which she had been reared.

"And then what?" asked Viva, anxiously.

"No matter! They may only gain surer sorcery over you; I forgot that you were feminine, my Waif! At any rate, your new friend means well; she can be of use to you, as poor old grand'mère never can; she shows great kindness in the mere interest she takes in you, because you are—what you are. You have grown impatient of the life you lead,—yes, and will grow more so, despite all your promises, which I know, for all that, were sincere. In the household of Madame de Lira you can see a little for yourself what the

greatness you covet is like. You can measure for yourself
the differences between the existence you lead through me,
and this existence in wealth and in pomp which you imagine
can have no cares. The opportunity offers: it is but right
you should take it. Come—there is nothing to wait for; I will
leave you there, and in eight days I will return for you."

Viva stood irresolute; something in his words, colder and
more brief than they had ever been to her, though still so
gentle, moved her with a certain fear, that dashed a chillness
over the prospect before her.

"But if I am not happy there?" she murmured, with a
sudden terror.

In an instant she saw the smile she knew so well beam in
its brightness, and its tenderness, over the face above her.

"Well!—you will know your refuge! Come to me in your
sorrows, if you forget me in your joys!"

For the first time some conception of the depth and
magnitude of this priceless love which succored her in all
things, and claimed nothing at her hands in recompense,
stole on her senses with a vague emotion of her own absolute
unworthiness of its sublimity. She could not measure its
height, more than the unaccustomed sight can gauge the
height of mountains; but in some way it moved and awed
her as the majesty of the everlasting hills will do those who
gaze upward to them.

She looked at him one moment, then threw herself into
his arms with all her childhood's abandonment.

"Ah! How selfish you must think me! If you had only
let me die when you first found me, what burden and what
trouble you had been spared!"

"Chut!" he said softly, though there was an infinite
sadness in his eyes as they looked down on her. "Where
two love, one of them is always selfish. And—as for the
other thing—not till you regret your life, my Waif, shall I
ever regret it for you. If you stain it, or learn to feel it
wearisome to bear, then indeed, but then only, shall I lament
the hour in which I saved it."

"But I have been only a care, a cost, a trouble to you? I have done nothing to repay you?"

"Pooh! little one!" he said lightly, for in that moment he felt too keenly to dare trust himself to earnest words. "Floating a Waif is a more innocent indulgence than most of our masculine extravagancies; and as for payment—when I hear you laugh that is quittance enough. And you have laughed often, I think, in your fifteen years of existence."

"Ah, yes!" sighed Viva; and for the moment that old life by the river side, that she had grown so impatient to get rid of for the "great world," looked wonderfully fair to her—transfigured as the golden light of distance alone can transfigure either the landscapes or the years we leave behind us.

"That is right," he said, briefly. "Whatever the future brings you, it will be well to have had that laughter. And now, make yourself ready; since this thing is to be done, do it quickly."

He moved to the window as he spoke; he was impatient of all bitter moments; his philosophies and his instincts alike rebelled against pain as the great foe of animal life and of mental peace; he was intolerant of depression, and resisted all calamity that strove to weigh him down, as he would have resisted a physical disease.

Opposite him, in the little casement under the gable, sat the grisette; her work had fallen in her lap; her tearful eyes were gazing vacantly out into the street.

Much the same pang ached in both their hearts; the woman brooded fondly over hers, the man thrust his passionately away. To her there was a lingering sweetness in it that she clung to; to him there was an intolerable weakness in it that he strove with all his force to uproot.

They both knew that they who go to the Rome of their desires never return to those whom they have loved and left in the old deserted land.

Viva was quickly ready, and at his side; she was in eager, tremulous excitement. She was glad that her desires had been granted thus; and yet she was fearful, after her past night's deception, of what vipers might lie curled in the purple passion-flowers of the world's pride and pleasure.

Tricotrin said little on their way, a way that led through country fields and the fragrance of the Ville d'Avrée woods, out toward where a summer villa stood, sheltered under reddening foliage that joined the forests of Versailles.

He lifted her from the covered wagon in which they had driven, and walked with her some little distance down a broad tree-shadowed lane. It was now almost dark. At the end of the road were the gates of her destination. In this sunny autumn weather the Duchess de Lirà preferred this light and pleasant place to either her great palaces in the Faubourg, or her château under the shadow of the eastern Pyrenees. Outside the gates he paused a moment; there was no one in sight save an old man sitting under one of the sycamores resting with a load of wood. He laid his hand on Viva's shoulder, and looked down into her eyes.

"My child, you have your heart's desire; you go among 'great people.' It may make your happiness; it may make your misery. Granted wishes are sometimes self-sown curses. Whichever it be, remember—go where you will, do what you may, you can always come back to me!"

The infinite tenderness of the words raised something akin to terror in her; her color went and came in rapid changes.

"But it is only for a little time!" she said, rapidly. "It is no separation? I shall be with you again so soon?"

He smiled: the smile that smote her heart with remorse, though why she could not tell.

"A week is an age sometimes at your years. I hardly think you will remain or return to me—the same. But that we must chance, grand'mère and I. Anyhow, love that has not been put to the test is no love; and the young bird that has never been allowed to fly, likes its cage from habit, not choice. Go within. I have rung; they will come to you. In eight days you shall see me again."

Before she could reply or resist he had closed the gate gently on her, leaving her standing within the enchanted ground of her new paradise, and had gone back, alone, through the checkered twilight shadow of the road. The echo of his steps upon the gravel, growing fainter and fainter as he passed away, filled her with a sudden sense of loneliness and of ingratitude.

"Oh, come back, come back!" she cried. "I do not want any one but you;—I do not wish to stay."

But the words did not pierce the metal gates that were now closed between them; and a servant, waiting for her, approached her with so courteous a deference, that she forced back her tears, and began to dream again that this was the commencement of that living fairy-tale, in which she, from the obscure chrysalis of a Waif and Stray, would change into the winged and glorious butterfly of an omnipotent Princess.

Through a wilderness of floral beauty, through gorgeous autumn flowers, blooming and blazing around snowy statues and sparkling fountain-spray, through aisles of scented bushes and of orange-trees powdered with their yellowing balls, she was led into the house. For the third time she was in an abode made luxurious and elegant by wealth; for the third time, the glow and shadow and subdued brilliancy of gold and silver, paintings and statuary, velvets and marbles, were about her as she moved; for the third time, the fragrance, the grace, the stillness, the indescribable beauties of good taste, and of choice art, filled the chambers through which she went. And they had lost none of the unutterable delight which at the château of Villiers and the house of Coriolis they had possessed for her. She drew a deep breath as she saw and felt their sorcery; she already forgot the echo of the steps, at whose retreating sound her tears had started but a few moments earlier.

She saw no one in any of the rooms and galleries she traversed. Her conductress, a creole woman, took her in silence through them, and only spoke when, at length, she threw one door open.

"Mademoiselle will wish to rest; this is Mademoiselle's chamber," she said, with one hand lifting up the silk curtains before the entrance.

Viva gave a cry of delight—the same childlike, eager, rapturous cry, as when in the wine country she had found a purple butterfly, or heard a new legend from grand'mère.

The small octagon chamber glistened with azure and white; a silver-winged angel hovered over the little sequestered bed; flowers in profusion filled each nook and corner; a little fragrant fountain played in a jasper basin; between the mirrors was a single picture, a Proserpine wandering among lilies and asphodels; beyond, through the open window, lay the gardens, and avenues, and orangeries.

Viva stood in a trance of enchantment, flushed, mute, beatified.

The curtain fell behind her; she was left alone. Her first impulse was to turn to the mirror; her next to gaze around the chamber that was "hers."

The little wooden chamber under the ivy-covered eaves in her old home had been kept for her at the cost of many a personal sacrifice, and the trifles that adorned it of quaint carving, or of oil sketches, had been the gifts of most tender pity or most generous love. This room, so fair to her sight, was but one among many similar in the house of a great personage, and all its beauties had been prepared, not for her, but for any other visitant who might be guest there.

Yet how mean and poor looked that little room of grand'-mère's! how exquisite and luxurious a nest was this!

"The fairies have remembered me at last!" she cried aloud, with her hands clasped above her head in breathless ecstasy.

And she—had forgotten one who never had forgotten her through all the years wherein the fairies had been silent to her call.

CHAPTER XXIV.

When he went thither again at the end of the eight days, the servants brought him a little note. It was very short, and like a child's.

"My best Friend,—I am so happy; I never dreamed that any life could be one-half so beautiful. They take me to-day to see a great review of soldiers. I fear that I shall miss you. If I do, will you leave word whether I may stay here three months? The duchess has asked me, and I hope very much you will say—yes. Your own

"Viva.

"My love to grand'mère and Mistigri. The duke is so good to me; and has bought me such magnificent things."

He read it, crushed it in his hand, and asked them for a pencil. Then on its little, torn envelope he wrote the one word of assent required.

"Give that to—Mademoiselle," he said simply, as he left it in the servant's hand, and went out from the gates.

Mistigri trembled as she looked up in his face that was white as with the whiteness of death.

The months went by, and Tricotrin might have been numbered among the dead for any sign that came to her from him. Where he went no one knew. The fishers of the western coast could have told, and they only.

The weather was wild and fierce; storms dashed the shores and beat the boats to pieces; the nights were filled with hurricanes, and the beach was strewn with driftwood and the flotsom and jetsom of barks broken on the rocks. All through that bitter time of the early winter he was with them. It was no new thing; and they were well used to see him in the driving gales,—with the winds tossing his hair, and the rains beating on his bare chest and shoulders, and the breakers leaping on him as on a granite block,—bring in some fishing-boat, whose load would be the sole support of some drowned sailor's widow, or launch some life-raft through the surge to reach the stricken vessel that, reeling and dismasted, plowed the blackened sea.

Few winters passed but brought him, in the time of peril, to the Biscay-beaten coasts. He loved sea and storm like some Norse viking of the old wild years; the rising of the sullen winds was to him as the trumpet-note to the war-horse; the exultant courage in him delighted in the contest with the waves; and he loved the brave, rough, patient, melancholy, great-souled people who lived beside the everlasting waters, and gained something of the grandeur and the poetry of those waters in the midst of so much rugged poverty, so hard a conflict for the bread of life. For many years he had appeared among them at such seasons; and in the superstition engendered by the mingled tragedy and simplicity of their existence, they looked upon him as on one of more than mortal strength and power, at whose bidding the seas released their prey, and delivered up their dead.

That he made music at their feasts, that he flung their nets over his shoulder, that he stacked sea-weed for their aged and infirm, that he mended their sails singing as he sat on the sands some of their old-world romances, that he laughed with their handsome fisher-maidens pushing a boat through the surf,—all these things had not made them the less deem him half a god, though his vigorous limbs were clothed in their garb, and he had been more than once dashed, bruised and senseless, on their rocks in vain effort to succor some sinking vessel.

These months in the late autumn he had passed among them, in the salt, hard, fresh seafaring life. If pain were on him he never let it brood on undisturbed; if regret or desire haunted him he exorcised them by some means or other; his whole temperament rebelled against the weight of care or sorrow, and sought light as instinctively as do the sunflowers.

Yet, against all his efforts and all the happy philosophies

that had kept youth so bright and ardent in him through years that bring the burdens of age to many men, against his will and his endeavor he could not turn his thoughts from Viva. He could not tear out from him the jealous, carking care that filled him when he thought of her in strangers' hands, the hot, senseless hope, which lived in him against all reason, that she would cling to him still in preference to the things of pomp and power. He grew to hate his love for her—but never to hate her. He knew that it had lost the purity and the peace which had sanctified it for so long; he knew that it was the love of a man for the fair eyes, and the smiling mouth, and the white limbs of the woman's beauty that tempts him. That love he had known oftentimes; but it had never been a gay, wind-tossed, chance-sown flower in his path; not a long-cherished blossom like this, with thorns hid in the heart of its sweet white leaves to wound the breast upon which it was clasped in caresses.

He hated the passion that had sprung up in him from out of the kindly and pitying care he had given her: it seemed to him to poison all the tenderness he had felt for her in the time when his hand had played with her hair, or his lips had touched her cheek in the unthinking and negligent fondness that he might have felt for a favorite dog. It was on the impulse of that hate for his own instinct of jealous possession that he had embraced the offer of a new life for her, dreading lest his love made him blind to what was best for her, dreading lest it warped him to injustice and to egotism.

He, careless and heedless in so much, watched with keenest scruple his own nature, lest, under the angelic guise of tenderness for her, there should be the hellish snake of envious desire. He had served her; all she had, and all she was, she owed to him; at his will he could have cast her out to the starvation of an unowned beggar-girl: for this cause he held himself debarred by all common law of honor from any shape of tyrannous usurpation over that which lay thus wholly at his mercy. The titles that other men might have thought gave him the rights to do with her as he would, were in his sight the strongest forbiddance from all such rights' despotic exercise.

Once he had saved a bird whose wing was broken; it had been in his earliest boyhood, and he had grown to love fervently the creature he had succored, whose shattered pinion he had bound, and whose food and water and sod of grass had been his daily care for months through a keen snow-laden winter. With the spring, just as its song grew music on his ear, and the brightness of its pretty eyes rewarded him, the little lark fluttered its feathers in impatient longing, and beat its beak against the cage that had so long been its sanctuary from the winds and the hail that had struck so many birds down, frozen, on the ice-bound earth.

He, a mere child, had wept grievously as he saw that feverish fretting of the lark which wished to leave him; some others standing by laughed to see his tears: "Silly lad!" they cried., "can the bird escape you? Bend its cage-wires closer; so shall you always have it with you."

But the boy had shaken his head.

"I have done it good, shall I do it evil? It must be free to stay or to go, else what is its love worth?"

And he had opened the door of the cage, and turned it toward the west where the sun was setting: then he waited and watched.

The lark saw the glow of the sun, and moved, and lighted awhile on the edge of its prison-house; then with one glorious burst of song soared upward, higher and higher, toward the golden radiance of the skies.

He looked after it as it flew, with the great tears blinding his eyes; but he smiled as he heard the hymn of its joy.

"It is happy," he said gently, as he hung the cage on the bough of an oak. "And—when the winter comes back perhaps it will be glad to come too."

But the bird never returned, though the empty cage stood open all the seasons through.

The same impulse as had moved him then, moved him

now. As he had given his lark its liberty, so he gave her freedom to his foundling. What was fidelity worth only born of coercion? The song of the lark had been sweet to him; but its melody would have been jarred forever had it come from the throat of a captive. The love of the child had been sweet to him; but its caress would have been embittered to him forever had it come from lips on whose breath there had hovered a sigh.

Let her go!—the child like the lark.

If the summer of other lands seemed fairer to her sight she must be free to take flight to them; if the old fostering care seemed dearer than the glow of foreign suns, then only would the love be willingly given, and not prison-born. Any way, the door was opened; and though the ingrate should wing swift way to vapor-palaces of sunlit cloud, still would the deserted refuge wait, unclosed; in case that storm, and snow, and driving blasts should ever bring the wanderer home, with drooping wing and breaking heart.

CHAPTER XXV.

The thirtieth day of the last month came. He passed once more up the linden-lined road. The bounteousness of color that had so late made the earth beautiful with fruit and flower had shriveled, dropped, and perished. Wild winds were tossing the russet leaves, and the great woods were bare and brown. There was winter in the air; and all the spikes of grass were white with frost. In so brief a space all the brilliancy and wealth of autumn had died away as though it had never been. Was the brief time long enough likewise to kill the young warmth of a girl's heart as it had killed the color of the earth?

He traversed the grounds unobserved; it was a wild and gloomy day, and no one was at work in the gardens. The house itself was long and low, with broad windows that nearly touched the ground, and had a terrace running beneath them. The rooms within, at all times visible, were doubly clearly seen from the bright light of wood fires inside them that glowed through their lozenge-shaped panes.

Instinctively before one he paused.

In the full illumination of ruddy color that was reflected back from the mirror-lined walls of the room, and glowed upon the rose hue of its velvet hangings, he saw her; and his heart beat thick with longing and with fear, with hope and with despair.

She stood upon the hearth, in the full warmth of the fire-flames, and was laughing, with her head thrown back, as she tossed to and fro in the air a pretty golden toy, a Protean Arlecchino jeweled and enameled, that went through changeful antics, as he was tossed or poised. Her face was radiant with laughter at the puppet's evolutions; dainty robes clothed her tall slender limbs, and trailed behind her on the floor; gold buckles glittered on her pretty feet; and her hair, turned backward in the Louis Quatorze fashion, was fastened by an arrow of gold half hidden in its rippling clusters; wealth and rank had set their seals on her; she looked no more a child, but a beautiful woman.

What need had he to enter? His question was answered by his first glance at her face.

Had the lark come back from its flight through the sunlight ether? Would the girl come back from her ascent into the luxury of riches?

His heart stood still, his hope died out, as he beheld her. With all that radiance on her face, where was the shade of one regret? With all that mirth upon her lips, where was the sigh of one remembrance? He had lost her forever. And he knew his loss as well as though he had seen her laid down in her grave.

Slowly, and with one long backward look, he turned and moved away toward the dark cold shelter of the woods; and she, unconscious all the while—laughed on, tossing her Arlecchino upward in the fire-glow till his jewels sparkled and his silvered bells rang again.

It was two hours later when Tricotrin returned, and the dark day was waning.

He desired, then, to see the Duke de Lirh. He was admitted at once, and conducted to where the nobleman spent most of his hours when in his mother's villa; a small, lofty, book-lined room, dusky even at midday, yet rich in bronze, and statuary, and antique things that gleamed curiously from out the twilight.

Tricotrin went quickly forward, and spoke ere his host could speak,

"I have kept my word: keep you yours. Let me see Viva. No! do not speak. Have patience with me. I desire to see her first and hear you later. I address the request to you since she is beneath your roof, but my right to her is not wholly gone; by it I come to claim her."

The Duke de Lirh looked at him in silence; his face was pale, his blouse was wet with night dews, his eyes were full of speechless woe, like the dumb woe of a dog. There was that in him which made his hearer obey the abrupt and fiery discourtesy of the command.

"I will send her to you here," he said as briefly as he rose, and passed out through the door of his chamber, and closed it behind him. Some moments drifted by, whether many or few he who waited could not have told; then the door reopened, and, with a light swift bound, the gay grace of her form came toward him, all luster and light in the gloom, with the shining Arlecchino still in her hand. It was with a cry of welcome and delight that she sprang to him; and it thrilled through him as the song of the lark had thrilled through his heart as a child.

He caught her with unconscious passion in his arms, and kissed her with kisses that burned her check like fire; then as suddenly he loosened her from his embrace and put her from him. He remembered that he had no right to force on her caresses, for which in a brief while she might blush with shame, no right to steal their virginity from lips that another might soon seek with a lover's or a husband's title.

She, all innocent of his thoughts, laughed up in his eyes: her hair had been ruffled by his touch, and her delicate dress stained by the night dews on his own; and the toy she held bruised and bent by the violence of his embrace.

"Oh the poor Arlecchino!" she cried, "how you have hurt him! And he cost a thousand francs in the Palais Royal yesterday."

With an inexpressible impulse he dashed the puppet from her hold on to the ground.

"That is how you greet me!"

She, who had never heard that bitter, burning passion in his voice before, stood silent, trembling, afraid, amazed, gazing at him with her bright large eyes. She did not know what she had done.

"I did not mean anything," she murmured, "it is only— the Arlecchino amused me so, and he is broken."

The words recalled him to himself, and roused him from the delirium of wounded love that had found its violence an issue in the toy's destruction. He stooped for the puppet, and raised it; his rival of tinsel and clockwork that was before him in the thoughts of the creature who owed him her salvation! His voice trembled, but was very gentle as he answered her.

"Forgive me, Viva: I erred greatly. I had no right to bruise your plaything, above all as I have not a thousand francs to give for any toy! But I have skill at these things, and I will mend his injuries; and—for my violence give me your pardon."

The words found their instant way to the still fond heart of the child.

"Oh, what do I care for the toy?" she cried. "The duke will buy me another. I was only afraid I had angered you; and—I am so glad to see you once more!"

He answered her nothing, but stooped his head over the Arlecchino. The welcome was little worth, it was the welcome of a playful unconcerned affection; and, already she looked to a rich man for the solace of her woes, the provision of her pleasures!

Viva looked at him earnestly, in some perplexity; she was afraid that she had pained him, but also she was irritated that he should have acted so strangely. Three months had been sufficient space for her to have learned to look upon herself as a thing of beauty and of witchery to whom all should bow and give way.

There was a long silence between them; a silence that she spent, almost instinctively in noting the stains of the grasses and the rains upon his linen, and thinking how much nobler he would look if he wore velvet, like the men whom she had seen of late. The feminine mind played with frivolities and caprices while the masculine soul suffered a mute martyrdom.

At last he looked up, laying the puppet down.

"The toy will be none the worse; I will remedy what is amiss. And now, have you forgotten, Viva, that this day is the last of those which you were asked to pass here?"

She started; and a flash of remembrance and of terror came over all her face.

"I had forgotten it," she murmured.

"And—you regret it?"

She looked down; and he saw her mouth quiver. She said nothing.

"You have been happy here then?" he asked.

"Oh!—happy?—yes!" she murmured, the flood-gates of her enthusiastic speech opened at last. "Happy? Why! it is like enchantment! You do not know how beautiful the life is! They have been so good to me. They have given me a little horse, snow-white, and a hundred pretty things like Arlecchino, and many dresses, all as beautiful as this, and some more so; and then every nook and corner of the house is like a picture; and one has never even to pour out a glass of water for one's self; and my own room is so exquisite, and the duke is always giving me some new surprise or pleasure; you do not know what it is! And then one feels so great too —like a princess—among it all!"

"And who loves you—whom do you love in it?"

The question was passionate in its scornful demand, its vehement reminder of the one thing lacking.

"Love?" she echoed. "Oh, no one! But then—it is all so magnificent; it does not matter about that."

"You have learnt the world's lesson swiftly!" he muttered, as he swung from her.

The heartless creed couched in the guileless words struck him with an intolerable suffering. What avail to have given her care and tenderness for all these years!—a month of luxury outweighed them all!

"I am very different to what I was!" Viva retorted, with a certain petulance and offended pride, as instinctively she glanced at herself in one of the mirrors. Although it was twilight she could see the gleam of her gold arrow in her hair, and the trailing grace of her azure skirts.

"You could not speak a sadder truth!"

The words were hoarse in his throat with the acuteness of disappointed mortification. Unconsciously he had hoped, far more than he knew, that the ties of old association and of gratitude might have been strong enough to withstand the temptations that sought to break them asunder. Unknown to himself the idea that the gilded restrictions of a lofty station would gall her, much as they would have galled him, had misled him; and, relying on the free-born temper of the child, he had forgotten the ambitious vanities that ran with it.

"A sad truth!" echoed Viva, with all her graceful petulance in arms against the attack upon her vanity, while her eyes sought the beloved reflection of herself in the mirror. "A very happy one, surely! You might as well say that it is sad that the exquisite little old duchess here, who is just like one of her own porcelain figures, does not resemble grand'mère clicking over the snow in her wooden shoes, or peeling onions to put in the soup-pot!"

"For shame, Viva!" he cried, vehemently. "Have you less gratitude than the stray lambs feel for the hands that fed them when they were motherless? Your duchess! I know little of her; but I know that if all her life through she have had the truth, and courage, and charity, and chastity of the brave old woman you despise, it will be well for her when her last hour comes. What think you the noble old soul, who wearies for a sight of your face as she sits by her lonely hearth, would feel if she had heard your words now?"

The rebuke was passionately uttered; it touched her to remembrance, contrition, and all the affection still strong in her beneath the selfishness that stifled it. She sprang to him with all the charming impulsive grace of her childhood.

"She would call me wicked and worthless, as I am. My tongue should have been cut out before it should have breathed a word against her. Dear, old grand'mère! I care for her so much, I do indeed. It is only everything here is so different: it makes me forget, I think; it turns my head dizzy like wine!"

"The wine of flattered vanity—yes! Heads wiser and older than yours grow drunk on it," he said, with a quick, impatient sigh as he turned slightly from her.

"You think me cruel and foolish then?" she murmured, with a touch of piteousness; her reverence and love for him were stronger than anything else as yet in her, and were making her odious in her own sight if she were unworthy in his.

He looked down on her with a smile, whose sadness and whose tenderness she could not measure, for they were beyond her knowledge.

"A little cruel—youth always is in its own intense self-absorption; and—as for foolishness, we cannot look for you to be very wise: but you follow the world's wisdom in choosing the things of the world. But—how will it be with you, Viva, if you be obliged to come back to the only life I can give you?"

He saw her turn pale, and she gave a swift, upward glance of alarm.

"I will try and be content," she said, softly; and her promise was sincere.

But scarcely any answer could have stung him more. He knew what content that has to be striven for is worth; he felt all the bitterness of such niggard return for the lavishness of his own donations. He repressed the words that rose to his lips. She had been so utterly and entirely his debtor that he would not bring against her the charge of her ingratitude, lest it should seem like a citation of his own benefits.

"You mean," he said, calmly, at length, though the calmness was very hard to attain, "that you could not be simply and sincerely happy in your own life, having once tasted the luxury and brilliancies of this? You mean, that if you have to return to grand'mère and her cottage you will rebel with ceaseless regret against them both?"

Viva hung her head, and her eyes went instinctively to the gleam of her golden arrow in the mirror.

"No, no," she said, with the tears trembling in her voice. "It is not that—I love you so dearly, and grand'mère too—but it is only——."

"Only what?"

"That I think I am born for this life! I always seemed, somehow, to *want* it so much, even when I did not know what it was like! The duchess herself, who is so terribly proud, says that she is sure I come from some great race or another. And it may be, you see,—why should it not be, when all this that is great seems to come to me by nature? You remember, that English lord with the beautiful face said just the same thing when he passed me?"

Tricotrin made no answer.

He stood in the shadow, where she could not tell what changes swept over his features. It cost him a long effort ere he could reply to her as he desired to do—without trace of the conflict that raged in him. It was a strange caprice of accident by which, in the very words with which she endeavored to exculpate herself, she thrust deeper into his soul the iron wherewith she so all unconsciously stabbed him.

"You may be right," he said, at length. "Though beware how you lean on the thought of some lofty origin; it will be but a broken reed at best. I see, however, plainly one thing,—that whether you come of prince or peasant, you will never again be happy in obscurity. You would sooner go away to Coriolis than back to grand'mère!"

Viva colored hotly.

"Only to Coriolis' fame: it has greatness in a way at least."

"Greatness! Good God! how irresistibly what is vile looks fair in the eyes of woman! Pshaw! What avail to rear you fickle exquisite things in innocency and solitude; you find your way to sin and its pomps as instinctively as mice steal out to honey!"

The violence of the words escaped him ere he knew it, in the insupportable anguish that it was to him to find her thus wedded to vain things, and turned from all that he had thought would grow but dearer to her by their absence.

She—ignorant of his meaning, but comprehending only that he deemed her inconstant and unworthy—stood with the tears in her eyes, half of sorrow, half of offense. She knew that she had been heartless and wrong, but also she felt herself aggrieved.

She could not tell that the feeling which moved him was the consciousness that she, unless lifted from temptation and encircled by the safeguards of a sure and lofty position, was precisely of the nature that would be swiftest drawn down to gilded evil, that would be easiest lured to drink of the perfumed wines which poison as they intoxicate. The very ignorance and purity of her mind would lay her open and unguarded to the seductions which would come to her with every appeal to her vanity and her tastes, and with all the darker traits veiled from her and unguessed. He saw that, had the desire of his heart been given him, and the creature of his love been his, there could have waited for him in the future no other fate than the fate of Bruno.

She did not know this.

The lovely, careless, graceful thing, thinking of her golden arrow in her hair, and the azure glisten of her dress, never even dreamed of the sharp despairing torture of the man. And he took heed, even in his torture, that she should not. Why vex the thoughtless heart of a child by letting her behold a wound which she could neither measure nor comprehend?

Not to pain her was his first thought; and he crushed the thorns into his own breast unseen, rather than let them touch the hand which she might have stretched out in pity, had she known that they were wounding him.

There was a long silence between them; when he spoke it was gently and gravely.

"I seem harsh to you, my child. I am not so, God knows. You have the foibles of your sex in a strong degree; but we should scarce expect you to be free from them, — with such a face as yours, and barely sixteen summers over your bright head! You are enamored of your life here, doubtless, though to my thinking the life you have led was far simpler, and freer, and happier. But there is one thing you seem to have forgot, Viva; your sojourn here was but for a visit. Though you have been given so many gifts, you are but a stranger?"

She was silent. He saw once more the quiver of disappointment on her mouth. She had never thought of this —to her belief it had been the fairies who had brought her to her rightful heritage.

"You have forgotten that?" he pursued. "You have forgotten then, also, that to-day you were to go back with me to your own old home; since no guest can outstay the limits of her invitation?"

Viva lifted her head, with an impetuous passion in the gesture.

"Oh, wait, wait!—hear me! It is not because I am ungrateful, not because I do not love you and grand'mère with all my soul; but, indeed, I must be something great somehow. If it be only charity here, I will not stay. I know I was born an aristocrat like themselves. I will not remain for their alms, however splendid they be. But do let me go on the stage. I need not be wicked, as that cruel Coriolis is. I will obey all you wish; I will do all you say; but there I could conquer the world—or what is the use of the beauty you all tell me I have? It is not because I am heartless, not because I do not feel all that you and grand'mère have done for me; but I *know* that if I go back to be shut up, all the long winter through, in our little room by the river, I shall die just with longing for some other world, like the Mexican bird that the sailor son of Sarazin brought his mother from over the seas!"

The whole pent-up passion of the girl's heart broke out in the vehement words. Under the terror that she would have to return to the monotony and peasant companionship of her home, the flood-gates of her impetuous desire were unloosed; and there poured out before him the turbulent stream of her long-repressed thoughts.

Of what the stage was in reality she had even yet little notion; it was only in her sight a means whereby women of beauty and genius soared their way from obscurity and poverty into the light of the world's adulation. Every sentence she uttered pierced him to the heart with the sharpness of steel; but she knew naught of that. She knew only that he loved her. Why, then, should he deny her this one yearning of her nature—to be great?

He let her speak on, answering her nothing. To answer her must have been to either condemn or affright her; and he dreaded lest she should see the tempest that raged in his heart of grief, and despair, and desire.

This was all that he had reared her for—to hear her speak of the river-nest that had sheltered her as of some prison-house, and beseech his permission to follow the steps of the vilest women of Paris!

But of what he suffered there was no trace in his voice when, at length, he replied to her,

"I have told you—I would rather see you in your grave than on the stage. But that may be a prejudice. You are right, an actress may be as noble and pure a woman as any other of her sex, but,—if she be, she is hissed off the boards! I see well that your heart is set on some far different life than any I can give you. I will think awhile on all you have said, and see you again. Meantime, go; and if you can, bid your host come to me."

She paused before him, wistfully.

"You are angered against me?"

He stooped to her, and there was an emotion in his voice that she had never heard before, as he answered her.

"Child—if with years you grow the guiltiest woman that ever shamed her sex, *I* shall have pardon for you. Can you not even dream what love is?"

She looked at him half fearfully, her great eyes wide-opened like a startled stag's. Of such a tenderness as this she had no conception; yet it stirred her to a vague terror and an intense sense of worthlessness and weakness beneath the divine greatness of such a gift.

With a sudden wild awakening to its strength and her own blindness, she stretched her hands out to him with a broken cry.

"Ah! Who will ever care for me like that again?"

For this one instant the supreme value of this priceless benediction outweighed with her all lower and baser things. She saw, in that one moment, that never, so long as her life should last, would such a love as this be hers again.

A delirious hope flashed on him. He caught her hands against his breast, and held them there with convulsive force.

"Would that love suffice to you, Viva? If you wandered with me always—were never severed from me—would you sigh then for the golden gifts of the rich, or the triumphs of Coriolis?"

His eyes fastened on her face with feverish longing, with thirsty dread and desire mingled, to read his answer there. She hesitated a moment, looking up at him with innocent wonder, knowing no meaning in his question save that she should go whithersoever he went in his wanderings, as, when a child, she had so often begged to do.

"I do not know," she said, tenderly, and with a tremor in the answer, for she loved him in return very fondly, though with a love, to him, well-nigh more cruel than her hate would have been. "I am always so happy when I am with you; only—only—it is to be great, too, that I want!"

He dropped her hands, and turned away. The hope of a moment's span was gone.

"Send your host to me," he said, briefly.

She went as he bade her slowly, musingly, with a certain terror and vague sense of loss and of remorse upon her. She forgot the errand on which he had sent her; but went almost mechanically to her own room, and curled herself among its velvet cushions, and buried her face among its hot-house flowers, and cried as if her heart would break—why she could scarce have told.

She had said the truth sincerely, yet she felt that she had been heartless and ungrateful; she felt too, though indefinitely, that in the answer she had given, she had in some way or another divorced her life from that of the one she loved best. Best, although it was the thoughtless and half-cruel child's love that she rendered him; best, although the riches and glamour of the world were before him in her sight.

In her solitude she thought more sadly and more gravely of him. To go with him in his wanderings as she had used to pray to do,—she wondered how it would be with her if she did so? She remembered many happy hours spent with him in careless freedom; among the yellow wheat or the ripened vines; drifting down the river in some great cumbrous boat, that was yet so darkly picturesque, with its heavy tawny sails and loads of corn or fruit; or sitting under the broad-leaved chestnut-trees before some farm-house door, listening while the delicate delicious music of the Straduarius echoed through the evening air, and made the very watch-dog lift his head to listen. She remembered so many of those joyous

seasons—life made up of them would surely be fair to the
sight and the senses?

And then with him she knew her better nature reigned as
it never did in his absence: she was purer, simpler, braver,
nobler, beneath his influence than under any other. She
knew as well as he that in this life that she now led she had
deteriorated. She knew that for sake of every better and
higher thing in her she should cast off all these desires for a
fate he could not give her, and surrender herself in innocence
and contentment to the safety and simplicity of her old life
beneath his will. He had been to her in the stead of country,
parentage, home, and brethren: he, he alone, as far as her
memory could reach, had bestowed on her everything she
had received, from the very bread that had appeased her
daily hunger. And all the reward that she had given him
had been to pine for an alien greatness, and to refuse to follow him through the years to come! She was hateful in her
own sight; hateful and full of guilt. Her heart went out to
him in childlike contrition and longing tenderness; but her
pride, and the lusts of her vanity drew her from him.

To wander with him always—what would it be but to be
always among the people? True, they loved and honored
him, and his step brought gladness and mirth at his coming,
as the foot of the wine-god sowed thyme and flowers where-
ever it fell.

But it was ever among the homes of the poor that he
dwelt, in their fields that he labored, in their festivities that
he shared. He laughed to scorn the palaces of the rich, and
would never break bread beneath a great man's roof. The
dome under which he worshiped was the blue of the starlit
sky; and the ears for which his melodies were breathed were
the ears that through long labor had only heard the moving
of scythes, or the beating of oars, or the whirling of steam-
wheels, and had been deadened and deaf to the sweet sermons
of music. To be with him was to be "of the people" forever; forever to be banished from the triumphs of greatness,
from the luxuries of wealth.

And though the graciousness of love, and courage, and poetry, and charity, and tolerance, and peace, would be with her in the life, she still recoiled from it because it would be without the dreamy splendors and sensualities of riches, and without brilliancy in the sight of men to whom she would still be but a Waif and Stray.

"I *must* be great!" she murmured, vehemently. "I am sure I came from greatness!"

She could not doubt it, as she raised her head and looked at her face in the mirror opposite; there were patrician pride and patrician blood in every line and hue of it, flushed though its hot cheeks were, and tear-laden its brimming eyes.

She felt herself the offspring of some mighty race, and destined to some mighty sovereignty: should she be false to these? No!—rather must she be false where every common bond of gratitude claimed fealty.

CHAPTER XXVI.

TRICOTRIN remained long where she had left him, his arms resting on a marble shelf beside him, and his head bent down on them.

The torture of doubt was ended; there remained in its stead the dullness of despair.

The bird chose to spread its wings toward the glistening golden roofs of kings' palaces;—let her go! If she came not of her own will to find her repose and safety in his bosom, not by lure nor by prayer would he recall her.

Nevertheless, the corpse of a dead hope lay heavy on him, and its coldness chilled to ice the strong and vivid blood within him.

Yet not now, even in his own heart, did he reproach her. It had been his own folly, he deemed, to think that the free, wandering, homeless life of a man who was poor could suffice to the fancy and needs of a fair woman-child. Yet not once did he wish he were rich or were great,—the love that would

not cling to him because he could not strew its path with
roses, and fill its hands with gold, was love worse than indifference in his eyes. Indifference might have been cold,
but love such as this was cowardly.

An hour passed, unwittingly to him; then the door once
more unclosed and his host entered. Tricotrin started and
raised himself erect; in the dusky ruddy light of the declining day the agitation on his face was veiled.

"I only this moment learned that Viva had left you," said
the Duke de Lirà. "It seems she forgot your bidding until
now. You find her——"

He paused; hesitating how to put the question that was
on his lips.

Tricotrin filled up the blank.

"Changed?—or well? Which would you ask? I find
her—as I thought to find her—ruined for the life with which
she had been hitherto content, and ready to hurl herself to
any depths from which it should be promised her she would
rise enriched and great! You have done what I foresaw
would be done: I do not blame you. You have only brought
out, under hot-house heat, the native evil that always sleeps
in such fair frail things as she. You have thought to do well
by her, doubtless; but how is it well to make a creature, half
infant and half woman, loathe all that is honestly hers, and
crave all that can never be hers except with dishonor?—how
is it well, to make the pure bread of life taste coarse and abhorrent to her, and only the honeyed gilded confections that
poison and cloy become the sole food she will feed on with
appetite?"

He spoke with the swift eloquence that was always natural
to him under emotion; what arrests the speech on most men's
lips brought it, burning and rapid as fire, to his. His hearer
listened without anger, though it was a bohemian who rebuked him for what the world would have called a generous
and most marvelous charity.

"You do us some wrong, I think," he said, patiently.
"Here, the tastes that were inherent in her have developed;

that is all. Is it not better they should do so, while yet her future is undecided and malleable, than that they should be discovered by herself and by others too late?"

"Too late!" echoed Tricotrin, with unconscious violence. "It is always too late for a child to discover that she is made for riches, and rank, and honor, when she is motherless, fatherless, nameless, and penniless! What avail is it ever for such an one to discover that she pines for a palace, and has the graces that empresses have not? What avail ever, except to lure her outward to the road where vice dresses itself as splendor, and disgrace thrones itself as a sovereign, and the woman who counts the most honors is the woman who counts the most sins! I see no end that is served, except such an end as this, by her learning that she passionately craves what is not hers by birth or by title, and can never be hers by purchase unless she barter her beauty for it!"

"You forget our covenant," interrupted the Duke de Lira, still gently, for he interpreted aright the despair and the dread which inspired words in themselves so pregnant of offense for him, had he so chosen to read them. "You cannot think us such barbarians that we can forsake this lovely child when once she has been under our roof? I gave you my word to provide in such measure as I could for her happiness. It is I who am her debtor for having brought so much of youth, of gladness, and of freshness into my own somber existence."

Tricotrin flashed a searching burning glance upon him: he said nothing, but in that glance he read the other's heart like a book,—his suspicions were confirmed.

"My mother has grown to attach herself to Viva," the nobleman pursued. "She would part from her with regret; of the girl's own contentment you can judge for yourself. This life suits her well—let her lead it."

"How?"—his teeth were set hard as he put the question.

"As she does now. I have no—absolutely no—kindred. I can do as it pleases me with my wealth without wronging any. I will guarantee to her such a fortune as shall raise her above all possible neglect or need. For a year or more she can spend her time in such studies as are pleasures to her; then when she is some few years older she shall enter the "great world" that she longs for, in such fashion as shall show to her only its brightest side. I know that for her to do this is for you to surrender all the claims on her which you justly hold as her sole friend and protector; but it is for her own happiness, which, I think, can ill be made in any other way. If I wound you by what I say you must remember that in saying it I only keep my word."

"I thank you; you are very generous."

That was all he answered as he turned and paced to and fro the length of the chamber. He knew that the words addressed to him were spoken in honor and liberality; the acknowledgment of them was wrung from his justice; yet he could have leapt on the man that uttered them and have strangled him, as wild beasts do their foes.

"You will prefer the assurance of her future from a woman than from a man," pursued the other; his sympathies were too true to let him misconstrue as offense to himself the pain that he knew his words caused. "My mother will say to you all that I say; in her name, not in mine, if you deem it better, can the conveyance of such wealth as we may decide on be made over to Viva. She has attached herself to the child: it will lend a charm to her last years to see so graceful a creature about her in all the brilliance of youth. What more can I add? Any pledge, any security, any bond you may wish I will give, and that life will go well with her I cannot doubt. She is not one of those formed to suffer; under calamity, or poverty, or shame, she might kill herself like enough, but exist in pain or want she would never."

"That is true,"—he paced still to and fro the chamber, his head sunk down on his chest. He knew that it was true; that this child whom he had rescued from the dreariness of death by hunger, thirst, and the chills of the night, was of that temperament to which existence must be sweet, rich, uncheckered, or else,—is cast off by rash passion in the first hour of desolation.

He knew that with himself happiness could not come to her, since in her sight that magic gift could only be summoned by a wand of gold. She desired these things which now were offered to her: though the effort were to kill him he would not seek to hold her through her gratitude, nor permit pity to approach him from those whom she selected in his stead. His pride arose to repress the evidence of pain before the man to whom her allegiance would henceforth be given, by choice and preference.

He came and stood before her host, grave, calm, with a haughty and patient composure, beneath which all passion and all pain were alike held down in silence.

"You make a great offer; a generous offer," he said briefly. "From you, moreover, it is dictated by no design of a libertine, no desire of a voluptuary. I comprehend your intention, and I honor its charity. Its acceptation or its refusal lies with her whom it concerns, not with me. It were idle to affect to doubt which it will receive. Were she my daughter I should refuse, in her name, a liberality which, however nobly tendered, must still be an alms. But, having no sort of title to her life, I can have no justification in forcing her away from your charity, which can bestow on her the magnificence she covets, to retain her under mine, which can scarcely at its best lift her above poverty. Let your mother state to her to-night what you have stated to me; let her, then, weighing well the two, choose betwixt you and me. A thing of so much moment should not be hastily adopted or rejected. I foresee many objections to your plan: many reasons why much trouble may come to you through it; we do not know whence she comes, nor who may some day claim her. But this is for your judgment; not for mine."

The Duke de Lira answered nothing. He stood, looking earnestly and with a curious wonder on the man who thus addressed him with all the tone of one gentleman to another, though speaking of poverty and clad in the guise of a laborer. With a sudden impulse he spoke aloud the perplexity that had baffled him from the hour when he had first seen the revolutionist, with the hymn of the Marseillaise in his lips, and the red flag above his head, drive back the plunderers from out his court of honor.

"Tricotrin! *what are you?* Forgive me the insolence, if insolent it be, for sake of the friendship I would bear you if you let me. A bohemian, a genius, a scholar, a democrat, a wanderer, a man who might be everything, and who chooses to be nothing. What can one make of you?"

Tricotrin's fine delicate lips laughed slightly.

"Sir—the people do not share your perplexity. I would make myself intelligible to your Order, if I cared for their comprehension. I am no mystery that I know of; save that truly a man who does not care for greed or for gain is an anomaly in this day! But I do not care to speak of myself. I thank you for your offer of friendship; but I make no friendships. And from your order to mine they would savor too much of patronage for my taste. Let us rather conclude the matter which alone unites us,—for a season. You desire absolutely to adopt Viva into your family and your station?"

"I do so."

"You remember that contingencies may arise that I cannot avert? No one knows whence she came, nor by whom she was born or begotten; there is the possibility at any time of claimants arising; specially so when she is of prominence in the world."

"That we must hazard. I think that there is little. I have had fresh inquiries instituted whence you discovered her; but there appears no clew whatever to her parentage or her abandonment. And the crime of such abandonment will keep silent its perpetrators. Moreover,—who has seen her in that little chalet by the Loire? A few peasants only. There are indeed Coriolis and her young lover, but we can guard her from their sight until such time as, with her womanhood, she shall have so changed that they would never dream of her identity. Unless you choose to reveal it, none need recognize her in the new life she will lead."

"I shall not do so. At the same time let it be understood that I cannot guard you or her from such possibilities. And I deem them more perilous than you do. Women like Coriolis never forget aught—save their God. Nor on the other hand will I surrender my right to have free access to her whenever I may deem fit. Account for my connection with her as you please: but I will not be debarred from some watch over her life."

"Heaven forbid you should be. If she ever forget what she owes to you——."

"She will forget it. It is not remembrance of that kind that I need. But I desire to have, always, the power to judge for myself of how far from, or how near to, happiness she be. You may trust me to exercise the power in such wise as will be best for her. As regards wealth,—it would not be just, that taking her to a glittering life, she should be abandoned to the chances of caprice; or left to poverty if your mother die. Therefore, let the Duchess de Lirà settle on her such sum as she shall deem just, if Viva decide—and there can be no question but she will so decide—on acceptance of your offer. Let her ponder well, understand fully, what it is she does. As she selects, then so be her future. If I do not thank you as you may deem you deserve, believe that I do not the less appreciate the gentleness and benevolence which move you. I leave you to acquaint her yourself of your will with her. You can then propose to her all that you desire, and see if she accept your guardianship: there can be no doubt that she will do so."

As he turned to move away, his host stretched out his hand to arrest him.

"Stay! Tricotrin, if it give you pain, if it cause you regret, to part with her to our keeping, I do but ill repay the debt I owe to you?"

"You owe me none. I forced my people from plunder and incendiarism: think you I should have done otherwise if they had attacked the house of my enemy?"

"No matter, I do not hold what you did so lightly. Well

as they loved you they were nigh turning on you for thwarting them, like tigers balked of their spoil. And if to lose the child you have cherished cause you one pang of regret——"

Tricotrin stopped the phrase on his lips with a smile that had an irony more mournful than tears.

"Pshaw! Is there aught that we love that does not stab us, somewise, soon or late? There is no serpent without, that can sting half so hard as the tenderness in us!"

Then, his pride forbidding him even so much as these words of reproach and lament, he laughed as he passed to the door.

"I am a wanderer, and have no ties to be ruptured. You solve a problem that began to grow knotted and vexatious in my hands. I should thank you more than I have done. Without you Viva would most likely have passed to the path of Coriolis. Her rescue is my obligation. Adieu!"

He was gone as the farewell was spoken: in his hand was the injured Arlecchino. Even a trifle that pleasured her had worth in his eyes; and a promise concerning a toy had its bond on him, even though the toy were his rival.

As he passed an open door, a soft, silvery, luminous thing sprang through it toward him; it was the form of Viva, in the airy grace of her evening appareling.

"You are not going?" she whispered. "Madame receives to-night, and they have dressed me early—I want you to look at me!"

His breath came and went, swift and hard. While his heart was breaking over her, this frivolous thing only heeded the sweep of laces and the shimmer of silks!

"You were fairer in your vine garland," he said briefly.

She gave a sigh of impatience.

"Oh! how can you say so? Just look at me, I am all snow and silver, like a fairy."

And she shook herself, and whirled round lightly, that the gossamer tissues might gleam in the light and float on the air. A strange dreamy memory of the German Willis of legend, who dances in the midsummer moonlight, and with whom whosoever dance also must perish ere dawn, came to him in the moment, as such weird fancies will come to minds of the strongest.

"Nature has given you beauty. Take heed how you use it," he said wearily. "But you are too young for these pleasures, Viva."

"Oh! They only let me go for one hour, just to see and be seen," she murmured, with the tears still wet on her flushed cheeks. "And it is so beautiful there! and the great ladies caress me, though I think that they hate me in their hearts! and the great nobles tell me they never saw anything half so lovely as I am. And I think it is true when I look in the mirrors: there is no one like me!"

The confession was so naive; the vanity, as yet so innocent; even in that hour he could not choose but smile at them, though the smile was very mournful.

"From the world they prepare you for, and the world of Coriolis there is little difference, save a glazing of lip honor! But—what can they call you in this house to their guests?"

"Only Viva: there is mystery kept up about me. It is thought that I am the grandchild of a dead friend of madame's, whom she has discovered in an obscure position. Nothing definite is told. Madame likes to have it all shadowy and vague, and to excite people's interest without conceding anything to their curiosity."

"So! You take kindly already to the lies of the great world?"

Viva colored: the dauntless haughty nature of the child was instinctively and inherently truthful, and he had trained her to look on falsehood as the disgrace of the coward.

"I do not say anything," she murmured. "It is supposed so, and I am not to contradict it. Madame tells me that it would never do to allow it to be divined that I am—a foundling."

The last abhorred word was very low; it could not be consoled to her even by her own convictions of her splendid though hidden lineage, which she never doubted would soon or late blossom out into some magnificence of heritage and celebrity.

"No!" he said, with a grave tenderness in his tone that moved her strangely. "And yet, though you will deem me cruelly harsh to say so, I doubt if it would not be better for your future if that one memory of what you were could be kept ever before you! I see you to-morrow—farewell."

She stood irresolute and remorseful as he passed away; then, a strain of music caught her ear, and she turned to a mirror near.

"I shall have no beauty if I cry!" she thought, and she choked back the sobs which were fast rising in her throat as she looked at her own reflection.

CHAPTER XXVII.

"She has accepted. It is quite natural she should have done so."

He spoke quietly, with a grave courtesy, where he stood on the morrow in the chamber of the Duchess de Lirà. He was quick to conceal all emotion, impassioned and impulsive though his nature was; and he came before them calm, careless, full of the ready wit and of the easy negligence of his habitual manner. His temper made him fling off pain; and, having once resolved to surrender her up to those who virtually purchased her by superior wealth, he was none the less resolved to conceal from them that the surrender cost him aught. The intelligence that she had thus chosen was no blow to him: he had not dreamed that she would choose otherwise. All that she desired they could bestow; nothing that she desired could he accord her; and he knew well how the affections of such feminine Caprices as Viva were guided by their sunny and unconscious egotism.

The old aristocrat studied him with well-concealed wonder. She knew of the debt that her son had owed to him in the times of the revolution; but she abhorred every form of revolution, and had imagined him a coarse eccentric man of the people who could be dismissed as soon as his Waif were purchased from him, as easily as the husk of a chestnut is thrown away, when the sweet snowy kernel is extracted. She was lost in the same amazement and wrath as had at the first moved her at finding in the bohemian whom she had thought to relieve by taking a burden from his hands, a man who dictated terms to her, and made the presence of a foundling in her house as grave a matter as the betrothal of a princess, and spoke to her with all the dignity and power of an equal, while he fascinated her by an irresistible charm she could neither analyze nor dispute.

Though worldly-wise and haughty to coldness, the aged duchess had a certain gentleness of heart, and a great generosity. The desire of her beloved and only living son was law to her; and although she had viewed at first with aversion and disgust his attraction toward a nameless, and doubtless bastard child, she had ended by feeling a woman's tenderness for the child herself; whose native grace, pride, and refinement, assimilated themselves so rapidly to her own. Her son's desire had been at first inexplicable and most unwelcome to her: but now, there had come into her thoughts a vague conception which she did not like to brood upon, yet which insensibly served to reconcile her to his wishes: the threatened extinction of his race was a great misery to her, her craving for its perpetuation still stronger than her pride; as it seemed he could never be wooed by those of his own rank,—since the days of his earliest youth when a cruel treachery had taught him his alienation from their sex,— would it not be better that he should wed even with a peasant than leave his name to perish?

If this were ever to be so, the preparation and commencement for it must be, she resolved, the absolute and unalterable banishment of all things connected with the girl's past life. Therefore her chagrin and her wrath were great, when in the man whom she projected to dismiss forever, she encountered as proud a spirit, and as resolute a will as her own, one who scarcely thanked her for her splendid offer, and who dictated conditions as though he, not she, were the patron and the donor.

At his last stipulation, she, had it not been for her son, would have bade him take back his foundling and make a servant, a gipsy, an actress of her, what he would: yet the last stipulation which offended her so deeply was but this:

"I have only one thing more to add," said Tricotrin, when their interview drew nigh its end. "It is to stipulate that I, myself, shall never be denied access to her. You can account for my knowledge of her as seems best to you. I have spoken my desire that she should never be painfully reminded of her past, or led to feel that she is deemed of an inferior class to that in which she will henceforth move; you may be certain therefore that my presence will never be forced on her, unadvisedly or inopportunely. But I will not surrender the right to judge for myself of her happiness or unhappiness. I will not relinquish the power of ascertaining the truth concerning her welfare. I will not consent to become as a stranger to her."

"It is impossible," commenced Madame de Lira; but her son, standing beside her chair, laid his hand on hers:

"Nay, madame, it is but just," he said quietly.

"It is but just," repeated Tricotrin, calmly, "to myself and to her. All that I know of her history you know; and that all is nothing. But I have taken, of my own will, the maintenance and direction of her life. Having once assumed those, I should err to her if I did not continue to hold, at least, the ability to know how life goes with her in her future. I have said, and I repeat it if that be needful, that I shall exercise the right with all due regard to her position or your prerogative; but the right itself I shall not relinquish. She will see me very rarely, very rarely indeed, if she be happy; but whenever she needs me—if ever she needs me—I shall be there."

"Surely!" interposed the duke, still with that gentle touch of his hand on hers, entreating silence from his mother.

"Do not think that we seek to teach her either ingratitude or oblivion."

"There will be no need to teach them. Both will come self-sown! Nay! Do not think I say this either in irony or blame. She is human; why should we expect her to be above humanity? I thank you for your kindness toward her I see in it a beneficence to myself. For evil would have touched her in obscurity and want of riches. You have saved her from the chance—the certainty—that in the only life she could have led through me she would one day have cursed me that I ever came between her and the death that was allotted to her in her infancy. To you, madame, I need say nothing. You are a woman,—I need not remind you that she is worse than motherless? You are of gentle blood,—I need not bid you remember that a scornful word, which is a jest to the well-born, can sting like a serpent what is desolate and dependent? You are aged,—I need not solicit from you sympathy and patience with the fanciful enthusiasms and wayward ways of youth? The gift of your gold will be the generosity that the world will appraise. It is the gift of your love and your gentleness that I would bespeak for Viva. An old peasant-woman gave them; they were all she had to give. But—unless they be added to your treasures likewise, the child, amid riches, will remain poor indeed. I will bid her farewell now; and then—she has her will, she is yours."

His voice was calm and unbroken throughout the words, yet there was an accent in them that thrilled through the hearts of his hearers; and, as she heard, dimmed with a strange unwonted emotion, the keen eyes of the chill, imperious, disdainful protectress of what had forever abandoned him.

"He dictated to *me!*" she murmured, as he quitted the chamber, moved as she had never been through many years, beneath whose ice the love she had borne her son had been the only living thing of warmth. "And you called him a man of the people, my son!"

"He calls himself so——"

"Of the people? Of the mob? Ridiculous! He has the voice of a man born to rule; he has the grace and the negligence of courts. What is there of the populace about him?"

"Nothing save his sympathies. They are wholly with the people."

"Bah! that is no rule. One is sometimes tired of one's self—of one's order. How else would you get your Egalités, your Mirabeaux? There are conservative work-people; there are democrative princes. You know nothing else of him?"

"Nothing. No one knows anything of Tricotrin."

"Tricotrin! Pshaw! Tricotrin! Is that a name? It means nothing!", answered the old patrician, with impatience. "That man has borne some other name; that man must have been noble once!"

"Why so? He is a scholar, an artist, a genius, but a bohemian, nevertheless, to the core. For the twenty years and more that I have heard of him he has been simply what he is, a lawless wanderer of the '*école buissonnière.*'"

Madame de Lira shook her silvered head.

"No matter! He must have *race* in him. Heraldry may lie; but voices do not. Low people make money, drive in state, throng to palaces, receive kings at their tables by the force of gold; but their antecedents always croak out in their voices. They either screech or purr; they have no clear modulations. Besides, their women always stumble over their train, and their men bow worse than their servants. But this man, look you,—he has high blood in his veins, however he come by it. And—he suffers."

Her acute, penetrative acumen had pierced to the truth, though with it she had never once seemed to have a pulse of sympathy. Her son paced slowly and musingly to and fro her chamber, with an anxious shadow on his face.

"I hope not," he said, with a pang of self-remorse. "I hope to heaven not! I have done for the best——"

"Bah!" murmured the duchess, with her delicate irony. "Do not use those words. Nobody ever takes refuge in them except when they divine they have—done wrong. Half the misery of this world is made by persons 'doing for the best,' instead of leaving others alone to do just as they choose! It is 'best' for her, of course—the pretty, heartless thing. But for the man,—it is a little bitter. Your silver Harlequin and my gold shoe-buckles outweigh him, and all his years of care, with her; it is a little bitter—that!"

"It must be so—indeed!" murmured her son; and for his good deed he felt a deeper remorse than many feel for brutal crimes.

He had gone to her where she had stayed during the hour of their converse, in a dainty, radiant little room that was called hers. She was kneeling by one of its couches, with her head bowed down upon the pile of cushions, as he entered. She had chosen as her desire and her ambition dictated, chosen as her vanity entreated, chosen as the evil spirit that her Prince Fainéant had awakened in her, tempted and urged her to do. And yet there were sorrow and shame on her; she felt unworthy in her own sight. In the moment of her triumph she felt humiliated; in the very seizure of her wishes she felt disappointed.

Though vain things too often obscured it, the core of her heart was pure and brave; its fibers were of nobler stuff than the egotisms and the frivolities that surrounded it. There were dauntlessness and truth enough there still to make her know that she had acted basely; that the humblest peasant-girl working in the vineyards in summer droughts for her own existence, was more near to true dignity and freedom than was she; that the coarsest shepherd or swineherd, keeping his herds upon the plains, and giving of his poor wage to the parent or the benefactor who had reared him, was nobler and more grateful than herself.

Her pride told her that she should refuse all alms however disguised in a magnificent liberality; her conscience told her that she should reject all temptations, however glittering and alluring, which would banish from her the lives that had sheltered and succored her own. She was well aware that she was won by the purples and fine linens, the brilliancies and the aggrandizements of the bribe by which she was enthralled; and she was worthless in her own eyes.

For the second time in her life she shrank from the presence of the only living creature that she loved; in his gaze she felt an accusation; in his voice she heard the accents of a judge. Though she had done naught against him she felt as though she had betrayed him; she had forsaken him; she had denied him; she had been ashamed of her allegiance to him. She knew that she had sinned as sinned the faithless disciple who denied his master.

The bread of life, and the food of the spirit, had alike come to her from his hand and from his voice; he had bestowed on her daily bread through his charity, and had raised her soul toward high imperishable things by his words. She owed him a greater debt than the nourishment of her mortal form; she owed him the rescue of her mind from the sloughs of ignorance and vice;—and the way that she paid this debt was to desert him for the bribes of wealth! Her truer nature told her that, although following in its flight the gilded arrow of ambition, she had in that desertion left the greatness which was pure and lofty for the greatness which was a toy of tinsel.

To be true, to preserve truth unstained at any cost, had been the one lesson he had ever taught her; and she would be henceforth a lie—delicate, sunlit, harmless indeed, but still a lie to herself and the world.

When the vine wreath had dropped, crushed and broken on the floor, Viva would have given the world, if she had owned it, to bring back the bloom and the freshness to the bright crown that she had scorned because the people had woven it, and a great man had seen her wear it. Her old child-life that she had despised and rebelled against because it was obscure and simple, and led amid peasantry,—would she sigh as vainly for it, she wondered, as she had done for the lost grape garland?

Yet she cast it from her heedlessly and willingly.

Until the vine leaves of youth are faded, who knows their value or sweetness? None, alas! while yet the violet down is on the grapes, while yet the hair that they crown is unsilvered by time.

Some vague sense of the bitter fact that corrodes all human life—the fact that desire is everything, fruition or possession but little—came to Viva, in the granting of her wish, as it comes to the lover, the monarch, the bride, the hero, the statesman, the poet, all alike, when that which they have sighed for, and thirsted for, lies feasted on to satiety within their tired grasp.

Viva had gained the "great world;" and because she had gained it all the old things of her lost past grew unalterably sweet to her now that they no longer could be hers. The brown, kind, homely, tender face of grand'mère; the gambols of white and frolicsome Bebée; the woods where, with every spring, she had filled her arms with sheaves of delicate primroses; the quaint little room with its strings of melons and sweet herbs; its glittering brass and pewter, its wood-fire with the soup-pot simmering above the flame; the glad free days in the vineyard, and on the river, with the winds blowing fragrance from over the clover, and flax, and the acacias and lindens; nay, even the old, quiet, sleepy hours within the convent-walls, lying on the lush unshaven grass, while the drowsy bells rang to vespers or compline;—all became suddenly precious and dear to her when once she knew that they had drifted away from her for evermore.

But never yet so dear or so precious that they made her waver in her choice. The young wood-dove fluttered her white wings in impatience for their flight from the forest-covert to the rose aisles of kings' gardens.

And he—thanked God that he had found strength, against himself, to bid her go where heart, and fancy, and desire had already taken flight, as he beheld her on that morning in which, for the last time, he was with her as the guide and guardian of her life.

She had been robbed from him, less by the tempting of

others than by the discontent of her own soul. It was cruel as the serpent's tooth to relinquish the grace of her caressing ways, the fairness of her perfect loveliness, the watch of her bright and wayward intellect, to others.

He who loved Mankind, but who had long had no special love within his heart, had grown in the last few months to passionately cherish and desire her. Yet to hold by force, what he could not gain from fidelity, would have been an egotism and a baseness impossible to him.

"You think me wicked!" she murmured, as he stood beside her. "You think me ungrateful—selfish—full of greed? I told you the other night that I would not take their charity, however splendid it might be—and I have taken it. I have——"

"Hush!" he said, gravely. "Speak of it no more—never more. You have chosen—chosen where your desire already had run before you. You have not known when you were happy; such ignorance is ingratitude to fate. You are happy now, with such happiness as comes from granted wishes; be wise enough to know it."

"Ah, yes!" she said, with a sudden vibration of passionate repentance in her voice. "I have my wishes; but I feel weak and guilty in the joy of them. Just so I longed for jewels; but when that young prince gave me them, although I loved them, I never felt at peace. And it is just so now!"

"Child,—what title have you, do you think, to escape the doom of all humanity? You desire—you possess—and you find repentance and satiety already lying, in wild justice, at the core of the thing you have coveted. You are no exception; you have the common fate of all mortality."

"But then it is because what I desired was wrong. When I wished for the vine-feast, when I wished for your coming, when I wished for the swallows' return, when I wished for a sail on the water, it was not so;—I was so happy when my wishes came——"

"Because your desires then were innocent. Nay, they are now no guilt, but they are corroded, they are born of envy and the lusts of wealth; and their advent is not peace, because your conscience is in unrest at their purchase."

"Because I know myself so false to you!" she cried, in that breathless terror of a sudden remorse. "Because, while I love all these things that I gain, I know myself so base, so unworthy, so unfaithful to you who have been to me in the stead of father, mother, brethren, friends, and home! Because I know that all my lifetime spent in service and fidelity to you could not repay you all the long years debt I owe! I choose the life they offer me,—I cannot help but choose it, it draws me to it with a sorcery. I pine, I long, I thirst to be in greatness, and if I had refused it and had gone back with you, the evil in me would have made me vile, the longing in me would have made me restless, the discontent in me would have made me your torture, not your blessing! I cannot help what I do. Forgive me for it if you can!"

The impetuosity, broken and vehement, of the words, but ill told the conflict in her heart; the conflict betwixt the irresistible delights of that new world which tempted her, and the remorseful clinging of her old affections to their severed ties. He heard in silence; the time was past when it could give him either hope or dread; when it could move him to expectation or disappointment.

Through all these years he had taken thought of her,—the young forsaken creature for whom no other cared,—he had denied himself that she might enjoy; he had put down the wine-cup untasted that she might have bread, oftentimes; he had broken in the careless laughter-loving indolence of his temper to the deliberate acceptance of labor, that the trust he had self-assumed might be borne out by her maintenance. And all this was counted as naught; all this was swept aside as though it had never been, by the first proffer of a rich man's gold!

But it was his nature to give lavishly and royally; it was his nature to appraise as nothing the good that he did to others; therefore no word of reproach escaped him where he stood alone with her, on this morning when she accepted as a charmed gift from a beauteous fate the life that would sever her from him forever. One thing only, in which would have been for her the deepest reproach of all, had not her self-absorption prevented her being stung by it, did he ask her. It was simply,

"Viva,—do not wholly forget me!"

As it was she felt in that one moment of its utterance a pang such as rarely struck through the playfulness and pride, the vanity and airy willfulness of her nature.

She looked upward with impassioned feeling.

"Forget you! If ever I do may God himself forget me!"

He shrank slightly, as though the future veiled from her was clear to him; as though oblivion of himself were so sure and so inevitable that in her words he heard her self-invocation of abandonment by her God.

"Make no rash vows," he said gently. "Do not touch the future; let it come as it will. Though you do utterly forget me may all that I wish for you be with you to your life's end."

"But how *could* I forget you!" she cried, as if in terror at that doom which to him seemed so certain, and to her so impossible. "Could I grow so base, so cruel, so vile, so brutally unworthy of all your love and pity?"

He smiled: the smile she had so often seen of late; of a sadness she could not gauge, of an irony she could not comprehend, of a bitterness she could not fathom.

"Nay; you will only grow—a beautiful woman and worldly. No more! An ingrate? Well! are you not that, my little one, to the good old creature you call grand'mère? Her heart hungers for you, you know that well, yet for sake of Madame la Duchesse, and the dresses, and the pleasures, and the jeweled toys, you will leave grand'mère to sorrow alone, and be solaced as best she may!"

Viva's face crimsoned.

"It is selfish, I know. It is wicked!" she murmured. "But grand'mère always said 'never mind me, my child; do what pleases you;' and in a little while I will get them to let me go and see her, and I will show her all my pretty things, and take her some presents, such as she would——"

"No!" he interrupted her with an accent that was almost savage in its intensity. "Do not insult what you desert! Your absence will shut the last lingering light out of her life; do not think to heal the wound that you have made by gifts bought with rich people's gold!"

She was frightened and stilled by his sudden violence; with it there seemed to break on her all the strength and the value of this great love, all its grandeur and its rarity, with which she had played, knowing no more of its force and its beauty than a little child playing with sapphires and diamonds knows of their worth. With a sudden impulse of remorse, and fear, and repentance, she nerved herself to sacrifice all her ambitions and all her delights.

"If you wish it let me go home!" she cried, in sudden and sincere renunciation. "If it pain you let me stay there always! I would not give you an hour's sorrow for all the bribes of France!"

But in the cry there was only a love that entreated to stay near him for his sake, not its own; a love as of a child's petulant pliant affection; a love that to the burning passions of the man was well-nigh worse than none; a drop of dew when he thirsted for the ocean, a gleam of light, making the darkness greater, a Tantalus touch upon the lips of the fruit denied to them, a ray of the pale moon when he longed for the full rich glow of southern suns.

But all that he felt he restrained.

"Not so," he answered her. "The die is cast and you must go, Viva. And—to wish for the time to come when you should desire to return would be to wish your dreams false, your faith betrayed, your paradise poisoned by the serpent, your glorious hopes all cheated and misled. It were to love you ill to wish you back at such a cost. No! As you are happy in your new life so will you forget your old; as you go nearer the fruition of your prayers so will you go further from me. So be it, if for your joy."

Once again there stole upon her with a sense of terror, and of guilt, in her own unworthiness, some perception of

the majesty and the purity of this martyred love passion
which asked nothing for itself but all for her. She trembled
greatly, like one who leaves hold of some long-tried and
never-failing support to plunge down into an unknown abyss.

He saw that, and in his infinite self-sacrifice hastened to
comfort her, and to lead her thoughts from what he suffered.

"Now listen to a few last words," he said softly, with an
effort, so successful, at his old familiar tone, that she was
stilled and reassured. "You go to what you desire: you will
have riches, luxuries, gayeties, brilliancies, all around you;
you will have indulgence, and in a year or two more, homage. But, Viva, none of these things will suffice to you unless your own heart be at peace. You have a noble nature
in much; but you have grave errors that will mar all the rest
if they be allowed to grow and to strengthen. You have delight in your loveliness,—that is natural: but the illness of a
week, as I have reminded you ere now, may sweep it away
forever. How will it be with you, then, if your soul has been
anchored on the allurements of your face? Win regard and
attachment on something surer. You are too proud, and
everything in your new existence will tend to heat and to
pamper that fault. If you have any tenderness for me you
will strive against that besetting sin of yours, or it will make
you very cold, very cruel, very arrogant, very avaricious! It
will kill all the divinity in you as surely as the frost kills the
flowers. Nor will it, like the frost, leave the good root below unseen, but still not slain, to blossom out again. For the
nature frozen by the ice of greed, and vanity, and unscrupulous ambition, there comes no spring: but all is night and
winter there. Keep only such pride as shall ever rise above
all taint of falsehood or of meanness, and gain you that true
dignity, a stainless name. To Madame de Lirà, who henceforth will have authority over you, you will be gentle, grateful, with such reverence as becomes the young to the old,
and never forgetful that you owe her very much more than
it will be in your power ever to repay. And for the rest,—
well!—the future must bring you what it will, but you will
have the surest shield to meet it, if you gain for yourself

that temper which adversity cannot appall, and prosperity cannot exalt, which knows not fear as it knows not vanity, and which in trial is dauntless, as in happiness it is gentle and pitiful of others. I have read you a homily, Viva mine, but I do not think it will be altogether forgotten; and if,- as you have said,—you deem that there is any question of debt betwixt you and me, and you would care to reward me, and to pleasure me for the little I have done for your childhood, show me thus thy sincerity and fidelity;—by curbing what I who love you best have blamed, and by keeping your glorious nature uncorrupted from the world. When you are tempted, Viva, by your beauty, and glad pride, and brilliant besetting sins, that seem to have no evil to you, because they are masked in such proud and witching disguises, think of this that I have asked of you;—if I have had place in your heart one hour you will have strength to resist temptation then."

His voice had deepened from the playfulness with which he had at first spoken, into a grave and earnest softness, but into no other tenderness than that which he had ever had of old with her; they were wise and gentle counsels, and all that he called, not unjustly, her more glorious nature awoke and stirred in instant and ardent response.

"I will, I will!" she murmured passionately. "I will remember every word; every time that I am proud, and wayward, and wicked, I will think of you; I will try to be all you will; I will pray night and day to God to make me so! And,—as for forgetting you,—Viva will never love any one in the wide world as she loves you. Never, never, never!"

Tricotrin did not answer, but he laid his hand on her fair, bowed head, with a smile infinitely beautiful, infinitely mournful.

He foresaw the future more clearly than she. There was a long silence in the little luxurious chamber; while the winter sun fell through the deep-hued painted panes, and touched them where they stood with light; then she clung to him with her old caressing grace: "Play to me once—once!"

He looked on her, still with the same smile.

"Child, however thy new life indulges thee, and strews thy path with roses, thou wilt not be more spoilt than thou hast been as a Waif!"

Then he bent his head, letting her desire be his law; and that music, which had given its hymn for the vintage feast of the Loire, and which had brought back the steps of the suicide from the river-brink in the darkness of the Paris night, which sovereigns could not command, and which held peasants entranced by its spell, thrilled through the stillness of the chamber.

Human in its sadness, more than human in its eloquence, now melancholy as the Miserere that sighs through the gloom of a cathedral midnight, now rich as the glory of the afterglow in Egypt, a poem beyond words, a prayer grand as that which seems to breathe from the hush of mountain solitudes when the eternal snows are lighted by the rising of the sun, —the melody of the violin filled the silence of the closing day.

The melancholy, ever latent in the vivid natures of men of genius, is betrayed and finds voice in their Art. Goethe laughs with the riotous revelers, and rejoices with the summer of the vines, and loves the glad abandonment of women's soft embraces, and with his last words prays for Light. But the profound sadness of the great and many-sided mastermind thrills through and breaks out in the intense humanity, the passionate despair of Faust; the melancholy and the yearning of the soul are there.

With Tricotrin they were uttered in his music.

Other arts Earth still mingles with and profanes; passion is in the poet's words, the senses wake with the painter's voluptuous hues, and the sculptor dreams but of the divine beauty of a woman's form; but with music the soul escapes all bondage, and rises where the world has no share, unclogged and uncompanioned. His heart spoke in those wild, pathetic, nameless, melodies as it never spoke in human language: he who should have read them aright would have read this man's life by its master-key.

As Viva listened to the harmonies which had been her dearest delight from her earliest years, the slow tears gathered in her eyes, the flush faded from her face, leaving it very pale, she pushed back the shining masses of hair off her brow, and stood as she had stood long before in her infancy, when the Straduarius had decided her destiny.

Her future seemed to float before her in the rich fantastic passionate waves of sound that filled the stillness,—that future of sunlight, that future of sovereignty!—and still ever, through all the glory of the melodies, one under-note of deepest sadness seemed to whisper that in all the life to which she went, she should find no love that would equal, in its measure and its sacrifice, this love that had sheltered and shone on her childhood, this love which she had now forsaken.

Then suddenly, the wondrous magic of the music ceased, and dropped, and died; and she threw herself on her knees before him.

"Ah! if I heard that music always, I should never be proud and vain and wayward; I should love and pity all the world; I should do your will, and God's!"

Tricotrin smiled, and the smile was like his melodies.

"Viva mine, were we all what we are in our holiest moments, we were all godlike! Treasure the music in thy heart then; so will it be thy guardian-angel. So shall I have one gift to give thee! And now—farewell!"

At that one word, all the anguish of severance came on her; she loved him with fervent, tender, clinging affection, though she loved yet more dearly her vanity and her pride. She had dwelt joyously away from him because she had been so sure she could go back to him; but now that she had to part with him, and from the home that he had given her, without power to return to them, the fondness that she bore for both conquered every other feeling, and she sobbed as though her very heart were breaking, her head bowed on his breast, her hair flung over his arms.

She did not feel the shudder that ran through him at her touch; she only heard the gentleness of the voice upon her ear.

"My child of chance! The fairies call thee to their Avillion where are no toil, no pain, no shame, to gall thy heart and fret thy pride. No poor grape garland to be heavy on thy brows, no lives of labor about thee to make thee dread a great man's sneer. Go with a happy heart, and spoil not thy present by looking backward at thy past. The past, however bright when it was 'present,' is ever dark with vain desire when it lies behind us, like the lands from whose sky the sun has long gone down. Remember that!"

She made him no reply; but silently clung to him weeping in a very convulsion of love and of repentance; a summer tempest soon to pass, yet none less vivid and desolating, because fated to be evanescent.

He looked mutely down upon her; and where her head was hidden on his breast she could not see the yearning passion that his eyes spoke, for one moment unrestrainedly, because it knew itself unread and unsuspected.

"Ah, true to thy sex!" he murmured bitterly. "Thou mournest me now, a day hence and I shall be forgotten!"

A burning flush dyed her face as she lifted it with impetuous eagerness of denial.

"Never, never, never! I shall never forget you till I die!"

The smile that made her tremble, why she could not have told, was still upon his lips -- the smile of so much tenderness, of such little faith.

"You will die early then! Nay! live in joy ever, though not a thought of me pass over thee. My child—my love! Farewell!"

He held her one moment longer in his embrace, one moment longer pressed his lips on hers: then, ere she knew it, drew her still closer yet, once more, thrust her quickly from his arms and left her; their lives were cut in twain forever.

CHAPTER XXVIII.

Wild winds were driving snow across the vineyards and the plains in blinding white sheets of powder; the swollen river was black and angry, rushing in stormy tide and eddy between its brimming banks; in spots where its torrent had overflowed, a dark sullen sheet of water spread over submerged meadows or ruined gardens; the night was tempestuous, starless, heavy-laden with snow; through it Tricotrin passed, insensible to the furious blasts, the icy cold, the perils of the flood, the fatigue of every step.

When here and there the dim reflection of some lantern, hung upon some wayside cross to guide the way of travelers fell upon his face, it was very pale, and his eyes looked straight forward into the unbroken gloom, unblinded by the sleet that drove against them: in his breast curled Mistigri, and with one arm he held her there and sheltered her from the night.

He made his way, by instinct and by habit, to one familiar place; the great chestnut branches were groaning in the gale, the rush of the river below the rocky slope was like the swelling hoarseness of the sea, the wind was tearing the ivy from the stones where it had clung so long, and scaring the birds in terror from its shelter.

There was a ray of yellow light streaming from an oval hole in the shutter; through it the homely interior was visible, ruddy with the cheerfulness of burning wood, and with the form of an old peasant-woman alone within it. Grand'mère sat, by the wood fire on her hearth, half asleep in the twilight, her high white head-dress nodding to and fro, the chestnuts cracking in the embers, the white cat Bébée purring in the warmth.

She started, and clicked across the floor in her wooden shoes, as a knock came on the door of her dwelling. She threw it wide open with her oil lamp held above her head, and gave a loud glad cry; then she trembled till the lamp rays flickered like a candle flame blown about in the wind.

"Where is the child?" she asked.

"The child is well, grand'mère."

Then he entered and shook off the snow that had fallen on his beard and blouse; and took the little shivering Mistigri from his bosom, and put her kindly down beside Bébée, and unstrapped his knapsack and laid it on a wooden settle. At last with an exceeding gentleness he turned and took the two old withered hands within his own, and looked down into the eyes that had watched him with such mute pathetic entreaty.

"You can bear pain, grand'mère?"

She gazed at him with a hard, fixed, agonized regard that searched his very heart.

"Paris has taken her!" she said slowly, with a terrible bitterness. "I have known it long. Paris is fed with all our blood, all our beauty, all our youth, all our innocence: Paris is never quieted. The children come to the birth and lie at the breast only to be devoured by her when they have fairness or strength in their frame!"

Then casting her serge gown over her head as a matron of Rome cast her robes, she turned from him and leaned against the wall, silent. To her there was no need to say more: Paris, that fatal, beautiful, cruel, pitiless thing that drew all lives within its murderous embrace, had taken the child—all was told.

Tricotrin laid his hand on her shoulder.

"Grand'mère, it is not so bad as you think. Believe me, it is well with Viva."

The old woman uncovered her head, and looked at him with all the fire of her youth flashing through the slow salt tears of age.

"So *they* said,—each one of them! My noble boys! It was well with them they thought—the city was so grand, and the wage so good, and the mirth so gay, how should they have deemed otherwise? Paris wore a smiling front to them; she smiles always, until she sucks the life out of their veins, like the bat that fans men to slumber to kill them. Antoine wrote me it was so well with him! He fought for liberty, he was kissed on the mouth by fair women who called him a hero; he dreamed of freedom for all France, and of the love and the patience of God breathed into the hard souls of men. That was how she lured him, that Paris, whose stones drank his blood. And he died in his youth, with the balls fired into his breast!"

"I know—I know! But Viva——"

"She has gone where he went!—where his brethren went!" she interrupted him fiercely, every line of her brown withered face quivering with grief and with passion. "They could never come back; nor could she, I know well. It is ever the same with Paris—she draws them all in, the youths and the maidens, and when she has got them, she pits them one against each other to ruin them all—the men to tempt the maidens, breathing lust in their ear, and pressing gold in their hands; the women to lure the youths, kissing them blind with bought kisses, and teaching them the pleasure that kills! How should she come back? Can the clay come unburnt from the furnace? Can the callow-bird return from the throat of the squirrel that has drawn down and devoured it? Why did you not slay her with your own hand rather than take her to that gilded and honeyed death that steals the soul with the body?"

Then, once more she turned her head from him, and wept —wept as the aged weep, without hope.

He waited awhile till her grief, wrought almost to frenzy, should have grown calmer.

In the light of the hearth Mistigri trembled, and watched them with her black and melancholy eyes, and stole closer to Bebée, who, himself, slept and purred on, indifferent, so long as the fire burned bright to warm him.

After awhile, Tricotrin spoke, and told her the truth as it stood, and strove to soften the blow, as best it could be softened, by tidings of the child's joy and safety.

Grand'mère heard him in unbroken silence; her gaze never leaving his face, and reading there that she did not suffer alone.

Of his own trial he said naught; he dwelt only on the brightness, on the security, on the eminence of the future that Viva had chosen. What was heartless in her conduct he left unrecorded; what was tender and generous he lingered over. Yet, despite himself, the story was told in weariness, and had the chill of grief in it, as the snow drifted up against the lattice-window, and the red flame grew low in its socket.

They knew that never again would the child's form—that
had lent such light and grace to the little homely chamber
with its blackened elm wainscots and its white-washed walls,
and its pendant strings of thyme, and onions, and pumpkins
swaying from the rafters—come thither to dance upon the
bare floor, and mirror itself in the burnished coppers.

The old peasant heard without answering a word; her
face did not even change when he spoke of the offer which
the duke, in considerate kindliness, had sent for her to make
her home near Viva's new resting-place.

"You need feel no sorrow, no separation," Tricotrin, giving the message, pursued. "They wish that you should live
in all comfort and peace near her. They desire that you
should go where she will go, and dwell on the Lira estates,
where you will see her most likely with every succeeding
autumn of each year. You——"

She rose and stopped him, and spoke for the first time
since her paroxysm of dread and of despair at Paris had
broken forth, in eloquent, quivering invective.

"Tricotrin—I am an old woman and poor, and the time
for my hand-labor is well-nigh passed. But—if so it be
willed that I live on and on through other desolate years, I
will go out and wash linen in the river, clear insects from the
vines, gather fruits for the markets, weed stones from the
trefoil, and beetroot, and sainfoin, ere ever I will take bit or
drop, log of wood or roof of house from those who have
robbed us of her!"

"Nay, it is no robbery. They mean aright——"

"Aright? Can it be aright to build the pile of her glories
on the stone of her ingratitude? Can it be aright to bid a
young child forget the one debt of her life? Can it be aright
to take her into high places, where she shall learn to blush to
tell truth of herself? But let that be! I have no wish to say
ill of her. She has been as the core of my heart for too long.
Only let them know this,—though I shall hunger like one in
famine for the sight of her face and the sound of her voice, I
will never go nigh those who have led her astray. I have no
title to dwell longer under this roof, which was only kept for

her sake; but I have strength still, and I will go and lie down with the oxen, and ask the fowls for their corn, before I will take alms at the hands of your spoilers. I have spoken!"

There was resolve, so strong and so proud, on her face, that it rendered almost beautiful the aged, weather-beaten, sun-bronzed features; her eyes kindled, her mouth set, her voice grew clearer; all the bold, hardy, peasant blood in her rose as it had risen when she was offered the government-alms she flung back, to the rulers who had sent out her first-born to perish in Africa.

Tricotrin saw and heard; and he bent his head with the reverence he ever gave to the pure honesty of this simple and undaunted nature.

"Grand'mère! There is no need to think of that. This place is yours so long as you shall will to have it so. You cannot deem so ill of me as to think that——"

"Tricotrin, you are a generous man; we know that well," she answered him, with the anguish and the wrath in her eyes softening away. "I have never been two leagues outside my own vine country, and shall not begin my travels now. But neither have I ever lived on alms, nor will I now. While I could serve—*her*, it was just that I should take your bread; but now that I am of no use, how should I justify myself to eat it?"

"Hush!" he said, gently, and his voice had an unutterable sweetness in it. "Every man owes a debt to his mother; mine died ere I knew her. I can only pay it to her sex. Do not fly from my shelter. Your hearth is the only home that I know. Keep it,—lest ever I wander to it weary and maimed. Keep it,—lest ever the child that you lose should find her visions fade as she pursues them, and learn to long for its refuge and pine for its peace."

As he spoke, the brave, strong, sunburnt face, on which the light from the fire played, grew paler and more tender, till all the passion died from it.

"Tricotrin,—you are a noble heart," she said, slowly. "You know how to cover your charities with the grace and the goodness of souls that give as God gives the sun and the fruits and the harvest. But think you she will ever come back?—nay, listen. I thought so too when my lads went forth; they flung their glad arms round me, and they kissed me with their honest lips, and they all whispered in my ear 'we shall be back so soon!' And the one would come as a great soldier with crosses on his breast; and the other would come as a rich man to wed the little yellow-haired girl at the water-mill, and rear up his young children around me; and Antoine—my handsome Antoine!—would come as a liberator, as a redeemer, as a chief of the people, to bind France in one vast brotherhood of peace. Well! one was slaughtered in African raids; and one was crushed by a building stone; and one was shot down by his countrymen's carbines. That is how they 'come back' to us—the children of our love!"

She turned away, and employed herself in her homely household cares, heaping the wood upon the flames, scalding some red wine in a copper stoup, brushing the snow down from off his outer garment. The peasant instinct and habit of her life led her to labor as the only palliative of woe.

"It is an awful night, Tricotrin," she said, spreading bread and chestnuts before him. "You must have felt the storm bitterly."

He bent his head in silence. The food and the steaming wine stood untouched beside him. Looking at him earnestly, as in the first hour of her anguish she had been too blinded by her grief to do, she saw that the fairness of his face had lost all color, and that the sun-hued waves of his hair were whitening with other silver than the silver of the snow.

And her heart hardened against the child whom she had nurtured and cherished from that early time when the tearful smiling eyes of the forsaken thing had first looked up at her from the ferns and the blue fraxinella. She laid her brown, wrinkled hand gently on his shoulder.

"Tricotrin,—when my sons went forth, one spoke of duty to his flag, and one spoke of duty to his betrothed, and one spoke of duty to his country; but not one of the three remembered that duty might lie nearer his own hearth; not one of the three remembered that I had endured the pangs of their birth, the woes of their infancy, the fret of their passions, the evils of their maintenance. The children never remember— they live in themselves. But when in turn they grow heartsick, and are betrayed, and hunger and thirst, desolate amid the wealth of the world, then they remember us, and yearn for us—then we are avenged. She forgets you now. In the day of her necessity she will pray for you, and, it may be, pray vainly."

A shiver, that was not of the cold of the night, shook him as he heard. The deep quivering voice of the speaker had the terror as of prophecy in it.

"God forbid," he answered her, "that ever my vengeance should come so!"

"It would be but justice," she muttered. "But the only justice we get upon earth breaks our own hearts when it falls."

And she left him, and went into her own chamber, and wept bitterly, as the aged alone weep, when the light of their eyes has passed from them for evermore, and none other can ever illumine the brief dark space that parts them from the grave.

CHAPTER XXIX.

"Write to me to the care of Mère Rose," he had said, when he had parted from her. "If thou art happy—keep silence. But when aught pains thee, write."

To the house in the Pays Latin, where she had once heard the grisette sigh for those who went to the Rome of their desires, her letters flew, for awhile, swiftly as carrier-pigeons. For the heart of the child was at unrest, and full of love, and therefore full of love's twin-brother, pain.

When the spring deepened to summer, the winged words came more seldom. They were carrier-birds made laggard by the tempting of warm suns and luscious fruits, and by the luring melody of winds and waters.

With the autumn but very few ever came. They were as doves that would not answer to those who murmured their

old familiar names, because they better loved the peace
and abundance of the palm-groves in a new and brighter land.

Through the year that followed they almost ceased; one,
here and there, in a stretch of many months, still coming,
like the single bird that bore the olive-branch of hope.

Not seldom he would make long pilgrimages from north
or south, from east or west, to ask that single question: "is
there any letter, Mère Rose?"

And when she, leaning from her lattice, would shake
her head, with tears in her brown comely eyes, he would turn
away.

"So best: it is well with her then."

But the woman would murmur fiercely and sadly, in her
throat: "Nay! it is ill."

And he knew that she was right.

With her body, with her beauty, with her youth it was
well: but with her soul?

At length, one day in a fragrant spring time, when all the
city blossomed and laughed with flower and song, Mère Rose
reached down from her casement, and in her hand lay a letter,
like a little, white, tired bird.

He took it with a light in his eyes that was not from the
bright noon sun: and when he had read it, and another one
that lay within it, he reeled slightly like a man under a blow,
and his lips grew white, and he stood staring blankly up at
the bright sun and seeing naught.

"Is she dead?" cried the woman, from the lattice above.

He looked up at her with blind eyes, and answered
nothing, but went slowly away down the long street, with
heavy staggering steps, as of one in whom there is no life left.

The city was filled with buds, and blossoms, and green
leaves, and with the singing of students and maidens, and
with the joyous laughter of children, and with the fragrance
of tossing lilacs, blue and white, that were flung upward by
boyish hands in the sunlight of the feast day.

But Mère Rose, leaning at her casement, heard nothing,
and saw nothing of these. She was looking down the street
after the man in whose hand the letter was hidden like a

snake that stings the hand which fed it; and from his form, as he passed away into the shadow cast by a dim old gothic church, her eyes wandered into the chamber of the opposite house. The casement stood open; and in the darkness stood the coffin of a woman within.

It waited for burial until the festal time of the Mayday had come and gone.

"Ah, thou saidst truly, poor little one!" murmured Mère Rose, gazing into the chamber of death, so quiet and so dark, amid the light and the song and the blossom of the world around. "'They come back from Rome—yes! But back to those whom they left—never!"

CHAPTER XXX.

"Is the child dead, grand'mère?" the people of the vine country asked with bated breath and anxious eyes.

"Yes—she is dead," the old woman answered ever: and would say no more to all the eager, curious, unceasing questions that were put to her by those who met her at the little chapel in the fields, or in the woods where she gathered her fuel; on the straight road across the plain, as they rode their mules to market, or by the towing-path as they walked above their slowly-laboring boats.

"She is dead," was all she answered: and they knew that it was just thus that she had spoken when the story had come from Paris, creeping tardily and terribly through the awe-stricken country in its hot hush of midsummer silence, that her youngest-born had fallen under the bullets, with the hymn of liberty on his lips.

"The child was dead," they murmured among themselves: they did not feel much wonder; she had never been one of them; she had never seemed of their mould and of their kind; she had always been invested to their sight with something rare and strange, and not of mortal birth. They had watched her careless, useless, cloudless life among the sunshine and the flowers, so unlike to their own hard, toilsome, and unlovely lives, as they might have watched some paradise-bird, had one flown, of a sudden, down amid the swallows of the hamlets, and the plovers of the fields, with all the colors of the east upon its gorgeous wings. "She was dead," they repeated among themselves; and broidered on the naked barren fact a thousand tales woven at evening with their women's flax upon the wheel, or passed from mouth to mouth with the stone-picking in the cornlands, and the insect-seeking amid the vines.

Louis Sarazin, at the ferry, knew the truth; but Sarazin never spoke of it. He only covered over with a piece of tarpaulin, the bench on which she had used to sit in the stern of his old black boat, and let no passenger be seated there. And he would stand very quietly at the door of his cottage, looking wistfully down the stream, hour after hour, if none disturbed him, with the broken oar or the torn sail in his hand, unmended.

"They all go down that river, see you?" he would mutter to his dog. "But none of them come back; I suppose they never want the old landing-place any more. Is it all smooth water there? Are there no shallows and no speats? Do they not have to row against the incoming tide at any time, I wonder? I suppose not, for they never want the old landing-place any more."

Those who heard him, said that in his great age his brain wandered, that his senses were gone, that he saw in his silent highway the highbroad of human life, and grew mad thereon. Only his dog was wiser; his dog only knew his meaning, and pressed more closely, and licked his withered bony hand in tender consolation.

"She was dead:" to all her little native world about the river, on which her glad eyes had opened with so many summer dawns. A few among them said prayers for her departed soul when they knelt down at the wayside cross, from which the thatched roof of the home that she had shared with the swallows was visible where it thrust itself through its cover of green leaves. But the greater number took the words as holding but a figurative meaning, and believed that the child of the fairies had gone to that strange land whence she came, and whispered marvelous things of her, where they sat by the light of the oak log of Noel, or brought the wagons of grapes to the wine-press in the shade of the autumn-browned boughs.

But away southward, when gossips met in the porch of the dairy-house that looked out over the broad, low-lying water-threaded pastures about Villiers, a great-limbed, brown-faced, tawny-skinned milkwoman, with her arms akimbo, and a brutal laugh on her mouth, scoffed at her neighbors' regret and mocked at their idiotcy.

"Dead? Dead? That is what they always say when one of their angels has fallen! Dead? She is no more dead than we are. She is gone to riches and shame, that I warrant you. Oh ho! have you forgot the little liar's story of the magic fruit and the sorcerer's ring on the Indian jasmine? And who was the sorcerer except our young lord?—and what do his dainty jewels always betoken? How blind ye are, blind as bats that butt themselves against a barn door when they are driven out of their nests at noonday! Dead? If she be dead, then are my cows dead where they graze yonder. She was bad, I tell you; bad, core through, like a gourd that has the worm. Did she not call us a set of senseless peasants? and she a bastard too, a bastard most like of the man that fed her! Well—I shall know that lily-white face of hers, with its mouth like yon carnation, and its hair like ripened wheat, a score years hence if ever my eyes light on it. Dead? she is no more dead than that mouse that skirries over the floor. She is only—gone to Paris!"

And she laughed again, cruelly, in the mellow waning evening time; for jealousy is lusty of life, and tenacious of it, and is as the toad which can lie stirless under a stone through many seasons, yet keep its sight and its venom unspent, to use when the stone that has held it down is rolled off it.

Now, which was the truer version, hers, or that gentler belief which mourned the child as innocent and lost, none could tell: for to all questions grand'mère answered ever, "She is dead."

And Tricotrin came no more into the vine country at the harvest-time.

The pipers piped, and the maidens danced, and the oxen drew their loaded wains crowned with green branches, and the ruddy blossoms of the declining years; but no more was heard that sweet, wild, rapturous music that had caught in it all the cadences that the fauns of old had danced to in the virgin forests, while yet the world and the gods had been young.

And to the people who had loved him, there seemed a silence through the land.

CHAPTER XXXI.

On the wild western seaboard, a little hamlet hung upon the rocks like a curlew's storm-swept nest, high in air, and overlooking the wide Biscayan waters.

The great black cliffs were dark as night; the chasms between them were yawning pits, of which no men living told the depth; the land for leagues on leagues inland was a desolate heath, a wilderness of thorny gorse, broken only by gray stones of shattered Druid altars.

Life was hard there; a long incessant struggle with all the forces of the earth and elements, a never-ending contest with the winds and waters to snatch the scanty bitter bread of bare subsistence from out the fishers' mouths. In the long, tempestuous, cruel winters, death entered well-nigh every household, and few boats returned with all those who, at their setting forth, had manned them. The children were early braced to peril, and scourged with the stripes of the sharp sea foam. The aged were old long ere their time, and toiled like mules up and down the steep stairs of rock, laden like mules with driftwood, or with weed flung upward by the storms.

There was a little chapel on one of the highest ridges of the rocks, where a light burned steadfastly all through the blackest nights of hurricane. There were a few huts that formed the village, all huddled together in the hollow of the cliff, like callow-birds fearful of coming ruin. There were men, melancholy, taciturn, rugged, of a hard simplicity, of a doglike fidelity, like most dwellers of the mountains or by the ocean. There were women with the old, iron heroism of amazonian times, whose naked limbs were beaten by the billows, and whose massive arms wrenched drowning bodies from the breakers, till nothing of womanhood remained in their aspect except in the sad steady gaze of their large brooding eyes.

They were a rough, and sometimes a brutal people. They were often beset with the torment of famine; their pitiless stony shores would yield them little, and in revenge they were, in many seasons, without mercy to those who were cast away upon their rocks. There were men among them who thought little of drawing a knife across the neck of a wrecked sailor, and robbing the dead of the gold rings in his ears. They were very lonely in their wind-beaten fastnesses, where their only mates were the seagulls and eagles; they grew half savage, as those who live in such isolation will. Hunger bit them sharply at times; and when they were famished they turned on any prey like lions.

There were higher natures among them, on which solitude and privation had not this influence, on which the noble sublimity and terrific grandeur of their shores produced only gravity and sadness; but there were others—and these were the larger number—who would fight over a drowned corpse, for the sake of the purse belted round its body, like wild beasts over a heap of offal, and who looked on the flotsam and jetsam of the seas as their own right divine, with which no living thing from the doomed ship should be left to dispute their title.

And,—yet darker deeds than these made their wild crest of rock a name of terror to mariners. Sometimes it was utterly in vain that the light of Mary and her Angels gleamed in the high spire of the chapel. Sometimes, on the darkest and dreadest nights of late autumn and midwinter, round a headland where the chapel lantern could not be discerned, high up among the blackest and steepest cliffs, a tar blaze would break into the darkness and send forth a flame that could be seen for leagues across the waters. So that any hapless vessel, laboring in the trough of a heavy sea, beholding the false signal, and by evil fortune mistaking it for that of the Church, came straightway to her ruin, and was dashed keel foremost on the pointed submerged rocks, and impaled upon them; and never again saw the light of daybreak steal over the seas.

Those who lit that beacon of murder were never brought to justice; safe in their caverns and defiles, the assassins crept safely, by subterranean ways, back to their hamlet and amid their people. It had been safer to thrust a hand into a hornet's nest than to follow and arraign them there. Even their comrades did not rightly know who did the work. It was only when some rarer jewel than common glittered in some fisherman's ear, or some richer-hued scarf was wound about the hips of his mistress, that the rest whispered together, half envious, half abhorrent, that he must be one of those who fired the flame.

In the beginning of one winter food was very scarce in this sea-den. The fisheries had brought little in; the weather had been calm though dull; there had been no wrecks; and though it was known in the hamlet that the death-beacon had thrice been lighted aloft, it had failed to lead any ship astray. They became fearfully impoverished; famine visited them; and the men were forced to bite the salt twine of their nets in their longing to devour something, and the children wasted to skeletons, and died, and were thrust hastily away into holes in the sand.

A horrible longing for the signs of the storms came on them. A murderous prayer for the rage of wind and water often rose to their tongues—a prayer reckless and godless.

At this season one of the wreckers, he whose brain and whose hand had first devised this thing, stole up one midnight through the crooked crevice, on the bare stone of the cliff, that served him as a stairway. His torch was in his hand, and his soul was set on murder. There were bitter north winds driving over the ocean; there were gray fogs and starless skies; there was a single ship striving heavily through a churning sea. It was a fair chance, as he muttered to himself.

In his shingle hut, in the village yonder, no fresh food had touched the lips, for months, of a woman whom he loved. The leathery skin of some salted fish had become too great a luxury for them to obtain; she had been driven to chew the broad ribbon of the seaweeds, and grind the fishbones into the likeness of flour to make bread: and never made murmur or moan at her privation, but only showed the gnawing of famine by the wolfish glance of her eyes and the drawn lines of her mouth.

There rode the ship,—doomed, surely, to perish, if lured here by the light. The rocks, sharp as needles, hard as iron, over which the sullen waters floated, would do his work for him unerringly. Refuse, that to him would be treasures, would be swept up on the in-flowing tide. Food, fuel, most likely raiment, possibly gold, would be hurled up on the foam: human creatures, too, dying or dead, who would, in the mad clinging of men to the riches that they cannot take with them beyond the grave, have bound about them some belt of value or some bag of coin. There would be wherewithal to eat, and to drink, and to be clothed in his darksome and desolate cabin. What matter a deathwail the more on the wind? What matter the ship sinking an hour soon, or an hour late, to her doom?

Ere now he had thrust back a shivering, striving frame into the blinding spray, from which it had well-nigh struggled; ere now he had stunned, with the blow of his club, a girl whose face had risen out of the breakers, with wide-opened eyes of awful appeal in the glare cast upon it from the lightning. He had done such things before, he could do them again, for the sake of an ounce of gold from a finger-ring, of a necklace of beads off a maiden's throat. Gold would buy brandy, the hot, strong, blessed, accursed drink of forgetfulness; and the necklace would show rarely on the long, stately, brown throat of his bona-roba. And in his fashion—tiger's love for tigress—he loved the woman who starved in his hut on the beach.

So he stole through the tortuous, narrow, cavernous way, winding upward, steep as a ladder, cramped as a coffin, going higher and higher, up and up, into the bowels of the rocks above. And every now and then, where he went creeping like a lizard, with the torch between his teeth, he stopped, and softly blew upon the flame that was dying down in the damp and noxious air of the chasm. It was the spark of life to him.

He felt a latent fear, that never before had touched him, of setting light to his bonfire. There had come one among them who had set his face steadfastly against this evil trade; who had sworn that if the false beacon blazed afresh he would unearth the man that fed and fired it, or perish like the ships himself; and these men of the western coast knew that their visitant would keep his word. Therefore the wrecker went with a certain terror at his heart, drawing himself slowly upward, as serpents crawl, through the perpendicular cliff toward his goal that hung two thousand feet and more above the level of the sea.

The fire was ready piled there. It was safe from all discovery. None, save those to whom the secret of those passages through the body of the solid rock was known, could ever attain that height, which rose, a sheer straight wall of stone, up from the shore, and was severed by deep abysses on either side from the adjacent rocks.

He raised himself tediously and painfully up the ascent, in whose narrowed space and fetid air he could scarcely breathe. His hands at last grasped the topmost ledge; he lifted himself gradually on to the highest point, where his beacon was set. The ridge of all the other cliffs, lofty though they were, sank far below him: countless fathoms downward there rolled the gray sullen mass of water. The roar of its waves ascended in a faint hoarse sound, and a dense mist covered all the surface of the sea.

There was no light except the glimmer of the slow match that he bore; no movement save his own, except when a night-bird flew by on the rushing of the north wind. He took sure footsteps on the jagged uneven peak; then set his match to the oil-soaked tow of the torch that he had carried in the grip of his teeth.

The tow caught and flared alight; he lifted his hand to fling the burning flax upon the piled dry touchwood, and the tar barrels of his beacon:—ere he had cast it his arm was seized, the torch was wrenched out of his hand, and thrown flame downward over the cliffs: a man closed with him.

The wrecker was supple and vigorous, sinewy of frame, and skilled in physical exercise,—a giant, whose limbs were braced by the strength of the waves, and whose nerves were trained in the daily habit of peril: but he had met his match in his unknown foe who wrestled with him in the blackness of the night. With the quenched flame of the torch all light had gone: the sailor struggled by sheer instinct, like a wild beast attacked when it is blinded, and strove to fling his opponent off him and over the rock, into the wailing waves below. The part on which they stood was narrow; a single overpoise would have thrown them down into the gulf beneath, locked in each other's grasp; yet neither thought once of letting loose his hold; both struggled for the mastery.

No word was uttered: it was an even combat of sheer strength, fought on that slender, jutting, slippery ledge, that overhung at such vast height the bottomless pit of the devouring sea.

Thrice the wrecker all but gained ascendency, and had his arms locked round his opponent's waist, and well-nigh lifted him up from the stone on which they stood, to fling him over the edge to meet his death. Thrice his antagonist resisted him, and kept his feet as though they had been rooted into the rock itself.

It was a darkness in which both were blind: both knew that with every moment they might be hurled down two thousand feet of air. Yet still,—neither loosened their grip one instant.

The curlews flew round their heads with shrill outcry; the noise of the sea boomed louder as the spring-tide rushed in;

the bitter north wind howled around the peak;—they strove together for dear life on a shelf of granite scarce wider than a horse's back.

The sailor, maddened and brutalized by rage and fear, at length made frantic effort to get free his arm, and draw the knife at his belt from out its sheath. His foe felt the movement that he could not see. With swift, keen science the foe closed in, nearer still, with the wrecker; twisted his arm backward as men twist a bough to break it; and seizing him round the loins with the true athlete's skill, shook him, swayed him, lifted him, and stretched him prostrate.

The sailor was stunned: his head had struck upon the granite. His antagonist stood awhile breathless, exhausted, with the sound of the winds and waters surging dully on his ear, and the blood in his veins beating like pulses. He could not tell whether he had dealt death or no: till he stooped, and passed his hand over the motionless body, he could not tell whether it had not swayed forward and been dashed into pieces on the rocks below.

The darkness was impenetrable: even the white flash of a roused seagull's wing could not be seen; he could not move a step lest he should out-tread the narrow limits of the ledge on which he stood. There was not even the ray of a single star through the storm-wrack of the clouds.

He had no means of lighting any of the touchwood that lay near; and if he had possessed any could not have used his means, lest the light should have lured the vessel to that very destruction which he had risked his own life to avert from her. He had no choice but to rest where he was; with his back against the pile of the beacon-timbers, and the northern blasts raging around him.

It had been past midnight when the wrecker had gone forth to his errand: he knew that a few hours would bring the dawn.

Therefore he waited, with the man who, for aught he knew, was dead, lying at his feet, and the hungry sea fretting and raging far down beneath, as though in fury, because cheated of her prey.

The moments seemed as years, bathed in that gloom, knowing that an unfathomable abyss yawned beneath his feet, with no sound but the thunder of the wind among the cavernous cliffs, with no companion save a creature whom he might have slain, or who, if living, might yet arise and fly at his throat.

As he stayed there, a faint spark dropped from the torch among the light pine-boughs that helped to make the beacon, blown by the wind gathered brilliancy, and increased into a flame.

The bright spot caught his eye; with cautious movement he leaned and caught the branch that was on fire; it burned slowly, but gave a dull ruddy glimmer, insufficient to be seen by those at sea, but enough to throw light on the place immediately around him.

He held it to the wrecker's face: the man's eyes changed and glared, his senses had revived, though he had not yet power to move.

"It is you!" he gasped.

"It is I,—move a limb, and I will shoot you dead."

The sailor, lying there half stunned yet, and dazed by the flicker light that was held against his sight, stared stupidly at the glitter of the pistol.

"Why did you not use that before?" he muttered, half conscious, half senseless.

"We should not have been equal: you had no fire-arms."

The man said nothing: he looked in sullen wonder at the face above him, on which the dim red gleam shone faintly. He was awed; and filled with a vague superstitious terror. He did not believe the foe that he had dealt with could be mortal.

"Can you rise?" his conqueror asked him.

He tried to lift himself, obediently: the fall had bruised him, but had broken no limbs. He moved his head with a gesture of assent; his eyes incessantly fastened on the steel glisten of the weapon that covered him.

"You can stir;—very well. Then rise up and lead the way down your accursed passages. Attempt to resist me,—

attempt to escape me,—and I will send a bullet through your brain. You know me: you know that I keep my word:—as I kept it to-night."

The wrecker stared at him with the same stupid amaze; as of one who beheld some being of another world than his own. Then, docilely as a dog, he gathered his aching limbs together, and crept slowly along the ledge, down to the aperture by which he had ascended, and into the hollow space that ran through the substance of the rock.

He dared not disobey; he essayed neither resistance nor evasion; he knew that the pistol was leveled at his head, and that its shot would pierce his brain if he attempted to go astray or to turn upon his victor.

The pine branch gave light enough to illumine the tortuous crevice as they dragged themselves through it; he could not turn aside because its narrow twisting tubes had no crannies, no outlets, no hiding-places, and he dared not endeavor to outstrip his pursuer, because he knew that his instant death would be the penalty of any attempt at flight. Once, pausing to take breath, he stole a hasty glance backward.

"How did you come there?" he muttered in his clinched teeth.

"I scaled the cliff."

"You could not! The face of it is as bare as a man's hand."

"That may be; but it is not more bare or more steep than the wall of an Alp."

"God! No living soul ever tried it, but one, and he was dashed to pieces on the shore below."

"So I have heard."

"You had heard that when you ventured it?"

"Yes."

"And yet you came?"

"To stop you from doing fresh murder. That is words enough. Pass on."

The wrecker's breath came hard and fast; his great frame shook slightly with a tremor as with cold; he spoke no more, but crept on his downward way, marveling greatly, and ashamed.

The way was long; the pine-branch had burned down to its last inch, the gray of the earliest dawn was breaking in the rain-swept stormy skies, when they emerged at length from the subterraneous path, and came out upon the low-lying level shore, on which the high tide of the sea was breaking. The dawn was misty, bitterly cold, ushered in by the wild north winds, that drove the sand along in clouds, and hurled the foam of the waves in their faces.

The sailor turned suddenly on him as they came forth into the open air.

"How did you tell I went to fire that thing to-night?"

"I saw you take a slow match in your hand as you left your hut: I had often thought you were the criminal?"

The man hung his head: his eyes still glancing like a cowed wolf's at the weapon that held him to obedience.

"I should not have done it if she had not been starving," he swore with a blasphemous oath. "You do not know what famine is!"

The gaze that kept such stern watch over him softened wistfully.

"Do I not?" he said gently.

Then without more words he went over the league's length of sand and stone that severed them from the fishing hamlet; driving the wrecker before him as a moor-dog drives a sheep.

"Where would you take me?" the man muttered, as they drew nigh the rugged stairway cut out of the face of the cliffs which led to the group of cabins.

"To your fellows;—for judgment."

"They will not let you touch me!"

"That we shall see."

With a quick agile movement, before the fisherman could resist, or scarce knew what was done, he had seized his elbows, drawn his arms behind his back, and bound the wrists tight in the knots of a strong rope he had carried:— the man was powerless.

"You do not know me quite well yet, Rioz," he said quietly: Rioz, gnashing his teeth in baffled fury, and cursing his own folly in letting himself be netted like a lassoed bull, looked at him with a look that through its sullen passion had something of admiration and of reverence.

"Know you!" he muttered. "How should one know you? Are you man, or devil, or god?"

"A little of all, perhaps; like everything else that is human."

Then with the rope in his left hand, and the pistol in his right, he forced the wrecker up on to the heights on which the cabins of his people hung.

In the early dawn the population—in all some hundred souls, not more—were stirring, though the raw mists of the late autumn night still hung over land and water, wrapping both in its dusky and icy shroud. As they were seen, there was a rush, a shout, a tumult, a shrill outcry, from men's and women's and children's voices; the boats, the nets, the huts, the rude beds of dried weed were all abandoned as by one single impulse; the little cluster of dwellings broke into agitated life, as a hive of bees breaks into violent movement when its swarm is stirred. A score of men were round them on the instant, naked knives flashing in their hands, yells and curses on their lips, wonder and eagerness and fury in their eyes.

The conqueror of Rioz stood unmoved in the din, holding the wrecker like a chained beast.

"This man is the assassin," he said briefly. "If there be any among you who would say fair words for a murderer, let him speak them. I will hear."

The tumult of the blaspheming and threatening voices sank on a sudden as a storm-wind lulls: hardened, brutalized, strong in clannish loyalty, and indifferent of bloodshed as they were, they did not care to take this guilt upon their own heads thus.

The man himself never spoke: he only watched, with intent and thirsty eyes, first the faces of his comrades, then the face of his accuser. There was a dead silence for a moment;

then the force of tribe-love and the brotherhood of common habit, common need, common peril, got stronger than their shame; they clamored in unison for his release. One of their brood should not be bound, not be arraigned, not be chastised; one of their race should not be subject to the laws of other men. They were free; they owned no ruler; they acknowledged no code; one of themselves should not be fettered while they had knives to free him. So they shouted, pressing forward in the white sulphurous mist, a throng of reckless, fearless, freeborn animals, who owned no kingdom save the ocean, and no master save the storm-wind. He heard them, in peace; knowing nothing more likely than that their knives would be sheathed in his own breast, but never letting loose his grasp on the bound wrists of his captive.

After awhile the rage of words died down once more into an ominous sullen muttering; in that instant's pause he spoke.

"You have had your speech; now give me mine. Night after night, for three winters, a lying light has blazed upon your coast to lure good ships to their destruction. You told me you were ignorant of which among you was the criminal. I believed you. You are brave men; and brave men do not lie. A blacker sin, one more treacherous, one more cowardly, never stained a human life. It was a reproach to your seaboard; a shame on your manhood, that such a guilt was harbored, and allowed to grow, and thrive, and continue, undetected and unavenged, among you. You did naught in it—whether from fear, whether from conspiracy, I leave to your own consciences. So the work seemed left to my hand, and I did it. I have watched many nights; in vain. To-night I seized Rioz, red-handed in the act; putting his flame to that infernal pile. That his greed might have some miserable spoil—some keg of wine, some bale of wool, some sack of wetted corn, some case of rotting fruit, he was about to light the blaze that would have brought a helpless vessel to her shipwreck, and murdered all the human lives she bore. It has been done many times ere this: more deaths than he could count lie on his soul. For sake of some wretched pillage to

sate his hunger or his wine lust, for sake of some glimmer of
gold to satisfy the miser's avarice within him, he has doomed
men and women and children to death under your waves.
You can be brutal enough; you can have scant pity for the
fleeting life; you can strip the gold off a woman's throat ere
yet her corpse is cold; but if you sanction such murders as
these, you are fiends and not men. By this crime you are all
disgraced. It is not enough that you may not have set your
own match to the wood, thrown your own beam to the pile.
That this thing has been done, and been pardoned, and been
protected among you, is sufficient to brand you all with its
infamy. The blood-thirst of Rioz must run in your veins,
though his arm alone had nerve to raise the torch and awake
the fire. There are noble souls among you; are they all dead
or sleeping, that this disgrace raises no wrath? that this
murderer has lived with his sin unvisited in your midst?"

They were silent, touched with remorse, and burnt with
shame; knowing that this sin had been harbored among them,
half in sympathy, half in desperation; knowing that they had
been willing that it should be sheltered in secrecy; knowing
that there were others in their community who had shared
its guilt and shared its spoils. They dared not claim the
murderer again from the hands of his accuser: they dared not
either denounce the blood guiltiness from which their own
souls were not pure. They hung together, stilled, enraged,
ashamed, uncertain—Rioz looked at them, and laughed.

"Ye are bold comrades at need! Well—I say naught. It
was an evil deed: but I am willing to bear its brunt. It was
my thought and my act; it was only the plunder ye shared!
Kill me,—and ye shall, in justice, kill also every man that
ever drank of my wine or borrowed my gold. There! Will
not that thin your numbers?"

The accusation and the irony, bearing the sting of truth
in them, inflamed against him every creature of the throng,
which a moment before had been clamorous to recover him
from chastisement. They rushed at him to strike their knives
at his half-bare body; they cried aloud for him to be given to
them; they hooted him, and reviled him, and demanded that

he should be theirs, that they might cast him down from the peak where his bonfire had blazed!

His captor beat them off, and flung them back; and smiled where he stood at bay.

"Rioz! I brought you for their judgment. You believed that they would not let a hair of your head be injured: see now what the fellowship of guilt is worth! Will you have my judgment or theirs?"

The wrecker ground his strong white teeth, and faced the brethren on whose loyalty he had counted.

"Ye curs! ye were willing enough to take a stoup of my rich red drinks for yourselves, and a roll of my bright silks for your light-o'-loves; ye were willing enough to have barrels of rice and tubs of salted meat rolled from the caves to your cabins, in the hard days of your hunger: ye were willing enough to have all that the beacon brought, and ye fed it, and fanned it, and called it a devil that was better than a god, many and many a time. And now ye are gone against me: now ye are clamoring for my body, that ye may fling it down on the rocks! Ye sharks! there is but one man on this shore this dawn. It is this man who has brought me rope-bound like a netted calf. Look you—he scaled that cliff that has no footing for a goat, just to stand between me and that ship; he periled his life fifty times because he had sworn that my bonfire should never redden the skies again; he could have shot me and flung me into the sea, and he never used his pistol, because I had no arms of that like about me. That was what he did—Tricotrin. And I say that I give my life to him; and I will be judged by him and not by you—ye spawn of the devil-fish, that will suck the dead men's bones but will cry out that ye never took life! He may throw me off the rock, if he will: but ye—come one inch nearer to me, and, bound though I be, I will find a means to brain the best among ye!"

They were men as bold as he, and of like passions; but for once they hung back in silence, and for once their knives were never lifted: conscience made cowards of them.

"Tricotrin," they muttered. "You have taken him, you must deal with him as you will."

Tricotrin looked at them awhile, and answered them nothing: then he turned to the wrecker.

"Follow me, Rioz."

The fisherman followed him without a word; he went down the side of the cliff and on to the flat yellow shore. The day had now broken, with a faint red flush changing the gray of the sky: in the tender shadowy light a single ship was gliding. The wild winds of the night had sunk to silence; the sea, though heavy still, rolled quietly; the vessel moved unharmed over its waters.

He looked at it, then looked at Rioz: the wrecker turned away with a shudder.

He was not altogether vile; though he had steeped his soul in murder he had not burnt out his conscience: if the woman he had loved had not hungered he would not have sinned.

His captor let him stand there awhile, with his hands bound in the knotted cords, and his head sunk on his breast, and his eyes afraid to look upon that innocent thing, afar there on the waters, which, had his guilt had its way, would now have been a shattered, shapeless, sinking mass, with the billows breaking over the place of its nameless grave.

Then he spoke.

"Rioz—you are content to abide by my judgment?"

The wrecker gave a motion of assent.

"You heard what your comrades' sentence would have been. They were willing to shelter your sin while it was safe in secrecy; but when it had been dragged to the light of day they would have cast your body from the rocks. That is ever the fellowship of sin; a parasite when the sin is successful, a traitor when the sin is discovered. If they had been just men, and stainless, their sentence on you had not been too severe: you have doomed others to perish, you could not deem it unjust if you suffered by the same death as your victims. If there had been no guilt among them there had been no marvel if they had cast you forth from them, and slain you, in loathing and in vengeance. But they have not the right to deal thus with you: their own hands are not unsoiled, their own souls are not pure. You have said that you would not rebel if I bade you leap from your beacon-point into the sea; that is to speak idly: you know I am not a murderer: but will you obey as passively if I send you to your rightful due—the galleys?"

The wrecker made no answer. He did not lift his head from his breast; but under his dusky, weather-beaten skin, the blood came and went in rapid flush and pallor, and his teeth were set like a mastiff's.

"So long as the galleys are the means whereby your country visits a criminal for his acts, you cannot claim exemption from them," pursued the grave, gentle accents of his judge. "For less than you have done, men have forfeited their lives upon the scaffold. If for one murder done, in rash passion or jealous wrath, the murderer perish, how shall you escape? You who cannot number the creatures that through you may have been stifled in those waters! you who have doomed the young with the old, the innocent with the guilty, to perish by a hideous death for this sake only:—that your hearth might have fuel, that your trencher might have bread! If your hand have never thrust any struggling body back into the waves—if your steel have never ended the throes of some quivering wretch,—none the less have you bloodguiltiness upon your soul; unredeemed even by such motive as the tyrannicide or the fanatic may plead for his crime. If I deliver you up to the tribunal; if I take you to the sentence of the galleys; if for all the rest of the years you shall live you shall toil in chains, eat and drink the bread and water of bitterness, be branded to every eye that looks on you, labor like the mill-horse under the threat of the whip, live in a hell of foul utterance and evil passion, never again see the leaping gladness of the ocean, never again breast the winds and the waves in all the exultation of your strength, never again look into the eyes or kiss the mouth of a woman you love,—tell me, will my judgment be more than justice?"

A great shudder shook the mighty limbs of the fettered man.

He was silent many moments. Then at length he answered—the truth, sullen yet resolute.

"No. It will be just."

Tricotrin looked at him long and earnestly.

"Brute and fiend though you are, you have greatness in you," he muttered. "For you have courage, and you have truth."

The wrecker did not hear; his eyes were fastened on the receding ship sailing through the soft, young light; his thoughts were fastened on the dull, drear, endless years that waited for him in the galley-slave's doom.

Tricotrin waited awhile, letting this thought fasten on and penetrate the long-brutalized conscience of the man with whom he dealt.

"If you had gone back from your word, and disputed the fairness of that doom, I should have abandoned you to it as a worthless and hopeless ruffian," he said, curtly. "But you are brave enough, true enough, to confess its justice. There must be some core of honesty in you yet. If the guillotine came down on your neck, you would have no more than justice still. But—I believe that there is that in you which may be worth the saving. The galleys will not save you; they will only cage you in, as a wild beast is caged, and deprive you of the power to do evil. It is a hard question,—how to disarm and punish crime; made so hard by such as you, that we cannot wonder that the world's wisdom utterly fails at solving it. The galleys will withhold you from doing added crime; but that will be all. They will make a sullen, venomous, half-mad, blasphemous outcast of you, with all the will to do tenfold worse than you have done, and only held back from action by the irons on your ankles and the scourge on your back. If I see you a score years hence, I shall see in you a man whose last state is a million times darker than his first. You will be a tiger, whose claws are cut indeed, but whose lusts to kill are fiercer than ever. They will paralyze your limbs, but they will only inflame your passions.

Well—if you have had no care for the better powers that are in you, why should your rulers have care? If you have chosen to strangle the higher life in you, why should they heed aught save your animal instinct to slay that it is their office to stifle and prevent? You will be treated like a caged wild-beast. Well—why not? since you have far viler savageness in you than the poor beasts, who never slaughter their kind?"

Rioz heard—with dogged patience.

"I do not resist," he said, slowly. "It is right, I dare say. And I said that you should do as you would."

Tricotrin's eyes filled with a great pity.

"Do as I would? Well, then hear what it is I would do. It is this: I would save you from yourself. The galleys would save others from you; but I would go further than that if I could. What lives you have wrecked you alone can tell; I know only that your false beacon has flamed many times, and would have brought yon ship to her death-throe to-night. Therefore I know you—a murderer. In full intent, if not in actual deed. There can be no plea, no palliation, for the vileness of your guilt. Viler, I think, there cannot be upon earth. But even for your deeds there can be atonement; even for your offenses there can be expiation. One life saved by you from those waters will be better amend for your crime than twenty years spent at the galleys. The galleys would simply waste your life, and render it powerless for evil. I would employ your life, and render it powerful for good. There is truth in you, and courage. They must be fit for other things than murder and pillage. Therefore, I will not drive you out to the doom that by law would await you. I will sentence you otherwise; if you have the force in you I think, you will bear it; if not, you must carry the galley-chain. You will live alone on that rock where your fire has blazed; you will hold no communion with your fellows; you will subsist as you may on the bare food you can glean from the shore and the sea; you are a strong swimmer, a bold sailor, you will do your uttermost to succor and to save all life that comes in peril off your headland. I give you—solitude, hardship, travail, atonement. Being of a brave temper, you will not flinch from the working out of your doom. Go,—you are free."

And he severed the cords that bound the wrecker's strong wrists together.

Rioz had lifted his head, and looked him hard in the eyes, as his condemnation was uttered. As the rope fell from his arms and left him at liberty, a great change passed over his face; its savage gloom passed away, its wolfish glance softened and lightened.

"You trust me?" he muttered. "You shall see, then,— I will do your bidding. It is bitter; yet it is just. I may go mad on that rock; it is like enough. Loneliness kills men's brain, they say. But while I have sense I will be true to you. And you are merciful, too—you leave me the sea, and the wind, and the air."

His voice died in his throat; he turned away to go out to his doom.

But the man who had judged him followed him, and laid his hand on his shoulder gently, yet with firm and tenacious touch.

"Nay—I give you not utter solitude. That were to be more brutal than the galleys. Nor will I leave you to work out my sentence unaided. We will dwell on that rock together."

Rioz stared blankly at him, with glazed, burning eyes wide upon.

"You!—you! *You* have done no evil? Why should you care whether I drown, or rot, or go mad? Why should you suffer to save me?"

Tricotrin smiled; the smile was weary, and more sad than tears.

"Chut! When you have famine, you cure it in one fashion; when I have famine, I cure it in another. There are two treasures we may both find on that bleak, wind-beaten headland —yours expiation, and mine peace."

And for three long years he dwelt there—sole companion of an assassin. There were many lives that he saved from the pitiless waters; but there was one life that he saved from a deeper abyss than the lowest depths of the ocean.

It was thus that he dealt with the sorrow within him. It was thus that he wrenched the iron from out his own soul, by wringing the blackness of guilt from the soul of another.

CHAPTER XXXII.

In midwinter all Paris was dancing.

Paris dances as nothing else can under the sun or the stars. Did she not dance when her stones ran blood; dance when dynasties fell at her word; dance on the icy glacis of Bréda; dance while the steel cut down through her loftiest throats; dance when the bastard son of Louis Quinze drowned with the roll of his drums the dying words of Louis Seize? Paris dances ever: beautiful, terrible thing, half child, half wanton, twin angel and assassinatress that she is; dances on under the million lights of her winter-nights as under the glorious suns of her summer-eves, under the fetters of tyrannies as under the banners of freedom.

They danced in the palaces, they danced in the mansions, they danced in every hall, and coffee-room, and concert place, and singing-booth, and covered garden, in this winter-time. In every spot feet flew, like autumn leaves blown by wild breezes; and laughter echoed like the chimes of sleigh-bells; and men and women went mad with the joyous delirium of motion. Specially they danced in an abandonment of revelry in the great hall of the Elysée Montmartre; grisettes, and students, and fruit-girls, and working men, and all that was maddest and brightest of the labor-world and the student-world of Paris. They lost all sense save that one sense of the hot, intoxicated delight of boundless, leaping, whirling, spinning, unceasing motion; like the whirlwind in its speed, like brandy in its strength, like tigers' frolic in its play. They danced as not even in Paris that night did any dance elsewhere. For above the noise of the hired bands, which, indeed, did sink hushed and abashed in rivalry by it, was the music that Paris loved best, the music that had in its marvelous melody all the color of a Titian, all the glow of strong wine, all the rush of a swift-running river, all the revelry of a royal carousal. One played for them who would not play at the bidding of monarchs; but who cast out, to those who had not gold to purchase pleasure, the lavish treasures of his genius.

That music could do with them as it would; and now it bade them dance on through the long winter's night. and forget that cold, and pain, and hunger, and toil and envy were their daily portions in the world that was white with its new year's virginal snows.

The player laughed oftentimes as he played, with rich gay laughter; but oftener still there came the look in his eyes as of the dreamy deep meditation, the awed surprise and yet serenity of one who beholds visions that none around him see. His face was the face of a poet; and it had but more fire, more force, more beauty for the silverwhite waves of the abundant hair, dashed back like a lion's mane. Hour after hour the music pealed out, untiring, exhaustless; music for which kings would have rained down their wealth, for which these dancers of the populace could only give their love. But this one gift they gave in lavish measure; and when at length the melodies ceased, the vast crowd pausing, shouted as with one throat such a cheer as years before had rung out for the great and beloved tribune of the people, when Gabriel Mirabeau had paused among them.

Such welcome, the cannon of royal entries, the troops of Imperial guard, the magnetized fear of a subject nation, cannot give, though trumpets call, and drums roll, and artillery thunder from dawn till sunset.

He could have led them where he would—these bright, wild, tender, ferocious children of Paris, so idolatrous in worship, so merciless in hate. He could have led them where he would, to hurl down the gates of palaces, to dash aside the serried ranks of guards, to scatter princes as chaff before the winds, to steep new-born liberties in a felt baptism of blood.

They tossed flowers high in the air; they flung up their arms in the bright light; they thronged about with passionate eagerness; the breasts of the women heaved like waves under a storm, the brows of the men burned red with the fires of freedom struck alight by his art in their souls. He looked down on their upturned faces and on their breathless, tumultuous homage, and smiled;—the smile whose meaning lay far beyond them.

"My children! No gratitude between *us*. Is there not love?"

Tricotrin—bohemian and wanderer, nameless and homeless among men—had a kingdom greater than monarchs held, a power greater than the scepter can command.

Through the bitter brilliant wintry night he walked, later on, straightly and swiftly, with the free long step of a forest animal, along the chill snow-covered streets of Paris. As he went he sang, in a voice that rang through the stillness, and made the sullen frozen patrol listen, with a smile on his face, to that joyous, drinking, and amorous carol, "*Sur deux levres roses:*"

> "I unlearn all my Latin
> On two red lips of satin,
> And study night and morning,
> All other science scorning,
> The art of those twin roses!
>
> High in air the sky-lark sings,
> As to me a maiden brings
> Fruit ripe as her breast is white,
> And wine that is full of light,
> And red as her cheek's roses!
>
> No chair of state can lure me,
> No classic bribe insure me,
> But all the lore of ages
> I glean from those sweet pages,
> Of Love's own leaves of roses!"

The snow was falling heavily, and was deep upon the earth: he went through it, and over it, with a step firm as a soldier's, light and free as a gipsy's. An old man dragging himself wearily and painfully along, shivering, glanced wistfully at his lighted meerschaum. He stopped, pulled a knot of tobacco and a pipe from his pocket, filled the bowl and lit it; then gave it to the aged creature.

"Smoke and forget, my friend! The pipe is our best comrade after death!"—then he went on chanting his rose-song.

A little child lay curled on a doorstep, blue, numb, almost

frozen, quite heart-broken, sobbing himself into a fatal slumber. Tricotrin paused again, lifted up the boy, and shook him from his trance: in the little, weary, whitened face there were exceeding innocence and grief.

"Have you no home?"

"No."

"No mother?"

"No."

"How old are you?"

"Six, I think."

"And all alone?"

"All alone."

"Not of Paris?"

"No. My father came from the west—very far away,—to get work; and there was none: they are ceasing to build, they say. So we starved; and my father killed himself. He is in that terrible black house by the river——"

"And has left you and Paris a legacy to one another? Scarcely fair; since without him you would have remained in the peaceful regions of the Unarrived: and disembodied souls neither want bread nor get blue with cold. Well! you see that passage, and the door under the third lamp? Run quick there; ask for the woman of the house. Tell her that Tricotrin has sent you: that you are to sleep on his bed, be warmed at his fire, have some milk and some bread, and forget yourself in dreamland till the morning. Then—well then we will see what substitute we can discover for this impolite father of yours, who sent you into this best of all possible worlds and never had the decent complaisance to secure you a crust in it. Off, little one—quick!"

The child stared up at him through the falling snow with wide-opened wondering eyes, thinking of the figures of the angels Gabriel and Michael that he had seen in churches, and marveling which of the twain this was that now had mercy on him in this bleak and brutal night. Then,—remembering him of the milk and bread of which this grand and pitiful angel had spoken, and moved by his famished desolate heart,—he looked up once swiftly, half afraid, then threw his arms about his benefactor's knees and covered his feet with kisses. Tricotrin shook him softly away.

"Chut! I am no god—only a stray thing like yourself. Go quick! you want the bread and milk, and the wood fire."

The child ran, with fresh life put in his chilled starved limbs: Tricotrin went on, singing his drinking-song.

A little way farther down the street there sat a small, brown, shaggy, shivering dog, of no value, of no beauty, shaking all over with the cold and howling piteously. He paused once more, and stroked it, and talked awhile to it, and its grief fell into a lower key, and became a plaintive sighing sound. Its bones were almost through its skin, its eyes were bleared and blind, its misery was great.

"Get out, you moaning brute!" cried a woman from a garret-lattice above, as she thrust her head into the darkness and aimed at the little dog a heavy billet of wood.

Tricotrin caught the wood as it came, and saved the cur the blow.

"Friend," he said, quietly glancing up, "if you had sent the famished thing a piece of a loaf, it had been softer to his stomach and to my hand!"

The woman peeped at him by the faint gas gleam.

"Is it you, Tricotrin?" she said, half sullenly, half ashamed. "I would not grudge the mongrel a bone; but it is such a wretched beast to howl. Look you: it belonged to a young man that lived here; a fool who was forever scribbling over every scrap of paper he could find, and thinking he was born to be a poet—God's mercy! Well—he could not buy a leek for his soup at last, and he had no shirts but the one he had on, and he could do nothing but scribble, scribble, scribble. So the other day we had to break his door open, and we found him stark and stiff on the mattress,—there was a charcoal pan just burned out, and all his poems were a little heap of rent paper. Now that cur you see there belonged to him: and drive it away how we will, it always comes back, and sits under his window, and howls like that. Who is to bear such a noise? It will not go away. And who is to feed it, a thing worth nothing? I will have it flung in the river, or sell it to a student to cut up with his dissecting knife."

Tricotrin took the little animal up in his arms, and stroked afresh the matted broken hair.

"Fidelity pays thee ill, poor little wretch!" he murmured. "Ah! thou art not alone!"

"You have none of that dead lad's writings?" he asked aloud.

"Not I," the woman answered from above. "He had torn them to bits, I tell you. There was one roll indeed, one on which he had writ that he had not had the courage to destroy it—he believed it would make his name live, though his body had been killed by hunger. But I burnt it in my stove as soon as I could: how could I tell it was not what would get me into trouble with the police?"

She shut her lattice sharply, unwilling to squander more time and more words on such poor things as a mongrel dog and a dead poet. Tricotrin again went on his way with the little shivering beast in the folds of his loose fur coat. It had ceased to moan, and was trying to lick his hand.

"So!" he murmured, half aloud. "The creature that thrusts the boy-poet's trust into her stove for fuel is called the immortal being, and you, who have a tenderer memory and a loyaler love than one woman in ten thousand, get kicked aside as a cur! How enormous is the vanity of humanity! The river or the dissecting knife—that is the only choice they give you. Little fool! you elected to love a man who had only intelligence, no gold; you elected to serve a life that had only high hopes, no practical pelf; you fastened your heart on a creature who knew the world so little that he fancied the legacy of a dream would be treasured like the legacy of a fortune: few women are so unwise as you were, my dog. And now, because you are a mongrel you are beaten; because you are faithful you are cursed; because you are only a thin, rough, ugly, hapless morsel, with a noble heart beating in your little hairy breast, and an immeasurable love consuming you, you are to be flung into the water with a stone round your neck, or quiver, and thrill, and gasp in torture, under the brutality men call Science! What magnificent justice we have! What appreciation of fidelity! Well—you shall come and have a share with Mistigri: and by-and-by when the chill of the winter has passed, you shall go into the green country places, and live on a Normandy farm that I know of, and blink your eyes all day in the sun, and roll in the long sweet grass, and sleep under the apple-tree boughs. If your master was really a poet, it must have been an added pain to him to think that he left you alone. Had he the divine afflatus, really, in him? Surely not, or he had never left a little desolate thing like you to starve and to pine in the streets. And yet—I do not know—poets are but men, men a little nearer to God and the Truth than are others; and when hunger is keen, and the world is cruel, the truth gets obscured to their sight, and they say that God is dead also—since he will not hear or give answer!"

The little dog nestled closer, comforted; and Tricotrin passed on through the network of the streets.

Ere long he drew near one which, in the late night, was still partially filled with vehicles and with foot-passengers, hurrying through the now fast-falling snow, and over the slippery icy pavements. In one spot a crowd had gathered; of artisans, women, soldiers, and idlers, under the light of a gas-lamp. In the midst of the throng some gendarmes had seized a young girl, accused by one of the by-standers of having stolen a broad silver piece from his pocket.

She offered no resistance; she stood like a stricken thing, speechless and motionless, as the men roughly laid hands on her.

Tricotrin crossed over the road, and with difficulty made his way into the throng of blouses and looked at her. Degraded she was; but scarcely above a child's years; and her features had a look as if innocence were in some sort still there, and sin still loathed in her soul. As he drew near he heard her mutter,—

"Mother, mother! She will die of hunger!—it was for her, only for her!"

He stooped in the snow, and letting fall, unperceived, a live-frank piece, picked it up again.

"Here is some silver," he said, turning to the infuriated owner, a lemonade seller, who could ill afford to lose it now that it was winter, and people were too cold for lemonade, and who seized it with rapturous delight.

"That is it, monsieur, that is it. Holy Jesus! how can I thank you? Ah, if I had convicted the poor creature—and all in error!—I should never have forgiven myself! Messieurs les gendarmes, let her go! It was my mistake. My silver piece was in the snow!"

The gendarmes reluctantly let quit their prey: they muttered, they hesitated, they gripped her arms tighter, and murmured of the prison-cell.

"Let her go," said Tricotrin, quietly: and in a little while they did so,—the girl stood bareheaded and motionless in the snow, like a frost-bound creature.

Soon the crowd dispersed: nothing can be still long in Paris, and since there had been no theft there was no interest: they were soon left almost alone, none were within hearing.

Then he stooped to her: she had never taken off him the wild, senseless, incredulous gaze of her great eyes.

"Were you guilty?" he asked her.

She caught his hands, she tried to bless him and to thank him, and broke down in hysterical sobs.

"I took it—yes! What would you have? I took it for my mother. She is old, and blind, and without food. It is for her that I came on the streets: but she does not know, it would kill her to know; she thinks my money honest; and she is so proud and glad with it! That was the first thing I stole! Oh God! are you an angel? If they had put me in prison my mother would have starved!"

He looked on her gently, and with a pity that fell upon her heart like balm.

"I saw it was your first theft. Hardened robbers do not wear your stricken face," he said softly, as he slipped two coins into her hand. "Ah, child! let your mother die rather than allow her to eat the bread of your dishonor: which choice between the twain do you not think a mother would make? And know your trade she must, soon or late. Sin no more, were it only for that love you bear her."

Then he passed from her swiftly, chanting still the burden of the roses.

The girl-criminal, the child-courtesan of sixteen summers, stood mute and paralyzed; her hand mechanically closing on the gold; her large dark heavy eyes gazed over the white stretches of the snow, and up at the black star-studded skies: hot tears rushed under her swollen lids, and she flung up her arms to the heavens with a sob that was prayer and oath in one.

He had ransomed her from more than the prison cell: he had bought her soul from sin.

And the joyous amorous song rang gayly through the night; for these were daily things that he did, and were nothing new in his life, which, if like the life of Desaugiers it was one perpetual fête, was also one continual benediction. Turn by turn, his life had been full of mirth, and passion, and poetry, and revelry, and pain, and all the delights of the senses and the soul in changeful sequence; but in it one thing reigned ever, never sleeping, never shadowed, never silent, never cold, a thing of which men have little, and saints have less,—charity.

By-and-by, through the streets of the old city and across the river, he came to where the great front of the Tuileries glittered all alive with light.

"Ah! I remember they are dancing here too," he murmured, as he glanced at the illumined palace. "So there is the eldest son of the church spending half a million to entertain the princes of the earth, while out in the street yonder filial piety must turn harlot to get a crust! Sublime crown of civilization!"

And he walked through the Carousel to the Court of Honor.

"No one passes," said one of the Cent Gardes, bringing his bayonet level, while his sky-blue and silver harness glittered in the gaslight.

"Bah! I pass; you know me, Petit Jean."

The guard looked, smiled, and let him enter. He knew that Tricotrin was privileged, by right of that love which the people openly bore him, and the fear which their rulers secretly felt of him.

He stood in the entrance among the fretting horses, shouting lackeys, flaring torches: they filled the vast court with movement and with color, while above-head the heavy snow whitened the roofs of palace, pavilion, and gallery.

The guests of the court were then leaving in the gray of

night that met morning: hundreds passed by him, women of beauty and birth, and men of every nation's nobility, the brilliant throng of a new-year ball, passing out to their equipages in the red tossing flamelight of ten thousand torches.

Among them came one whose loveliness had had no peer even among all that was loveliest in Europe:—a woman of a perfect beauty, moving with slow sweeping step; a woman of lofty slender stature like a palm; of voluptuous and exquisite grace; with eyes dark as night, full of languor and luster, and a skin like the snow, and hair of lightest gold, in which stars of diamonds shone; a woman with the dignity of an empress, the glance of a sorceress, the face of an angel.

And the running footmen, with their torches blazing, cleared a wide way before her, and called aloud for the carriage of,—"Madame la Duchesse de Lira."

He, standing there beyond the torch-glare, started and went forward, the blood flushing his forehead, his eyes lighting to eager passion.

Once this beautiful sovereign had said, "If I forget you then may God forget me;"—now her careless imperial glance sweeping over the throng passed over him and did not even see him.

His head dropped as if he had been struck a sharp blow; a keen anguish, like the anguish in the bold faithful eyes of a hound wounded by the hand that it loves, came into his: not without need and prescience had he once answered her, —"thy sins to me I shall forgive thee: for what else have I given thee love?"

The carriage rolled away with noise and royal ceremony; bearing her from the scene of her victories; and he went slowly forth back over the river into the haunts of the old city with the stray dog in his bosom.

With the riches of his genius had he made the hearts of the poor and heavy-laden to rejoice that night in innocent and natural delight: with the stripes of human ingratitude and oblivion was he scourged that night himself.

"What matter? what matter?" he murmured, as he went through the driving sheets of snow. "What matter?—she is happy."

END OF VOL. I.

www.ingramcontent.com/pod-product-compliance
Lightning Source LLC
Chambersburg PA
CBHW030306240426
43673CB00040B/1074